THE
CAPTIVE
AMERICAN

———————————— ★ ————————————

THE
CAPTIVE
AMERICAN

———————— ★ ————————

LEE BRANDENBURG
with Andrew Lewis Shepherd

Library of Congress Cataloging-in-Publication Data

Brandenburg, Lee, 1930-
    The captive American.
    Bibliography: p.
    Includes index.
    1. United States—Politics and government—
1981-   .   2. United States—Economic policy—
1981-   .   3. Political participation—United States.
I. Shepherd, Andrew Lewis, 1959-   .   II. Title.
JK271.B649   1988   973.927   88-81159
ISBN 0-929158-00-8

Text design: David Crossman
Jacket design: Robert Pawlak
Production management: BMR, Mill Valley, CA

Printed in the United States of America

10 9 8 7 6 5 4 3 2 1

Acknowledgment is given to Random House, Inc., for permission to reprint
selected excerpts from *Man of the House*, copyright © 1987 by Thomas P.
O'Neill, with William Novak.
Acknowledgment is given to Little, Brown, and Company, Inc., for permission to reprint selected excerpts from *Khrushchev Remembers*, translated and
edited by Strobe Talbott, copyright © 1970 by Little, Brown and Company, Inc.

Hampton Books
San Jose, California

To three generations who have seen many changes, not all for the better:

> my mom and dad, Jessie and Mel

> my wife and best friend, Diane

> my kids, Karen, Eric, Gary and Bill

And to the generation I know will see a brighter future:

> my granddaughter, Diana Lee

ACKNOWLEDGMENTS

---------------------------------- ★ ----------------------------------

I owe George Parker and Anne Holliday warm thanks for their guidance through the book world and their constant advice to a novice.

At Stanford University I was able to persuade Janet Spitz, doctoral student at the Graduate School of Business, that this was an important project. Together we managed to convince Daniel Abbasi, James Babb, Mark Peceny and Lewis Shepherd, all doctoral students in the Political Science department. Wayne Camard also came aboard from the Economics department. I want to thank all of them for helping me get started.

My research team and I conducted a number of interviews with people around the country. While some interviewees declined to let their names be used, I'd like to thank each individual for the time and insights they were willing to share with me. They may not all agree with my conclusions or suggestions, but each contributed to my journey of discovery. Special thanks to Vernon Christina, an original member of Ronald Reagan's kitchen cabinet; Michael Closson, executive director, Center for Economic Conversion; Don Edwards, United States Congress, California; John Hannah, research fellow, Washington Institute for Near East Policy and doctoral fellow, Berkeley/Stanford Program on Soviet International Behavior; Gene Holley, former majority leader, Georgia state legislature; William Lowry, research fellow, Brookings Institution; Sam Nunn, United States Senate, Georgia; Lee Prussia, former chairman, BankAmerica Corporation; and Grant Rogers, regional trustee, Outward Bound program.

A number of my friends deserve recognition for reading through manuscripts and giving helpful and insightful suggestions: Charles C. Ellis, Mel Morgan, Bill Baron, Ron Pine, Alfred Fromm, Dick Pfaff and Arthur Tarlow. The book is infinitely better because of their comments, and would be better still if I had followed all their advice.

The following people gave me expert editorial advice and brought new perspectives to the material: Milton Moskowitz, Charles Seib and Renee Renouf Hall.

To Jack Jennings and his team at BMR, to Amy Rood, Karryll Nason, Ann Helstrup and Ron Helstrup, I also want to say thanks for their support and hard work on the mechanics of getting this book out.

My constant appreciation goes to my executive assistant, Melodee Dunlap, for her relentless efforts and positive input throughout this tortuous project.

Kira Sturney, vice president of Hampton Books, deserves my thanks for bringing all the diverse elements of publishing and distribution together.

And lastly, extra thanks to Lewis Shepherd, who followed my concept of the four steps of success:

—Put yourself at the right place at the right time

—Recognize that you are there

—Take appropriate action, one logical step after another from beginning to end

—Wrap up with the same thought and enthusiasm that you started with.

Nobody could be more dedicated and committed to our book than Lewis.

Somebody had to do it; I hope we succeeded.

C O N T E N T S

---------------------- ★ ----------------------

FOREWORD

This is a thoroughly delightful book which describes, more accurately than could any Washington insider, many of the deplorable failures of our political system in recent years.

Politicians are properly shown as the frauds that most of us are...or tend to become the longer we stay in politics.

Of equal worth are the author's insights into the three great professions, law, business and academia, which have traditionally furnished American decision-makers.

The author is an angry man and understandably so. He has seen in his lifetime the decline of much of what America held dear in his youth. His anger is properly directed at the privileged in our society, who have done nothing to halt that decline.

In this, he is particularly qualified to write this modern version of *Parkinson's Law*, coming as he does from one of the wealthiest and most environmentally blessed communities in America.

The author is the classic case of a sophisticated, enormously successful, wealthy American who has done absolutely nothing to halt the decline in the system he treasures—until writing this book. *The Captive American* is a cry of anguish...a truthful cry that Americans are captive only because of their own apathy. The author's call "Wake up America" is timely and from the heart.

I hope it will be read by every caring citizen and used in every college political science course. I intend to use it in my own.

Paul N. McCloskey
Palo Alto, California

WHY I FINALLY
WROTE THIS BOOK

──────────────── ★ ────────────────

I've never considered myself a very political man. I have always had a strong distaste for politics and politicians. Like a lot of people, I was content to watch the passing political parade. I worked hard at my real estate development business, and I became very good at making money. I guess I'm an American success story.

About twenty years ago, though, I started to see that politics *was* affecting my life. At first, it was only an awareness that I had a lot of unanswered questions. Why are good and bad business cycles affected by elections?

Why were we involved in Vietnam? How could we have homeless on our streets but send millions of dollars to foreign dictators? And why does Dick Nixon never disappear from the political scene?

So I started reading intensively about politics, foreign affairs and the economy, hoping that I could find some answers. The more I read, the madder I got.

Our problems seemed horrendous then, back in the late 1960s, and they were. I began to wonder why we didn't choose good, honest and competent leadership to handle them. I even thought about writing a book, to be called *The Best Man,* and I began doing the research, collecting newspaper and magazine articles. I met some resistance (not only on the sexist title). "There are plenty of books on politics," I was told. But the people who said that had never read them.

And for good reason: most of those **books** are written by boring academics, superficial journalists, or self-serving politicians. You know the books I'm talking about. Those authors don't have the answers. In fact, they're part of the problem!

No one had written the kind of book I wanted to write: a book for the average American. A book for the steelworker, the single mother, or the young couple without much education but with a lot of questions about their finances, their future. I told myself I could write a short, clear, no-nonsense book to demystify economics and politics, and maybe make some suggestions along the way.

But my business became incredibly successful and I was kept busy building what some have called a "real estate empire." Also, I was raising a family with Diane, my lovely wife of 36 years. We have a beautiful daughter and three great sons, and now I even have a gorgeous granddaughter to spoil. I didn't have time to write my book.

This past year, despite being busier than ever, I began thinking more about our national problems. They seemed immense, much more complex than ever before. I went back to my old clippings and compared some of the headlines with those of today. You know what? They were no different.

We were facing the same problems then: economic mismanagement, political incompetence, international bungling. But now they are worse! As a nation, we owe more, we've lost more and we're in far greater danger than we were 20 years ago of losing it all. I knew then, before one more election passed, I had to write this book.

Even a year ago, the ideas in this book might have seemed too radical for widespread acceptance. Since then, thinking people have been jarred out of their mental comfort zones.

I love my country, and it has been very good to me. I'm not here to bad-mouth America. Last year I paid over a million dollars in personal income taxes—okay, I did very well. But I want to know where that money went. I really want to know where we lost our way and how we can get back on course.

Why is our country's strength on the wane, even though we still claim the responsibilities of world leadership? Why does administration after administration solemnly pledge to address our crises, only to leave a trail of bigger problems? Our "leaders" apply band-aid remedies to cancerous problems and we get PR rather than solutions. Government has become the antithesis of the old town meeting; people feel overwhelmed.

I'm not a man on a white horse, but I am trying to rouse my fellow citizens from their apathy. When we get complacent, we get ripped off. The American people must love that, because we're ripped off so royally and with such finesse.

A scholar once wrote that Tom Paine's *Common Sense*, the pamphlet that sparked our first revolution, "opened the eyes of thousands of Americans to the realities of British politics." Too many of us have been blind to the realities of American politics. We are paranoid about what we put into our bodies, but we couldn't care less what goes into our minds.

It's as if we're passengers in a runaway car, speeding down the highway with the hood up. We *know* there's a brick wall somewhere up ahead, but we can't find the brakes and we're afraid to grab the steering wheel.

Let's stop talking about what great gas mileage we're getting. I say we slam the hood down on the runaway car and hit the brakes before it's too late!

Why would you read my book—and not one by a celebrity author? I'm not a political scientist, and I'm no Wall Street insider. But outsider status has its advantages; you see things from a more realistic angle. For too long, we've been told that national issues are too complex for us to understand, leaving the field wide open to political manipulation and bureaucratic stupidity.

This book's different. It can do something for you. Never again will a politician or so-called expert be able to pull the wool over your eyes.

The unwillingness of experts to address real problems surprised me when I began my research. My first thought was, go to the specialists, and they were right down the road at top-ranked Stanford University. I sent off letters to professors in the political science department and at the Hoover Institution on campus, asking them to suggest some bright graduate students to help me out. I thought it was strange that I didn't get a single response.

Finally one young woman, a doctoral student in the Graduate Business School, called me. She thought my project seemed eccentric, but with her help I was able to recruit some other grad students in political science. They all seemed a bit nervous about working on this venture. I couldn't understand that. Here was a wealthy businessman who had gained a conscience and wanted to write an informative book about our country's problems. I wanted to pay them handsomely to boot. That may not happen every day, but to me it seemed straightforward enough. I started to wonder why the young woman always spoke in hushed tones when she called me from her office on campus.

After getting to know me, the young scholars began to speak frankly. They were reluctant to get involved because my book was going to deal too directly with current political issues and the problems of the real world. They feared their professors might learn of this unorthodox activity with an outsider, and that their careers in the isolated ivory tower would be affected. Some didn't even want me to use their names in the acknowledgments.

Finally I persuaded a group of outstanding graduate students, some of the brightest minds in the nation, to help me. They gave direction to my search for "the truth"—and I think I gave them a few insights into the real world.

I have tried to approach even the most complex national problems in a common-sense and honest way. Unlike politicians, I don't pretend to provide all the solutions. (When was the last time you heard a politician say, "I don't know"?) But I do point the way to reform.

I'll leave the nit-picking to candidates and political pundits. This book isn't an endorsement for any political party or candidate. As you read, forget labels like liberal, conservative, Democrat, Republican. Labels aren't answers, and in fact the narrow-minded thinking they represent is part of the problem. I consider myself a pragmatist, liberal on some issues and conservative on others. I enjoy merrily bouncing left and right of center, for that tells me my mind is free and open.

I'm proud to admit I have only two qualifications to write this book. First, I had the money and the time it took to research and write it. Second, and more important, I am an American citizen just like you, with the same concerns and anxieties you face. We have both had our pockets picked by corrupt official-dom. We have both lost friends and relatives in senseless foreign interventions. We both care about this country.

There are many who could have written this book, and someone definitely should have. The fact that no one has until now is just another symptom of our malaise.

If you share my concerns, read on. The thought may come to you as it comes to me: what would our Founding Fathers think of us today?

Lee Brandenburg
Woodside, California

A NOTE FROM THE AUTHOR

---------------------------------- ★ ----------------------------------

To make my book as readable and unintimidating as possible, I decided to leave out footnotes. If you're like me, nothing spoils a good read like wading through lots of notes on obscure sources—even though that helps the book's credibility. Noel Coward once said that encountering a footnote "is like going downstairs to answer the doorbell while making love."

The information in the figures and tables came from various sources, including: the U.S. Census Bureau, the *New York Times*, the Office of Management and Budget, the Federal Deposit Insurance Corporation, *Business, Money and Power* by Michael Kidron and Ronald Segal, the U.S. Department of Defense, and the Congressional Research Service.

Wherever I quote someone directly, I mention the source in the text. The list of suggested readings at the end also refers to many books I found helpful. If you are interested in the complete list of sources I have used for this book, write to me and I'll send you a copy.

PART I

★

LEADERSHIP LOST AND FOUND

C H A P T E R   1
★
A People Betrayed

In the last year of the Reagan presidency, a year of great political uncertainty and turmoil, Americans became briefly obsessed—and amused—by a scandal involving astrology. The astrology disclosure helped sell hundreds of thousands of copies of an otherwise dull, self-serving book by former White House staffer Donald Regan. I was among the amused. I was also furious.

What do you suppose historians will conclude about America in the 1980s, when they discover that our national decisions were influenced by image-makers and star-gazers at the elbow of the President? What will they think of our politics, our judgment, our taste in books?

The politics of our time have produced a ton of kiss-and-tell books. It's not new; we got the same thing after Watergate, from Haldeman, Liddy, Colson and Dean. Even Nixon keeps writing. What I find disquieting, and so should you, is the deeper meaning of these books. Only in America is failure rewarded twice.

First we pay these people to go to Washington, abuse their power, bungle their jobs and complicate our lives. Then we let them sell their mistakes back to us as history.

THE ROAD TO WASHINGTON

Have you ever wondered how certain individuals wind up in the seat of power, deciding issues that hit us right in the stomach? I have some insight into one such ascent.

In 1961, I was a recent graduate of San Jose State, and had also recently moved up from real estate broker to land developer in the Santa Clara Valley. Sometimes I would revisit my old campus haunts, including one cocktail lounge in particular, the Interlude.

The piano player there developed a small following. He was another State alumnus, who had belonged to the fraternity next to mine. His name was Mike Deaver.

One night the piano player didn't show up. Turns out Deaver had lost his daytime job.

I learned the rest of the story from one of his frat brothers. Deaver had been accepted by IBM for a six-month training program (people were just beginning to call the area Silicon Valley). One condition of the job was no part-time employment. One night, during the probationary period, his supervisor at IBM happened to walk into the Interlude and caught Mike at the keyboard.

With a career at IBM down the tubes, he studied his options. There was no real job in sight, and the prospect of playing the lounge circuit did not appeal to him. So he settled for politics. I heard that he went to work for the Republican party in Santa Clara County, made connections in Sacramento and wound up on the staff of the new governor of California, Ronald Reagan.

From time to time, I would notice his name or picture in the papers. Then I saw he became special assistant to the President, at the pinnacle of the American government. As far as anyone could tell, he made it without ever holding a real job.

I was amused when I saw in his autobiography that Deaver said he went into politics "after I went to work for IBM in sales and concluded that the corporate world was not for me."

The Reagans came to depend on him so fully after 20 years that Deaver was asked to select a gravesite for the couple—and to ask one of Reagan's wealthy supporters to pay for it.

In his later activities as a lobbyist, Deaver joined the list of more than 100 Reagan appointees to be accused of misconduct. Our politicians are really building a legacy for us. No one can say the words "public servant" anymore without laughing. Today a statesman is just a politician who has gray hair and is not presently under indictment.

WHO'S TO BLAME?

Remember that we don't have a pure "democracy" where the people decide everything themselves. We're not like Switzerland, with referendums on almost every decision that needs to be made.

As a representative democracy, we elect a small number of our fellow citizens to go to Washington (or the state capital or city hall) and make the day-to-day decisions for us. The people we elect are our "leaders." They form our government—and we expect them to have goals, strategies to achieve them and the ability to rally the public around those goals and strategies.

Good leaders tell the people, as John F. Kennedy did, "ask what you can do for your country." Instead, today's politicians take an easier route, telling people fairytales and avoiding any hint of hard work or self-sacrifice for the common good. Instead of leaders who might place demands on us, we have "leaders" like Jack Kemp, who appeals to the selfishness in young Americans by saying that "at the age of 18, you should be focusing on your dreams and ambitions, not picking up cans in Yellowstone." These modern politicians like things that way. They're most comfortable when a majority of us don't vote or pay attention to public affairs, leaving the field open to those voters under party control. They want people to "focus on their dreams and ambitions" and ignore what goes on in Washington.

THE SCANDAL INSIDE THE BELTWAY

The Beltway is Interstate 495, which encircles the District of Columbia, and the city inside is the scandal.

At first glance, Washington is a place where thousands of public servants do their jobs honestly and according to the rules. But those workers, buried in massive bureaucracies, are hostage to the same political forces as the rest of us. They have little authority of their own, and their good work is often undermined by the abuses of those who do.

The deeper truth is that Washington has become the heart of American political decay. It is a city where a permanent elite holds sway, politicians and their accomplices controlling the money, prestige and power that political supremacy can bring.

There are two groups in our democracy: those who have power, and those who don't. "They" have power, and they have a lock on it. "We" are powerless, partly by default, and we apparently don't care. If we did care, we would use the means available to us to vote the villains out. But half of us don't even vote. The fact is, we have abandoned the principle of accountability that the Founding Fathers laid down as a guiding principle of our democracy.

The average American in the 1980s gives little thought to the philosophy of government we enjoy; for years I never really appreciated the importance of the tenets of democracy. But the straits we are now in make me look back to the efforts made by concerned individuals in another time of American political crisis: the authors of the Constitution.

Wary of an all-powerful state, the Founding Fathers wisely established a government of laws, not men. They were suspicious of centralized, long-held power, and they had no truck with career public "servants." They did everything they could to limit the power that any politician or government bureaucracy could exercise over the American people.

For fights within the government—say, a battle between the executive and the legislative branches over particular functions—the Founding Fathers devised a separation of powers and a system of checks and balances that still holds today. And for the never-ending battle between "us" and "them," the people and the politicians, they built in democratic elections as the ultimate accountability.

In the early days of this country, politicians were on a short leash. When election day came around, the people could yank power-hungry politicians out of Washington before they became entrenched. But in contemporary politics that leash has stretched and weakened, and the natural suspicion that most of us feel about politicians is only getting worse. We feel powerless and betrayed.

THE POLITICS OF DISTRUST

As long ago as 1869, Mark Twain wrote, "I always did hate politics." A century later, John Wayne, in his crusty seventies, summed up the feelings of many Americans when he told a reporter:

> I hate politics. I regard it as a necessary evil, a citizen's responsibility. There's no way, even if you went back to the days of the Inquisition, that you could get me to run for political office. Politics in the old days was fun. But now it's become an awesome monster and is apt to ruin the country. Politicians don't do what's good for the country. They do what helps them get elected. I just can't get enthused about politics anymore. I've got to keep making a living.

Wayne's words sound very much like the criticisms that another old actor, Ronald Reagan, used to make of politics. But is it politics we find so ugly or is it the *politicians* we really can't stand? We like "politics" when it enables us to fight for and achieve the policies we believe in or when it delivers the benefits we need—that government check in the mail, for example. We despise the "politicians" for the things they get away with, their blatant self-interest and the perks they enjoy at our expense.

It didn't surprise me to find out that Americans have always looked down on politicians, for the same reasons we do today. Mark Twain zeroed in on the target, saying he was "disgusted with the prevailing political methods, the low ambitions and ideals, of the politicians; dishonesty in office; corruption, and frank distribution of appointments among characterless and incompetent men as pay for party service; the evasion and sometimes straight-out violation of the civil-service laws...."

Twain might just as well be writing today. The corruption may not be as blatant—the subtle perks of power have replaced the brown envelope stuffed with cash—but we have always had incompetent and corrupt politicians. Now we just can't seem to get rid of them.

ELECTED FOR LIFE—OR LONGER

There is nothing wrong with our democratic institutions; there is something wrong with the people within them. The key feature of contemporary politics is something we have never had before in America: a class of *Lifetime Politicians*. Once they get into office, it is nearly impossible to remove them.

The problem is most obvious in our biggest political fraternity, the U.S. House of Representatives. From 1956 to 1980, incumbents in the House who sought reelection held their seats 92 percent of the time. In the 1982 elections, the percentage of incumbents returned to Congress was 95 percent. In other words, only 5 percent of incumbent Representatives actually lost their jobs to an opponent.

In the House elections in 1986, that high return rose to *98 percent*. Out of 435 total incumbents, 393 ran for reelection (the rest had either died or were retiring). Only 8 of 393 went down to defeat.

Let those numbers sink in. In 1986—with all the ills in the economy, our foreign policy debacles, social dislocations—only 2 percent of the incumbents lost re-election. We re-elected the same clowns whose hands were on the rudder as our ship listed toward the shoals! That's not accountability. *That* is the scandal inside the Beltway!

As I sat down to write this book, 1988 was shaping up to be a repeat story. The *Wall Street Journal* reported in April 1988 that in 78 percent of the nation's congressional districts, the incumbent was either unopposed or faced token opposition for the fall.

ONCE UPON A TIME IN AMERICA...

It wasn't always this way. I repeat: *IT WASN'T ALWAYS THIS WAY*. Modern pols are engaged in a careerist pattern which would have been viewed as very peculiar, even un-American, in earlier days. From the start of the Republic right through the 19th century, most Representatives served only *one* term. Turnover at each election averaged around 45 percent, often ranging up to 60 percent. When our great-grandfathers said, "Throw the rascals out," they did it.

Did you know that, before the turn of this century, only a handful of men had made a career of Congress, and they were often ridiculed? The founders intended our system to work that way, with average citizens taking their turns serving in Congress, then returning to their real jobs. In the 19th century, Congress was a part-time body.

Once Upon a Time in Italy

In the early days of the century, before Mussolini's fascism came to town, Milan ran its municipal government by lottery. That's right, city leaders were chosen randomly from the population at large, to serve for a year or two. The jobs they left were guaranteed at the end of their service. Did they know something we don't?

Two changes occurred in the first half of the 20th century, one in Congress and one in the way we thought of it. First, Representatives grew more and more frustrated at the ability of the Speaker of the House to appoint committee members and chairmen arbitrarily. In the 1800s high turnover meant "seniority" didn't count for much, so Speakers had a free hand with appointments.

In 1911 new and returning members of Congress revolted and took away the Speaker's powers of appointment, instead installing the seniority system. They wanted to feel they had earned their seats on committees, and the change gave them an . incentive to run for reelection...and keep running.

The other change came a few decades later, in response to the societal upheavals of the 1930s and 1940s. The New Deal era was a trying time for the country. People everywhere felt overwhelmed by the enormity of the Great Depression, and then by the dark days of World War II. Americans needed to rely on Washington's ability to handle our problems, and they wanted continuity in government. While they were electing Franklin D. Roosevelt to an unprecedented four terms in office, they began to reelect Senators and Representatives to third terms, fourth terms, fifth terms.

...AND THEY LIVED HAPPILY EVER AFTER

Right now, barely 10 percent of the U.S. House are first-term members. In fact, 385 out of 435 are veterans. The numbers are not much better in the Senate. In 1986, with 34 Senate seats up for grabs, 21 incumbents won reelection while only seven lost. When you add in the winners in states where incumbents had died or retired, the Senate welcomed only 13 new faces that year. (And of course we gave Ronald Reagan another four years in 1984.)

Today's politicians would be bewildered if we forced them out of the halls of the House and Senate into real jobs.

How can we expect fresh and innovative thinking in that kind of system? My local Representative, Don Edwards, is a wonderful guy, but 25 years have passed since he first went to Congress! The Tenth District is now just another safe seat, so safe that the Republicans couldn't even persuade anyone to challenge Edwards (a Democrat) in 1988.

The syndrome reaches down to lower levels, too. *California* magazine reported that in the 1986 election, every single incumbent who ran for reelection to our state legislature was victorious. The magazine concluded, "There's a dirty little secret of congressional politics in California: hardly anyone loses anymore."

What on earth is going on? To hear the politicians tell it, we simply keep endorsing their work. A local incumbent explained to the *San Jose Mercury News* that voters "think we're doing a marvelous job."

But you and I know that's not why they get reelected. Incumbents are simply better at running for office than they are at running the government. I'll show in later chapters exactly how reelection has been made into a sure thing. But I should point out first that you and I share part of the blame.

POLLS APART

I don't mean to get personal, but I'm betting that you didn't vote in the last election. That's a pretty good wager. American voter turnout is a disgrace, and it's getting worse. In 1960, 64 percent of the eligible voters went to the polls. By 1980, barely a majority of eligible American voters cast a ballot. In 1984 the figure was slightly better, but still only around 53 percent (see Figure 1). The weather was fair that day in most of the country; people don't seem to mind participating in democracy if it's sunny outside. Mind you, those were all Presidential election years.

In 1986, admittedly a non-Presidential year, only 37 percent of the eligible electorate even bothered showing up! That is the lowest figure since 1942.

Lifetime Politicians are happy with these numbers, and there is no reason to think the percentages will improve. Our

Figure 1—How many of us are voting?

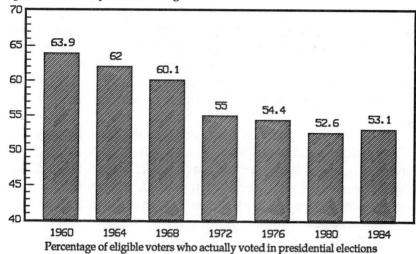

Percentage of eligible voters who actually voted in presidential elections

young people are even less interested in voting than their elders. In 1986 only *17 percent of those eligible under 30 voted.*

Arthur Hadley's book, *The Empty Polling Booth,* reveals that the United States has the worst voter turnout of all the democracies. Sweden, for example, has 88 percent, Britain, 72 percent. We make fun of Italians for their tendency to change their government; they have a national election on average more than once every year, so you would think they would be bored or frustrated with voting. Nope. They get a turnout of better than 90 percent. Even if their politicians don't do a great job when they're in, at least they are punished with removal from office by a responsible voting citizenry.

Hadley found that among Americans who stayed away from the polls, 70 percent said they "felt the act meaningless or they lacked a reason to go to the polls." That doesn't explain why the cycle gets worse and worse, though. The way I see it, this continuing decline is a circular problem:

First, you stop voting because you feel frustrated. You feel your vote doesn't make a difference. Second, the Lifetime Politicians don't feel the need to respond to your frustrations, since you don't vote. Third, as government policies become less reflective of your interests, your frustration and concerns deepen. Fourth, your dissatisfaction and alienation are multiplied. The result? More of us give up on voting.

You might ask what difference it makes to average citizens that they get perpetual incumbents. I'll tell you. Politicians who focus on reelection have little time to deal with issues; great campaigners make lousy leaders. And their experience as incumbents isn't as valuable as they'd like us to believe. In fact, perpetual incumbents see most problems through the lens of their ultimate concern: staying in office. So why do we play into their hands?

I have concluded that there are two big reasons why the Lifetime Politicians have gained such a grip on power. First, we have degenerated into a society that is easily duped. Second, the political system doesn't work as it should, any more than our present-day legal system works as it should. Let's look first at how we have been duped.

CHAPTER 2

★

Media and Mindsets

Think back to the Iran-*contra* hearings of 1987. There was Lieutenant-Colonel Oliver North, the clean Marine and American hero, sanctified by TV. He wore that fine-looking uniform every day. He had an appealing catch in his throat as he protected the flag from the evil Congressmen. Millions of Americans were moved.

But do you remember what he was saying? The substance of his testimony was about lying to Congress and the public, skimming public funds off arms sales to a terrorist nation. Nevertheless, the American people ate it up. There he was, riding high in the polls. Why?

Here's a clue to the answer. Some polls showed that those who listened to him on the radio were not as favorably impressed as those who watched on TV. Also, only days later, Admiral Poindexter gave virtually the same testimony, often in the same terms, as his junior officer. Yet North caused a sensation, while Poindexter caused snores.

Another clue: According to *New York Times*/CBS News polls, before North testified only 33 percent of Americans favored military aid to the Nicaraguan *contras*. During his TV appearances that figure rose to a majority of the public in some polls. But then, curiously, after the "Ollie Show" was over, support for the *contras* slid back to the 33 percent level.

The only conclusion I can make for these gyrations is that we were sucked in by television, by the attractiveness of the images we saw on the screen, rather than by North's argument or reasoning. Oliver North was the epitome of form over substance, and his popularity shows how the American people can be turned into willing sheep by the symbols and images of the mass-tranquilizing media.

Fortunately, he only appeared for two weeks, and his influence was short lived. Presidents and Lifetime Politicians, however, are on our screens every night.

LOW-CAL NEWS: HOMOGENIZED INFORMATION

Did you ever wonder why most people prefer the "fast-food" news that TV and some of the print press feed them to the more thoughtful and analytical information you get on, say, PBS? Have you ever sat down one night and watched a network-news program (one of the biggies), and then flipped channels to see "The McNeil/Lehrer News Show" on PBS? Why, they're worlds apart! The PBS program has the time and the programming freedom to cover stories in depth, and to present both sides of issues. The hosts provoke genuine debate on important topics, and the viewer is treated to a wealth of news and insight unavailable anywhere else.

But most of us don't watch McNeil/Lehrer, or the other news specials and documentaries on PBS. We don't like it when a channel continually asks for something from us—not our money, but our minds. We resent PBS's demand that we *think* about the news, and we don't want to take the responsibility for national affairs that comes with being informed. We'd rather not know. Most of us sit back and assume the couch-potato position, turning to the channels that leave us alone.

While some media executives often try to blame the public for the degeneration of information into symbols and pap, their argument that "we're only giving people what they want" is only half the story. Nobody forces reporters and editors to do a superficial job. The fact is, the gatekeepers of the media make conscious decisions every day to focus on the trivial or the titillating. Bill Moyers, who worked at CBS but in frustration moved to public broadcasting in 1986, recently described a revealing incident to the *Christian Science Monitor:*

I walked into the fishbowl [control room] for the "CBS Evening News" one afternoon, and they were looking at a feed from overseas. One producer said, "That's not news!" Another producer said, "But it looks like news." The executive producer said, "Then we'll use it!" And they did that night.

Obviously, no one was handcuffing those journalists into such a decision. We are captive to these media gatekeepers and their decisions on what will be declared "news" on a given evening. Today, it's expensive to make the effort to stay well informed. The expense is in terms of time and attention. The average person doesn't want to spend a lot of time watching or reading the often boring details about complex issues and events, even though that is the only way to stay truly informed.

They take their news in small doses, so it won't interfere with the mind-numbing nonsense that passes for entertainment on prime-time TV. Newspapers and television are only too happy to oblige, since it is cheaper to report the public antics of a Gary Hart than to produce a hard-hitting investigation of our public finances.

As a result, important issues are ignored. In December 1987, NBC received many calls complaining that Tom Brokaw's historic interview with Mikhail Gorbachev, on the eve of the Washington summit, had preempted "Alf." I can't believe how low the level of television fare has sunk! An informative PBS piece doesn't stand a chance against ABC's "Hooperman," which features a farting dog. A farting dog!

The media do provide some hard news, but for most people the primary concern each day is keeping their heads above water. They are working so hard to get food on the table that they can't be expected to make a real effort to be informed. So what do we end up with? The 20-minute newscast, with 20-second stories:

"The deficit grew bigger today, and Wall Street took a dive. Now over to you, Chuck!" "Thanks, Suzanne. Hey, what a day it was in Washington, nuclear warheads raining all around. What's that going to mean for the weather, Biff?" "Whoa, not so good—film at eleven."

It is a fact of life that people quickly tire of bad news, so we receive an onslaught of tranquilizing messages. The American mind is bombarded by a multiplicity of commercial signals, suggesting what to eat, what to drive, what to wear—but *not* what to know about politics and the issues of the day. Commercials are big business, of course. Thirty seconds on "The Cosby Show" in the 1987-88 season sold for $410,000!

Successful advertising panders to our yearnings for the ingredients of the good life: security, prosperity, sexual allure and fulfillment, the aura of success and higher social status. These messages radiate happiness and a "feel-good" mindset. And they have to be getting through; the television set, the "dope of the masses," stays on seven hours a day in the average American household.

It's not only TV, of course. Newspapers share the responsibility for the decline in public awareness of important issues. *USA Today* is a fine paper, in its way, but I don't feel comfortable with the fact that thousands of Americans may be using it as their only source of information about politics, national affairs and world issues. Its news is dished out in nugget-sized "factoids" rather than in depth, so the larger context is missing. There's an informal policy at *USA Today* which many staffers call the "Peter Meter": a story can't be longer than six inches.

The media (press and television) consider themselves watchdogs over government, and of course they do, from time to time, uncover scandals and inform the public. In fact, it is hard to imagine what this country would be like without the watchdog press. Thomas Jefferson once said that he would much prefer a press without a government to a government without a press.

I realize that I have been painting with a very broad brush here, and I want to acknowledge the fine investigative reporting and astute analysis provided by some newspapers, magazines and broadcasters. What does disturb me, however, is that the mainstream media—the major metropolitan papers, and the three major networks—all too often cave in on their job of watchdog.

NEWSHOUNDS OR LAPDOGS?

To hear politicians tell it, the press is a vicious pack of attack dogs, sniffing out any damaging story however trivial or beside the point. That cry comes from both liberals and conservatives; the Carter administration used to complain just as bitterly as the Reagan administration about media bias.

But my criticism of the media is more fundamental than political bias. I believe the media functions as *part* of the power elite I cited previously. I said there is an "us" and a "them." Mainstream media belongs to the "them" side—and "themness" transcends normal political labels.

The tendency of the media to side with the powers-that-be stems in part from their ownership structure. Many fine studies have been published pointing out the corporate character of the *New York Times*, the *Washington Post*, CBS and so on. Ben Bagdikian, dean of the journalism school at the University of California at Berkeley, showed in his book, *The Media Monopoly*, that in 1981 only 46 companies controlled a majority of the nation's information media: TV, newspapers, magazines, book publishing and movies. By 1986, that number had fallen to 29. The urge to merge for market control is rampant in American business as a whole, but nowhere is it more dangerous than in the media. It's not so critical that Coke and Pepsi dominate the supermarket shelf-space, but we can't let a few corporations dominate our mind-space.

When an information medium is dominated by a corporate mindset, certain things, like bottom-line profits, become more important than others, like the caliber of the reporting. We only have to look at what happened after 1982, when the Federal Communications Commission (FCC) abolished the rule requiring new owners of TV stations to hold on to them for three years. The rule was designed to ensure that owners had some stake in the station as a provider of information. When this piece of deregulation went into effect, the profit instincts of station owners surfaced immediately. By 1986, half of the nation's TV and radio stations had changed hands. So we end up with huge chains like Knight-Ridder, which owns 30 newspapers, eight TV stations and assorted cable systems, or Gannett, which publishes 129 newspapers and operates eight TV and 15 radio stations.

Ever wonder why journalists like Dan Rather, Tom Brokaw and Sam Donaldson are celebrities, earning million-dollar salaries and attracting media attention themselves? When ABC's "Nightline" does a story about Dan Rather, we get to watch the media covering the media covering the.... Such royal treatment can influence the way they do their jobs. They become insiders, while we, the audience, remain outsiders.

George Will, the syndicated columnist, was particularly annoying in his almost sycophantic attitude toward President Reagan. Among his media peers, he made no secret that he "lunched" regularly with Nancy Reagan at swanky Washington restaurants, and that he was a frequent guest at the Reagan White House. But he didn't feel it necessary to make these connections plain when he appeared on "Nightline" or "This Week with David Brinkley." He passes himself off there as just another objective, journalistic observer.

Will's Washington media colleagues may have known that he coached Reagan in his warm-up for the 1980 campaign debates with President Carter. But the television public didn't know that when they saw him on television later, rendering the opinion that Reagan had "won" a debate. With cozy relationships like those, it's no wonder Reagan was called "the Teflon President." He might have attracted criticism, but there were always members of the media ready to scrub him clean with electronic Brillo pads!

MOMMY, WHERE DOES TEFLON COME FROM?

Many liberals accused the networks of being soft on Ronald Reagan, but the truth is more subtle. It wasn't fear of political retaliation that made the media gutless during the Reagan era. More important was the fact that the network news organizations had never before dealt with a political character like Ronald Reagan, who proved so personally appealing to the public. Remember, for most people politicians are slimy creatures. In the first four years of the Reagan presidency, members of the media were astounded by his ability to retain high levels of public support while his policies were under sharp attack.

As a result, criticism of the President was muted even though those early years were marked by unbalanced federal budgets and a sharp rise in government borrowing, two "evils" that candidate Reagan had pledged to eliminate. In a comment echoed by other reporters, George Skelton, the White House correspondent for the *Los Angeles Times*, explained, "I used to spend a lot of time writing those stories, but I just gave up. You write the stories once, twice, and you get a lot of mail saying, 'You're picking on the guy'.... And editors respond to that, so after a while the stories didn't run anymore. We were intimidated."

Most segments of the mainstream media have abdicated any responsibility for providing the crucial coverage we really need on our political candidates. The media focus is not on qualification but on nomination; reporters love to pass on the horse-race aspects of campaigns. As soon as 1984 was over, the media starting reporting on the 1988 Presidential race without giving people what they really needed to know—not who's ahead, but who's *good*.

PRISONERS OF OUR OWN MINDSETS

We have the idea in American politics that people come in only two flavors: liberal and conservative. I think we need to examine whether this is as natural and inevitable as it seems.

For decades, academics in sociology and political science have studied what determines political mindsets, without arriving at any clear answers. The best they can do is point to a complex of factors with some influence on the philosophical and ideological makeup of the individual. Family background is known to be important—your upbringing, the traditional ways of thinking in your family. On the other hand, it's not uncommon for a child to rebel and think along directly opposite lines from a parent. I know lots of former hippies whose kids are like the character Alex Keaton on the TV show, "Family Ties"—little Republican stockbrokers. Education is also influential, although it often seems to reinforce opinions rather than open new vistas.

The more I began to think about politics in preparation for this book, and to discuss current issues with friends, the more I noticed that people seem to acquire information according to predisposition. Two intelligent people can read the exact same story—say, the 241 Marines killed in the 1983 Beirut barracks bombing—and each will interpret it differently. Even when given the *exact same information*, each mind will filter and bend it to make the lessons fit preconceptions.

For example, a conservative would say this about the Beirut bombing: "Well, that was too bad. The commanders in the field must have screwed up with the security barriers. But, dammit, that's why we sent the Marines instead of the Peace Corps.

Marines are trained to die." (I actually heard someone say this.) Then the conservative would demand that steps be taken so that it doesn't happen again.

A liberal's reaction seems more emotional—shock, horror, anguish, anger. The focus would be on the human toll among the soldiers, not on their identities as tough Marines. The lesson learned would be to examine the rationale for putting troops in such a vulnerable, unprotected position.

Now, I'll admit that my portrayals are a bit stereotyped. So let's try to examine the mindsets objectively. Conservative minds have innate respect for authority. Once a decision is made, they stick by it. Conservatives stress constancy of principle. They have difficulty changing their minds for fear that they will look weak and vacillating. Also, given their respect for strength and authority, any mishap can't be the authority figure's fault, because might makes right. Therefore conservatives often seem to search for some other cause, either a lower-level scapegoat or preferably some outside agent (in the Beirut case the Libyans, the Iranians, or better yet, the Russians).

The liberal's ties to tenets are less rigid. He or she feels a need to question authority, to reexamine first principles. This is not necessarily good, you understand; such uncertainty can lead to vacillation and to compromises of both policy and purpose. Also, there is a tendency among liberals to be bleeding hearts, to throw money at problems and to seek utopian solutions, always finding fault with the real-world efforts of earthly authorities.

Conservatives and liberals prefer to stay within their narrow bands of thinking. When we say that a conservative is for the status quo, or a liberal for change, we are really identifying basic differences between human beings—like the basic difference among people in how much they like to take risks in life. Is someone likely to take a risk, given the opportunity of greater gain in the future? Or is he or she willing only to keep what is comfortable, what is already held? That difference is very close to different political and ideological mindsets, and it is not new. John Adams, a cynical old "realist," wrote in a letter to that old idealist Thomas Jefferson, "Your taste is judicious in liking better the dreams of the future than the history of the past."

There's nothing wrong, of course, with diversity. It's one of the great strengths of our country. And whether those differences are God-given or have their roots in childhood trauma or other causes, really doesn't matter. All sorts of factors are surely involved.

The problem comes when people are so locked into their ideological mindsets that they don't hear what the other person is saying. For a democratic society, where we supposedly rely on popular decisions made after calm and thoughtful reflection, that can be disastrous.

ALL ALONE IN THE COMFORT ZONE

Most people never stray from their Comfort Zones. People find safety in the certainty that a mindset, conservative or liberal, gives them in struggling with the floods of information our society produces. The individual strains incoming information through a mental colander, protecting long-held beliefs and preconceptions by screening out conflicting data—what psychologists call "cognitive dissonance."

Without such a filtering process, a lot of us would be overwhelmed by the crush of facts, often contradictory and confusing, that besiege the mind in the media age. In extreme cases, the Comfort Zone is so small that a person can be a self-made "know-nothing," refusing to be bothered by any facts and resting secure in unchallenged biases and preconceptions. (I think a lot of people become more know-nothing as they get older.) Filtering is a self-protective process, needed to prevent restless days and nights of paranoid anxiety about the murky and mysterious ways of the world. Most of us don't even realize that we are wrapped in a Comfort Zone, because it's so darn enjoyable to be certain about things.

But the downside is that the filtering process diminishes our ability to distinguish what is true and what is false, to discern the real outlines of political reality and to visualize creative solutions. Our refusal to build and maintain a background of knowledge sufficiently deep on both sides of an issue sabotages our ability to make informed judgments. A Comfort Zone society does not expose itself to different points of view. Any American would have to admit that we are not well read as a society. Even worse, though, is not the amount we read, but the narrow spectrum of material with which we are content. Before I started thinking about this book, I dabbled in a lot of reading, but I never deliberately set out to expose myself to different viewpoints. I just kept an open mind.

Liberals subscribe to magazines like *Nation*, *New Republic* and *Washington Monthly*. Conservatives subscribe to magazines like *Commentary*, *American Spectator* and *National Review*. Very rarely, though, will one person read magazines from both camps. (Most Americans never read *any* of these magazines, but that doesn't mean they are not captive to their own deep-seated prejudices.)

The only way to escape rigid ideologies is to make an effort to read and listen to people with whom you disagree. Because we don't make that effort, we hold ourselves captive, and doom our minds to the narrow bounds of prejudice.

The political consequences of our rigid mindsets ensure that we do not enjoy a healthy discussion of issues. Opponents end up talking right past each other. A conservative like James Watt, Reagan's first Secretary of the Interior, can say to a group of voters, "I never use the words Republicans and Democrats. It's liberals and Americans." A liberal like Tip O'Neill can say of Ronald Reagan that, when it came to compassion, he had "ice water for blood." Hey, I may think that Comfort Zones are bad, but politicians sure seem to like them. They love to stroke our Comfort Zones. That sways public opinion, and eventually it sways our votes.

If you want to test for the presence of these "filter-out-what-I-don't-want-to-hear" mind processes, simply bring up the Soviet Union in a discussion. And then listen to the responses. Liberals almost always favor a soft line, conservatives a hard one. No matter what may have happened recently in the Soviet Union, I'll bet that you will find people responding from their gut as if there was no difference between Joseph Stalin and Mikhail Gorbachev (for conservatives), or Gorbachev and JFK (for liberals). We all rest safe within our mindsets and the automatic responses they trigger. We don't listen to incoming information—we reduce it to symbols we're comfortable with, familiar heroes or villains. Unfortunately, this is not just a matter or personal failings or character flaws. It enables ideologues and demagogues to treat us like sheep, to their great profit. We're not all walking zombies. But I think we have to recognize that political discourse has changed, for the worse, in this century.

People who are willing to think and explore, in an open-minded way, avoid political involvement. They disdain the narrow vision of those who claim to have "all the answers." I've been like that for 20 years, deliberately giving up my right as a citizen to have my say in politics, simply because I was so fed up. At the same time, others with minds locked into their Comfort Zones are incapable of engaging in the kind of argument and debate that a healthy democracy requires. The result: pervasive apathy and nonparticipation—a tranquilized democracy.

Finally, I woke up. And when I first began to ask people my original questions about politics, they would always respond, "Well, the academics say...." So I looked to members of academia for answers. They should be an independent group of "experts" who will give us straight answers. Now I'm not sure that I trust their judgments either. You'll see why in the next chapter.

C H A P T E R   3

★

The Moat Around the Ivory Tower

I live in Woodside, a small town near San Francisco, and from a balcony of our house you can look down Sand Hill Road and see the spire of Stanford University's Hoover Tower. Living so close to a beautiful campus, I have had some contact with the highly regarded university. In 1969, one of my companies built a campus housing complex, which still houses some 350 students. And since Stanford is one of the Bay Area's prime tourist attractions, I like to play tour guide for visiting friends who haven't seen the university's impressive Spanish-modern architecture.

But when you talk about intellectual contact between most of us locals and Stanford academics, the university might as well be on Mars. Stanford, like our other great institutions of higher learning, fails to provide answers to our political and social problems. The "political science" approach within the ivy walls separates our best and brightest minds further and further from reality, just when we need them most.

I first learned about the moat around the ivory tower from the doctoral students who helped with my original research for this book. I discovered that two strong forces are fueling this academic isolation. The first is specialization, and the second might be called scientification. One examines politics through historical research and case studies; the other focuses on theories and tries to uncover "eternal" political patterns. Each helps to undermine the relevance of political science to those of us in the real world.

HOW MANY ANGELS CAN DANCE IN BOTSWANA?

Specialization is rampant throughout academia. Young graduate students are taught that to be successful in an academic career they should concentrate on a field or subfield sparsely populated by others—the easier to make a name for themselves. As professors, many write articles or books on subjects so obscure that the average reader—even the average academic reader—can only wonder at their meaning and significance.

Some examples: at the 1987 annual convention of the American Political Science Association (APSA) in Chicago, a professor from the University of Illinois presented a paper on "Vector Autoregression Modeling of the Macro-Political Economy," while a University of Minnesota scholar wowed the crowd with a paper titled, "The North-South Conflict and the Fetishism of Sovereignty: Towards a Critical-Structural Theory of International Politics."

You would think that such narrow concentrations would mean less tension among colleagues, but the reverse is true. There's an old saying among academics that the less important an issue, the more vicious the academic infighting. Nothing is less important than some of the "current debates" in ivory-tower political science. Rivalries and factions are sometimes so intense that specialists in a particular subfield aren't even on speaking terms with one another.

The dynamics of the academic profession push scholars toward ever more exotic topics. To keep an academic career alive, a university professor has to gain tenure (guaranteed job security) by publishing books and articles that are well received by his or her peers—people who already have tenure. The more specialized your particular field, the fewer outside experts you need to please—and the harder it becomes for anyone who doesn't share your expertise to criticize your work. Scholars therefore narrow their focus until they are in a very tight group, studying not just the Third World, but Africa; not just Africa, but Botswana...and not just Botswana, but civil-military relations and differential political elite socialization in Botswana's northeast region.

Whether you're a graduate student with a dissertation on that subject, or an established professor well along in your career, you feel secure in the knowledge that only 50 people in the United States (or even in Botswana) will know what you're talking about. To the world at large, you have little to prove – and little to say. This rarefied atmosphere makes academia a very comfortable club despite the rivalries, a sweet life of conferences, travel (often abroad), sporadic office hours, and little hard work.

All the pressures within the ivory tower's cloistered environment encourage the academic to choose intense specialization, rather than rewarding him or her for work that is understandable and useful to the outside world. Policy-makers in the real world get little help from these reservoirs of intellectual power.

THE DRAWBRIDGE TO THE TOWER

Scientification is the second force alienating academic political science from real world politics. The problem is indicated by the name itself: is the study of politics really a "science?" Can it be a systematic investigation according to established rules, with logical theories, experimentation and the testing of hard evidence? Or is it instead a "soft science," like psychology or sociology, with lots of intuition, opinion and trial and error? Maybe political science is really no science at all.

More than 2000 years ago Aristotle was the first thinker to discuss a "science of politics," yet for centuries most scholars avoided a scientific approach. Instead, they were interested in immediate answers to political issues of the day: who would rule, how much money should be spent and what laws should be passed to govern society. Machiavelli wrote *The Prince* in the 16th century as a handbook for Italian rulers, and the images he used to describe politics were not of science but of real-life struggles.

In the last years of the 19th century, however, many American academics began to divorce the study of politics from the practice of politics by making their work more objective, deductive and "scientific." Never mind that issues in politics too frequently come down to value judgments. Scholars liked the status accorded the scientist in society, and took their lead from

German "social scientists," who were rapidly gaining prestige in European intellectual circles.

Colleges and universities went along with the trend. In the early 20th century many college and university departments changed their names from "Department of Government" or "Department of Politics," to "Department of Political Science." The American Political Science Association was formed shortly after the turn of the century, accelerating efforts to impose scientific standards and exactitude.

Today, many political scientists are more statisticians than students of politics. They spend their time, and their foundation grant money, searching for things like "deductive models and axiomatic governance principles." (That's something I won't even try to explain!) They stress quantitative methods—the use of numbers and advanced statistical techniques to "prove" political theories. Most political science graduate schools now require students to use powerful computers to solve complex equations.

In the traditional sciences, like physics and chemistry, many scholars have been disturbed by this trend and criticize this use of quantitative methods to cloak what are really opinions. In 1987, the National Academy of Sciences voted to deny membership to Harvard Professor Samuel Huntington, then President of the APSA. While Huntington is one of the most influential political scientists alive, his work came under intense attack from "hard" scientists for Huntington's claims to use scientific standards when writing about democracy, foreign policy and American politics.

Many political scientists go even further than Huntington in using statistics, calculus and computer programs in their work. Visit your local library, and look at a recent copy of the *American Political Science Review* (the top journal in the field, published by the APSA). I defy any layman to read through an entire article without becoming lost in the forest of statistical equations and computer jargon. You will think you're reading from Albert Einstein's lab notebooks.

One article published in the March 1987 issue, "The Institutional Foundations of Committee Power" by Kenneth Shepsle of Harvard and Barry Weingast of Stanford, examined congressional committees, a very important topic. The authors began with the statement, "We seek to explain why committees are powerful." Fair enough. After reading their article, I'm still not sure if they succeeded. I got lost in their jungle of "agents"—members of Congress—operating in each committee's "dimensional subspace." Under "General Framework," they wrote:

> The legislature consists of n *agents* ($N = \{1,...,n\}$), each possessing well-defined preferences (continuous and strictly quasiconvex) over the points of an m-dimensional Euclidean space....For any $x \in X$, agent i's *preferred-to set* is defined as $P_i(x) = \{x' \in X \mid x' \cdot >_i x\}$, where $\cdot >_i$ is i's preference...."

This wasn't just some wacko-fringe article. It was a very influential piece—but only within academia.

Where's the Politics in Political Science?

I don't think the average member of Congress would learn anything from reading in the *American Political Science Review* that, according to Kenneth Shepsle and Barry Weingast, "House majorities constrain changes in x°. Likewise, in the Senate $W_{S(x)}$ is a constraint set. To pass, therefore, the conference outcome [a legislative bill] must be an element of $F_{(x)} = W_{H(x)} \cap W_{S(x)}$."

Does such research by our best Harvard and Stanford scholars really help the average Congressman or voter to find solutions to pressing real life political dilemmas? Is that even what they want to do? What do you think?

Today's academics are too hung up on how neat their equations are, how cryptic their vocabulary has become and how far above the gutter of real politics they have risen. Those political science or economic Ph.D.'s who feel differently end up leaving for the real world of business, law or public affairs.

It took an intellectual outside the ivory tower, Richard K. Betts of the Brookings Institution, to ask of his colleagues in a paper delivered at ASPA's 1987 convention, "Does Academic Research Have Influence in the Policy Community?" His answer had a large helping of wishful thinking, but expressed real disappointment in how little attention policy-makers pay to current academic debates. No wonder—the ivory tower has willfully built an almost impenetrable moat swimming with jargon and disdain for the critical problems of our day.

Only rarely is a drawbridge lowered to span that moat. John F. Kennedy, a Harvard graduate, was able to attract top academics to government service, almost relocating Harvard to Washington. But the experience of Vietnam scarred them and ended the brain-drain from academia, and soon they were back in their libraries.

We, the people, are left without an independent body of expertise to rely on for advice and intellectual leadership in the vital areas of politics and government. And so our uninformed preconceptions and flawed thinking harden unchecked into the mindsets that hold us captive.

Without intellectual stimulation and guidance we are vulnerable to manipulation by politicians. Slick candidates know how to lay you right down in your Comfort Zone, tuck you in and lull you to sleep. And it is the votes of the slumberers, either uncast or cast by prejudice rather than knowledge, that let them stay in permanent power.

In the next chapter, I want to focus directly on the political elite, identifying them for who they are and how they operate. Let's meet the people who hold us captive.

C H A P T E R   4

*

The Seven Political Tribes

When I was younger, I shared the common perception of our political leaders as demi-gods, people who were called to rule over us by their superior merits.

Then I met some of them.

I remember the first time I met a President of the United States. It was just a fluke, really, but very thrilling for a young kid of 22. In December 1952 I was in the Army, stationed at Fort Gordon in Georgia, when I heard that President-elect Eisenhower was going to be visiting the state and playing golf at the Augusta National nearby. Not wanting to miss this opportunity to catch a glimpse of the great war hero and now Commander-in-Chief, a buddy and I piled into my old Studebaker and took off.

We found the golf club surrounded by fences, Secret Service agents and 7-foot-tall Georgia Highway Patrol officers. Unfazed, I drove slowly until I noticed an unguarded dirt road ending at a fairway near a green. We boldly parked by a tree and wandered onto the fairway.

Wouldn't you know it, it turned out to be the first hole, and Ike was approaching the green with his playing partner. Before we could think of what to do, we saw two Secret Servicemen heading for us, their rifles poking up from golf bags slung preposterously on their shoulders.

I suppose they understood that these two kids in uniform just wanted to get a good look at the great Eisenhower, and one told us that we could "wait until the General putts out" before we had to scram. Just at that moment, though, Ike looked our way. The politician in him must have taken over, or maybe he was just curious how two young second lieutenants could be on an exclusive course that was closed even to members. He walked over and stuck out his hand.

A few minutes chatting with Dwight Eisenhower was not exactly an intellectual experience, but the overall episode was memorable. Having penetrated the buffers around our political elite, the man at the top suddenly seemed much less imposing. Over the course of 30 years, I've met five of the last seven Presidents, dozens of Senators and members of Congress and countless state and local officials. I've worked with some of them, and (the age-old story) my wealth has given me access to others. I even talked with a few while writing this book. But I have some bad news.

They know no more than the rest of us about our problems. They may have more factual information available to them, but they're no less confused than we are about solutions. So how come they are the "elite"? To learn how the political tribes hold their turfs, we first have to know exactly who they are.

We really have two sets of political leaders—those we elect and those we don't. I'll look at each set in turn. First, our elected officials, who fit into three major categories.

THE FIRST TRIBE: LAWYERS

The most popular notion about politicians is that they're all lawyers. People think that for a reason: roughly half those we elect are attorneys or have law degrees. How better to maintain and even expand their powerful role in society than by electing their own kind to Congress? There is a simplistic assumption that law schools turn out better legislators because their job is to write laws. I feel that Congress needs less legalistic thinking and more common sense.

In the 1987-1988 Congress, 188 of the 435 Representatives had law degrees, along with 65 of the 100 Senators. That works out to 253 of the 535 members. One effect of this concentration is an ever-expanding stream of overly complicated legislation, certain to provide work for their brethren and for judges on the outside.

THE SECOND TRIBE: BUSINESSMEN

The next best road to political office is business. It helps to be a small local businessman or businesswoman if you are running for a House seat, or the scion of a prominent big business family if you're running for the Senate. The Senate is loaded with telegenic millionaire clones who have ready access to the kind of money it takes to run a serious campaign these days.

Even the White House attracts its share of corporate types who'd like the title Chief Executive. New York real estate tycoon Donald Trump makes no secret of his interest in running. Bill Farley, the "Fruit of the Loom" underwear king who almost ran for the Senate from Illinois in 1986, thought seriously about running for the Oval Office in 1988. In the fall of 1987 he bombarded Iowa with corporate advertising promoting his name and political views. But he was something of a flake; in 1986 he said he was a Republican, but the very next year he was thinking of running for President as a Democrat—probably because the competition didn't look as stiff.

THE THIRD TRIBE: DYNASTIES

For some clans, politics is the family business. This is nothing new—the Adams family gave us two of our early Presidents. The Lodges, Longs, Roosevelts and Tafts gave us many political leaders in this century. The Rockefellers have produced three Governors since World War II (one of them is now a Senator). And Kennedys from a new generation are already entering the political arena.

In the 1987-1988 Congress you could find 13 sons and two daughters of former Senators or Representatives. 1988 Presidential candidate Albert Gore, Jr., Senator from Tennessee, is the son of (you guessed it) Albert Gore, Sr., former Senator from Tennessee. These are just some of the more striking examples of family tradition; there are plenty more.

Alongside these tribes you'll find some national heroes (Eisenhower, John Glenn), sports figures (Jack Kemp, Jim Bunning and Tom McMillen in the House, Bill Bradley in the Senate), and a few actors (Iowa sent Love Boat's "Gopher" to Congress in 1986). Pretty soon the Congressional Record will read like the National Enquirer.

Actors in Politics

Actors are an interesting political group, if not a full tribe. Not only have we had one in the White House, but our society is so entertainment-oriented that the big and little screens have become our windows on the world. I don't mean to say that famous actors or actresses always make bad politicians. Clint Eastwood, a friend from Carmel, California, is a respectable example. Clint got involved in his own community at the mayoral level instead of taking advantage of his national name recognition. He proved to be a fine mayor. And he exemplified the type of new politician we need—who sees local problems and performs a community service by running for political office. He didn't make a career of it, and after one term he refused to run for reelection.

Not all actors are so exemplary. Charleton Heston toyed with the idea of running for the Senate in California a couple of years ago. Then he held a press conference to announce that he had considered the race seriously, but was taking a role on the TV soap "Hotel" instead—as if the two were equivalent positions in society!

THE ELECTED ELITE: NOT SO DIFFERENT AFTER ALL

I often hear people defending their Representative or Senator as a "good guy." And they're usually right. Gene Holley, a friend of mine in Georgia, was a long-time politician, even serving as the majority leader of the state legislature. He's a wonderful fellow, and has quite a life story, but what always interests me is how convincing he is when he tells me that "politicians are just folk."

The representatives we send to Washington, or to the state capital, are always to some extent "representative" of the communities that elect them. They can exemplify the best and the worst of the American people. A politician might be brilliant, and he might be as much of a horse's ass as my Uncle Jack.

British historian Lord Acton wrote a long time ago that power tends to corrupt, and we know from our own history how on the mark he was. Scandals involving public officials are endemic in American political life. It's impossible to be sure who in politics is honest and who isn't. No one seems above temptation. Mario Biaggi, the Bronx Congressman convicted in 1987 on a

THE SEVEN POLITICAL TRIBES ★ 35

whole variety of corruption charges, had been a career New York City cop before he went to Washington. In fact, in his 23 years on the police force, he was the city's most decorated officer. I'm not going to argue that New York cops are choir boys. I've seen them when they were on strike, and believe me—they can get ugly! But I am inclined to believe that there was something in the nature of his position in Congress that lured Biaggi to start dipping into the till. The permanency of the job is the most disturbing aspect. The longer you are in office, the more corners you might be inclined to cut, and the fewer restraints you feel from your constituents. Why, in 1956 Congressman Thomas Lane (a Massachusetts Democrat) spent four months in jail for evading $38,000 in income taxes—but he was reelected later that fall!

Politicians with skeletons rattling in their closets can count on the Beltway mindset to kick in, ensuring that an exposé of corruption is not carried too far. Each malefactor is scared that another has something on him, and it becomes in everyone's interest to protect the status quo. No one rocks the boat, no one gets hurt. When a Congressman like Biaggi is actually indicted and convicted, the others are reluctant to toss him out and start an anticorruption avalanche.

So those are our elected elite. By giving them our votes, we share in their guilt. Sometimes we're even happy that way. A Louisiana voter, asked about Governor Edwin Edwards by the New York Times, said: "Look, he's a crook, but he's an honest crook."

But there are four more elite tribes in Washington. These unelected tribes don't rely on our direct endorsement to gain and maintain their positions behind the scenes at the center of power. Often we don't even know who they are.

THE FOURTH TRIBE: NATIONAL SECURITY EXPERTS

These individuals are often described as the wise old men of Washington (there are women among them, too). Some are executives for multinational corporations and defense contractors, while many work for the various think-tanks like the Rand Corporation or the Brookings Institution. They are the self-appointed guardians of our foreign and defense policy.

Only the experts, they claim, can understand the mysteries of containment, deterrence and being tough with the Russians. They rest easy in their think-tanks and corporate suites, assured that the President or Congress will call on their expertise.

Henry Kissinger and Zbigniew Brzezinski belong to this elite corps. Each began his career in academia (Harvard and Columbia respectively), moved into the White House as National Security Adviser, and now makes a handsome salary as a quasi-academic "consultant," just waiting for that call back to power.

Meanwhile, from the business world, the best and brightest of the Bechtel Corporation—George Shultz and Cap Weinberger—came to Washington to run Reagan's foreign and military policies.

Sometimes these "experts" rise through military ranks, and we later see them shuttling between the Pentagon and "Beltway Bandit" consulting firms. Richard Secord of Iran-*contra* fame was a promising young whiz in these circles before he got caught in the tar pit, having traded on his Air Force credentials to turn a buck.

Like many in this elite tribe, Secord exhibited a real contempt for the American public and for our constitutional provisions for the open handling of foreign policy matters. As a midlevel military officer, Secord had written a master's thesis on "covert operations," arguing that opposition to such escapades from the "press, Congress, academia and others...should be dismissed out of hand" by the military and the White House.

Of course, we know where those beliefs led him (and us). But that logic represents the behind-closed-doors attitude that the "experts" use to keep pulling the strings of foreign policy.

THE FIFTH TRIBE: LOBBYISTS

These extremely influential creatures exist for only one purpose: obtaining favorable government decisions for their clients. Lobbyists are full-time professionals who use a mixture of persuasion, coercion, political skill and flat-out pressure to lean on members of Congress, the President and his staff.

Lobbyists have been around as long as legislatures have written laws. They're named after the lobbies of legislative office buildings, where they hang around all day hoping to catch Senators and Representatives on their way to and from votes. The corridor outside the House Ways and Means Committee, for example, is nicknamed "Gucci Gulch" after the dozens of high-paid, well-dressed lobbyists who congregate there, waiting to exert leverage over the Representatives inside who are writing the nation's tax laws.

We need to distinguish between two types of lobbyists. The first group is what we traditionally think of when we hear the word: lobbyists who serve economic interests (corporations, trade associations, unions)—the "Gucci Gulch" crowd. They argue how important their clients are to the economy. In return, they ask favors for their clients with the implicit understanding that these groups control a lot of money, and if members of Congress will go along, they might see some of those funds diverted to their next reelection campaign. Since the rise of political action committees, which we'll discuss in the next chapter, these lobbyists have not had to concentrate so much on passing money directly to politicians. Instead, they rely on good old-fashioned arm-twisting and back-scratching.

FISH WATCHERS, UNITE!

The second type of lobbyist likes to be euphemistically called a representative of a "public interest group." These lobbyists will tell you that they represent the interests of an important sector of American society: let's say, fish watchers. (There is a professional lobbying group for bird-watching, but as far as I know, my example is hypothetical—for now.)

Their primary tactic would be to persuade a Congressman, say, that there are x number of people in his district who enjoy watching fish, and who would enjoy it even more if fish-watching supplies could be made tax deductible. Whether this group's appeal will be successful or not depends on how many fish watchers there may be and whether they are a powerful bloc of organized voters. This is not surprising, since the Congressman's first question will be, "What's in it for me?"

The Constitution guarantees the right of citizens to form groups and press their cause with government. However, the Founding Fathers didn't anticipate that lobbying would become such a huge business in its own right, or that the lure of votes-for-sale would even attract foreign countries seeking American favors.

The problem for good government is that the number of lobbyists in Washington has exploded since the 1970s and is now estimated at almost 25,000. Almost every Fortune 500 corporation and hundreds of trade associations have full-time Washington lobbying staffs. The AFL-CIO has over 200 lobbyists, and most trade unions have busy Washington offices as well.

Many foreign countries have hired American lobbyists, trying to persuade Congress to vote foreign aid funds and preferential trade terms. It should be no surprise that Mike Deaver was accused of having improperly lobbied for foreign countries after he left his White House job.

Deaver had been in the same line of work before going into the White House, his firm pulling in $5,000-a-month as a registered agent for the government of Taiwan. It was only natural that as soon as he left, Deaver would be tempted to use his influence on behalf of foreign powers seeking favors. He quickly signed on to represent the Korean government, which paid him $475,000 to arrange a two-minute ceremonial meeting with President Reagan for a visiting Korean trade official.

Every year, according to Mark Green's book, *Who Runs Congress*, lobbyists spend over $2 billion to influence Congress, the White House and bureaucracies. But the problem isn't only the dollars they scatter around. It's also the success they have interfering with the political process and influencing the tough decisions lawmakers ought to be making. With "gimme, gimme" as their slogan, they press for more and more preferential treatment until incumbents and other officials lose the political will to say no to budget-busting handouts. We can't just blame the politicians. Own lobbyists, yours and mine, keep asking for too much.

THE SIXTH TRIBE: POLITICAL CONSULTANTS

Campaign wizards are the third batch of elitists we don't elect. Every politician has his cadre of political image consultants because only they understand the magic of getting elected. With their surveys and research, they tell their clients precisely what to say and do to win.

Illinois Senator Paul Simon, in campaigning for the Democratic nomination for President in 1988, said: "There have been PR people in every one of my campaigns who have told me, get rid of the horn-rimmed glasses, get rid of the bow ties; and mostly they tell me to get rid of my views on the issues. They want me to change my image." Paul Simon may have told these guys to take a hike, but then again maybe he didn't. His campaign of "I look like a nerd, so I'm natural," could have been a consultant's idea of an anticonsultant campaign.

We know that others took these wizards' advice and changed not only their looks but their stands on issues. "Some candidates just won't listen, they won't do what they are told," Republican polling consultant Vincent Breglio told political scientist Larry Sabato for his book, *The Rise of Political Consultants*. Breglio's irritation made it clear that he and his peers are used to getting what they want—not only control over candidates' images but control over their positions on vital issues.

Just think what present-day consultants could have done with, say, Tom Dewey in 1948, who lost by a nose to Harry Truman. They would have had a field day with Dewey, who was described as looking like the little man on a wedding cake. "Shave the mustache, get rid of the patrician accent, blow dry the slicked-down hair, get a pair of overalls for a commercial aimed at the farm vote." The greatest political upset in American history might never have happened, and "Dewey Defeats Truman" would have been no joke.

The focus on selling the candidate underscores the essential truth about the role of consultants in elections today: they are advertising men. Joe McGinniss's book, *The Selling of the Presidency 1968*, showed how account executives from Madison Avenue's biggest ad agencies swarmed into Richard Nixon's campaign and dictated how he would look, sound... and think.

In some cases, the candidate becomes almost irrelevant to the campaign. Back in 1966, the real George Bush became an inconsequential factor in his first congressional campaign in Texas when his new advertising director, Harry Treleaven, undertook to create and sell a new Bush image. Treleaven was recruited from the huge advertising firm of J. Walter Thompson, and confronted the job the way he had his ad campaigns for RCA and Lark cigarettes. As McGinniss reported, Treleaven devoted three-fourths of the campaign budget to TV commercials, and saw no reason why issues would "have to be involved in the campaign. There was no issue when it came to selling Ford automobiles; there was only the product, the competition and the advertising. He saw no reason why politics should be any different."

We may come to miss the days of the old-time pol, a back-room boy who showed himself to the public, warts and all. Even the crude old system of political patronage, with the spoils of office—jobs, government contracts—going to campaign workers was in some ways more honorable than the advertising-led campaigns of today. Today's slick public relations experts strive to sell the voter an image of a candidate and, just like their Madison Avenue peers, they don't pay a lot of attention to the product. They deal in emotion.

Democrats are just as eager as Republicans to use image doctors. Jimmy Carter may have been the first President to appoint a political media consultant (Gerald Rafshoon) to his top staff in the White House. The track record of one prominent Democratic consultant, Patrick Caddell, shows how the breed is gaining more and more control over the electoral process. Caddell told journalist Edwin Graham, "We are the preselectors. We determine who shall run for office." And Caddell did just that. A pioneer of sophisticated polling for George McGovern in 1972, Caddell was instrumental four years later in helping the unknown Jimmy Carter rise to national prominence. Caddell helped Gary Hart run for President in 1984. Four years later he helped push Joe Biden into the race.

These candidates weren't very reluctant, of course. Each had his own ambitions. But Caddell played a significant role in their decisions and in the formulation of their campaign "messages." It's reassuring that with all his wizardry, Caddell failed to do much for McGovern, Hart or Biden. (Caddell was also a consultant to the Coca-Cola Corporation on their disastrous New Coke advertising campaign).

On the other hand, remember that the opponents in each of those races had wizards of their own. It's the process that has become institutionalized, changing the nature of our political campaigns. Candidates are content to be treated as marionettes.

One thing you'd better watch out for: this tribe is headed for your town. The national consultants have discovered that the big bucks are not really in national Presidential campaigns, but in running dozens of state campaigns for senatorial, congressional, gubernatorial or even local candidates. Ray Strother, a chief in this elite tribe who ran Gary Hart's TV advertising, made over $2 million in 1986 alone by working for Democrats at the state level in Louisiana, Minnesota, Kansas and Connecticut, according to *U.S. News & World Report*. Roger Ailes, a top Republican consultant, worked for candidates in Oklahoma, South Dakota and Washington state among others.

The sixth tribe is pushing out on all frontiers, and we're paying for their expansion. The contribution checks you sent to your candidate helped the top 10 consultants in 1986 gross over $1.5 million *each*.

THE SEVENTH TRIBE: GOVERNMENT BUREAUCRATS

Government bureaucrats form an invisible "old boy network." Naturally, this group is only a small minority of the hundreds of thousands of government employees. But at higher levels within government departments, they exercise perpetual power.

Many enter government "service" at an early age, not out of a desire to serve but because it seems the surest nonelective ladder to the power centers of Washington. Every one of them thinks his or her job is the most important in the capital. You've never seen a power trip as obnoxious as these guys can muster.

Because of their positions and because it is darn near impossible to fire them, these empire builders can be even more insidious than politicians. They have no ties whatsoever to real people (i.e., the electorate). Members of Congress at least have to make a pretense of frugality and concern for the public good in case a constituent is watching.

Some of these "less-than-zerocrats" also keep a sharp eye out for opportunities on the outside of the compound, places where they can use the inside knowledge they have accumulated as bureaucrats. So you see them participate in the "revolving door syndrome," moving into Wall Street, public relations, the defense industry and the "consulting" business.

One example sticks in my craw. Robert Watkins, one of many Reagan administration officials accused of personal greed, was a deputy assistant secretary of commerce. As such, he was a political appointee, but also a bureaucrat. While in office, he negotiated with Japan to protect the American automobile industry.

It turns out he also secretly circulated a resume to Nissan, Honda and Toyota, begging for a lobbyist's job with one of those companies! He told them that he would be an effective lobbyist for their interests, pointing out that he had urged, successfully, that the President not push for voluntary Japanese restraint in auto exports to the United States. Watkins left office under a cloud, but as a Democratic Congresswoman noted, "I can understand now why he was such a weak negotiator."

THE LOST TRIBE

Those seven tribes, and assorted hangers-on, together form the pernicious, parasitic political class that runs our country. The elected and unelected elites all share one fundamental trait: they prosper at our expense. Mark Twain once again scored a bull's-eye when he said, "I think I might have developed into a very capable pickpocket if I had remained in public service a year or two."

Have you noticed that in this list of political tribes there isn't one called "Citizens"? We are outsiders—in a system that is supposed to be a democracy! We need to change the rules of the game. But before we know just what to change, we need to examine today's rules which let the politicians hold their power over the Lost Tribe. The next two chapters examine the two things Lifetime Politicians live on—money and votes.

Keep your hand on your wallet, because right now we're heading into expensive territory: the picking fields of campaign finance.

C H A P T E R   5

★

Money: The Mother's Milk
of Politics

After the recent sex-and-finances scandals involving TV evangelists (they should write a book: "Preachers Do More Than Lay People"), a lot of Americans wondered who could be naive enough to give their hard-earned dollars to such characters. My answer: the same people who are dumb enough to give a single dollar to an incumbent Lifetime Politician.

The late Jesse Unruh, Speaker of the California State Assembly in the 1960s (out here we called him "Big Daddy"), used to say that money was the "mother's milk of politics." Do politicians really "need" to raise huge sums of money to win reelection? William Proxmire, the veteran Wisconsin Senator who stepped down in 1988 after more than 30 years in the Senate, says no. Proxmire argues that the power of incumbency is so overwhelming in campaigns that "I think fully two-thirds of the Senators could get reelected without spending a penny."

Proxmire, to his credit, acted on that belief. After 1974 he took no outside contributions, financing his campaigns from his own pocket. His experience testifies powerfully to the benefits of incumbency. According to *The New York Times*, in 1976 he spent only $177.75 on his reelection, mostly for postage returning contribution checks to would-be donors. In 1982 he only spent $145.10.

A BIGGER BANG FOR A BIGGER BUCK

Not all incumbents are as thrifty—or as honest—as William Prox-mire was on the subject of money. In fact, most use financial over-kill to get reelected. According to the Congressional Research Service, the average cost of winning a seat in the Senate in 1986 was about $3 million, up from $610,000 only 10 years before.

Figure 2—Are congressional elections becoming more lopsided?

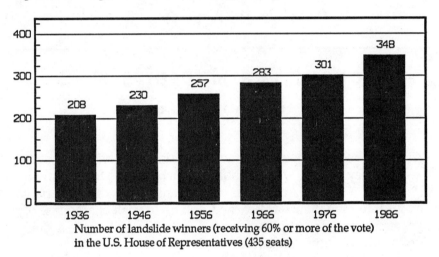

Number of landslide winners (receiving 60% or more of the vote)
in the U.S. House of Representatives (435 seats)

That's a lot of money, but the shocking fact is that it's mostly being spent on one side, by the incumbents. With figures sup-plied by the Federal Election Commission (FEC), I've calculated that in their latest campaigns 119 incumbent U.S. Representatives (almost a third of the total running) spent 10 times as much as their opponents. And nineteen Senators, or almost one in five, outspent their opponents by the same margin. Ten times! That ratio is hardly the mark of a fair race.

North Carolina Senator Jesse Helms holds the dubious dis-tinction of having won the most expensive political race in American history (not including Presidential campaigns). He spent over $16 million in his 1984 reelection campaign. Helms has vowed to raise and spend $20 million in his next race in 1990, "if it's necessary." Helms poured out nearly twice as much money as his opponent last time, and won only 52 percent of the vote. Incumbents don't like races to be that close, so they rev up the fund-raising drive even higher for the next go-round.

As of March 31, 1988, the 27 Senate incumbents who were running for reelection in 1988 had raised a total of $63.4 million, while their main challengers had raised only $15.9 million—incumbents were raking in bucks at a ratio of almost four to one! The biggest money-raiser? My own Senator, Pete Wilson of California, who had raised over $7 million, and that was with seven months left in the campaign.

Good men and women who might otherwise decide to challenge an office-holder don't because the amounts of money necessary keep rising and rising. One of our local city council members in San Jose, Shirley Lewis, began raising funds for her 1988 reelection campaign almost a year in advance, saying, "I'm trying to get enough money in the bank that any potential candidates will look at me and say, 'She's unbeatable.'"

INCUMBENT PROTECTION PLANS

One of the primary advantages of incumbency is that campaign financing rules are set by Congress, and incumbents prefer laws where they come off as an endangered species. The national Democratic Party even has an official "Incumbent Protection Program"—a fund-raising effort—for its members of Congress. (The Republicans have the same thing, but aren't as honest in what they call it.) Election results indicate that the Lifetime Politicians are doing a super job of providing "incumbent protection plans" in the laws governing campaign finances. More and more races are becoming lopsided victories for incumbents (see Figure 2), as qualified challengers are deterred from running by the staggering amounts of money needed to win. The landslides are getting steeper, and so things never change (see Table 1).

Table 1—Current U.S. Representatives in their most recent race
273 (63%) ran unopposed in their primary elections 48 (11%) ran unopposed in the general election 263 (60%) won in the general election with more than 66% of the vote 89 (20%) won in the general election with more than 80% of the vote

In California, I've watched incumbents try to maximize their financial advantage over challengers. Howard Berman, the

Democratic Congressman from Los Angeles County, whipped his Republican opponent in 1984 by using the "big stick" of money. According to the FEC, Berman spent $204,227 to his opponent's measly $6,545. In the 1986 campaign, while his opponent mustered $10,314, Berman spent a whopping $272,956. Over a quarter-million dollars for the incumbent, barely ten thousand for the challenger. A fair fight, wouldn't you say? Berman won—65 to 35 percent.

The bad old days of money in politics meant under-the-table payoffs. Some of you may be too young to remember the infamous "Milk Deal" of 1971 when the dairy lobbies actually "bought" a government decision by contributing tens of thousands of dollars to the Nixon-Agnew reelection campaign and other Republican campaign committees. In return they received the Secretary of Agriculture's assurance that he would raise the price supports on milk, which he did, resulting in consumers paying $500 to $700 million more per year for milk, butter and cheese.

Those days may be over, but now—even with disclosure and above-board contributions as the rule rather than the exception—influence-buying seems to be just as prevalent. Only the method has shifted, from the brown paper envelope stuffed with $20 bills to the perfectly legal campaign contribution by political action committees (PACs).

FACTS ON PACS

The formation of PACs was authorized by Congress in 1974 as the above-ground, legalized way to channel money into politicians' coffers. In the old days, secret contributions and slush funds came from corporations, unions and fat-cat individuals. They went straight into the pockets of politicians, without anyone being able to follow the trail. A corporate executive would take money from the company's till and slip it to a candidate. Union leaders skimmed cash from members' dues and did the same thing.

The 1974 Federal Election Campaign Act, designed to restrict the role of money in politics, set limits on contributions and opened the money trail to public inspection. Here's how it works. A corporation, for example, now has to set up a separate entity, a political action committee with its own officers, to raise funds from employees. The PAC, and not the company's management itself, openly solicits contributions. Employees now know where their PAC money goes. Union PACs operate in the same way. The rules protect a member's right not to contribute any money.

The 1974 reforms were designed to limit the amount of secret money streaming into campaigns. They did that. Money from PACs is publicly counted to the dollar. But the legitimate PACs have proven to be highly fruitful money machines. The money trail still flows—and that trail, while no longer hidden, bears more and more traffic all the time.

The number of PACs mushroomed from 600 in 1974 to 2,800 in 1982, and to more than 3,500 in 1984. At the beginning of 1988, there were more than 4,200! Seventeen percent of all PACs are affiliated with labor unions, but a whopping 68 percent are tied to corporations—around 300 of the Fortune 500 companies have PACs—or trade associations like the National Association of Manufacturers and the U.S. Chamber of Commerce.

Since each PAC is essentially a lobbying organization for its sponsoring body, it focuses on pouring money into the campaigns of candidates who will support the sponsor's cause in Congress. The money comes from within the sponsoring organization—executives and employees of a company, union members, trade association affiliates. In 1986, PACs kicked in almost $140 million to congressional campaigns—almost one-third of all the money candidates raised!

A GOOD POLITICIAN STAYS BOUGHT

PACs aren't concerned with party politics. They are looking for influence and results. They therefore contribute heavily to incumbents, often without regard to party. It's much easier for them to deal with old friends. As Representative John Bryant of Texas admitted in 1983, "Anytime someone, whether a person or a PAC, gives you a large sum of money, you can't help but feel the need to give them extra attention, whether it is access to your time or, subconsciously, the obligation to vote with them."

The result is incumbent Representatives and Senators have been getting a bigger and bigger share of that $140 million, leaving their challengers choking in the dust of inadequately funded campaigns. The imbalance is widening. In the early 1970s about half of all PAC dollars went to incumbents. By 1982 more than two-thirds (68 percent) went to the office-holders. And in 1986, incumbents got 88 percent, meaning that only twelve percent of the $140 million in PAC money went to challengers. The *New York Times* reported that 51 current U.S. Senators have each received at least $1 million from PACs during their congressional careers. (The *Times* called these the "PAC-Men" of the Senate.)

The easiest way to see if PACs are buying the votes of incumbent members of Congress is to look at who gives how much to whom. The public interest group Common Cause has traced PAC money for over a decade, showing how a particular company's PAC will target the congressional committee that oversees its industry—and then flood the committee's members with donations.

For example, in 1986 the political action committees of the top 10 defense contractors gave almost $3 million to candidates, with more than 40 percent going to incumbents sitting on the House and Senate Armed Services committees and Defense Appropriations subcommittees. These are the bodies that decide who'll build what weapons and for how much. Who would believe that those contributions have nothing to do with the decisions then made by the Senators and Representatives who need those dollars to win reelection?

Thanks to a recent anonymous survey of 114 members of Congress (conducted by the Center for Responsive Politics), we've learned that at least 20 percent of them admitted that campaign contributions do compromise the policy-making process.

So, with PACs as the vehicle, the power balance in the United States appears to be shifting, from those with the votes to those with the bucks. A politician is supposed to be responsible to the people who elected him. But with campaigns costing so much money, it's easy to understand why he or she will feel responsible to the funders. Not only have we citizens lost control over our own representatives, we've lost it to behind-the-scenes moneymen. Welcome back to the days of the "back-room bosses"—or more accurately, the "PAC-room bosses."

MUZZLED WATCHDOGS

Most of the figures in this book on campaign funds were gathered with the assistance of the FEC, which does a highly creditable job in collecting and publicizing the money trails of candidates. But the FEC has proven to be a toothless hound when it comes to the other side of its mission: enforcement against violations of existing campaign finance laws.

In his 1984 race for the Democratic nomination, Walter Mondale kept spending in New Hampshire even after he had exceeded the dollar limit for the primary. His staff figured that even if they were caught, winning would make any penalty worthwhile. The state limit was $404,000, but the Mondale campaign spent $2.85 million! Admitting that fact to *Harper's* magazine, Mondale's campaign manager Bob Beckel chuckled that the fine they had to pay was only $400,000: "It wasn't a lot, and that's the whole point. You think George Bush has a wimp problem? The FEC is not one of the great enforcement agencies of modern politics."

But there are even worse signs that our political system is out of whack. Turn to the next chapter and I'll peel back the cover over the biggest scam in American politics. You're about to read the inside story on how Lifetime Politicians capture your vote.

C H A P T E R   6

★

You Can Fool All of the People

Bob Dole thinks I'm a good friend of his. So do Jack Kemp, George Bush and Mike Dukakis. Like you, probably, I got "personal" letters from all of them during the latest campaign, and I was flattered. Bob Dole even sent me a personal and confidential "Presidential Issues Survey," with tough questions like "Does America need a Constitutional amendment to balance the budget so the liberal Congress won't spend more than it can afford?" (Gee, I thought Bob Dole was a member of Congress....)

A survey! Here was my chance to determine the issues for a major Presidential candidate, since Bob's letter said, "I want to know what you think....Frankly, I need your advice." Sure, it asked for money, too. But Dole wanted my opinions, and the official-looking package proclaimed, "Registered in the name of Lee H. Brandenburg, Registration #471962."

Imagine my surprise when I read *The Wall Street Journal* a month later, and saw an article about Presidential fund-raising. The article mentioned the Bob Dole survey as an example, and the reporter even mentioned that his survey carried personal registration #471962. Well, that sounded familiar.

Apathy isn't the only political problem we have. Even when Americans *want* to get involved, we are up against some of the greatest brains in the world—human and electronic.

"HI. I'M NOT A PRESIDENT, BUT I PLAY ONE ON TV."

In the old days, politicians campaigned from the "stump"—literally. They would speak to small groups from a tree stump or small platform, and they were immediately confronted with a popular response. Abraham Lincoln couldn't get away with evading a question or lying, because he would be instantly challenged.

It's different today. Presidents have long used the majesty of the office to set themselves on high, trying to escape criticism. Modern campaign techniques combined with security precautions remove candidates (particularly incumbents) from any personal contact whatsoever with ordinary people. Bob Dole's survey is just one example of the games politicians play with our minds, trying to keep us ignorant and quiet about the true state of affairs.

After he was inaugurated in 1981, Ronald Reagan had little contact with people. His press conferences were few—and he was rarely challenged. No one challenges our leaders directly because no one can get near them.

The media isn't entirely to blame for Reagan's invulnerability, since they were going up against the most powerful public relations juggernaut ever devised in the history of politics. James Reston of the *New York Times* estimates that by the end of the Reagan years, the administration was spending $2 billion a year on public relations activities, using the bulk of the 320-strong White House staff to propagate political messages as they saw fit. The Reagan team of media advisers (members of the Sixth Tribe we saw in Chapter 4) used the same slick, manipulative techniques used in the commercial advertising world and met with huge success.

FEEL-GOODISM MAKES ME FEEL SICK

In 1976 Ronald Reagan was beaten in the Republican Presidential primaries by incumbent Jerry Ford. Ford's advisers devised a campaign theme (even a campaign song) called, "I'm Feeling Good About America." That type of message has long been a theme in political campaigns; the Democrats like to blare the song "Happy Days Are Here Again" over and over at their conventions.

Reagan learned his lesson after 1976, and his consultants went to work fashioning a "feel-good" philosophy for future campaigns. The strategy worked in 1980, but their masterpiece was the "It's Morning Again in America" series of commercials for the Reagan 1984 campaign, which pandered to the emotional desires of viewers. What political message was transmitted in that slogan? None. But a very strong emotional message was conveyed, that you could feel good and leave your troubles behind.

Michael Deaver was the master of the new style. In the White House, each day at 8:15 A.M., he chaired a "line of the day" meeting, followed by a meeting with the President's communications and public relations staff. The agenda was simple: what are we going to do today to enhance the image of the President? And, what do we want the press to cover today, and how do we want it packaged?

As the architect of the Reagan campaign, Deaver concentrated on media events, especially large campaign rallies designed to provide television with sweeping shots of large, happy, partisan crowds and thousands of red, white and blue balloons, to give an image of Reagan associated with a hopeful American future—"America Standing Tall." Real voters were kept a safe distance from the candidate. Deaver simply found the buttons that had to be pushed and pushed them, day after day. The press corps and TV crews following Reagan on the campaign trail became a personal political entourage and publicity machine, since actual contact between reporters and the candidate was kept to a minimum.

The Reagan team's sophisticated strategy worked miracles. The dark problems of the night (an enormous deficit for example) magically disappeared with a new dawn. Have a nice day!

The feel-good genre of political advertising is extremely dangerous, and I'm disturbed that so many of us are taken in by it. But it's just a political extension of the thousands of TV ads assaulting the minds of America. What would happen if a fascist or communist extremist showed the same skill and ingenuity in using the media as mainstream candidates now show? When one politician succeeds, you know others won't be far behind. In 1988 a number of mainstream candidates tried to create their own Teflon. Gary Hart's reborn campaign may have been the most clever attempt to do so. Hart forced the media to cover his attacks on the media, trying to make them the issue—not Gary Hart.

Technology has also helped politicians devise new ways to get votes from otherwise free-thinking individuals. Two innovations—the TelePrompTer and the computer—have proven remarkably effective at fund-raising and vote-getting while actually reducing a candidate's contact with the public.

SEEING IS BELIEVING, BUT READING IS MISLEADING

One political insider tells me that, in her opinion, the most important technological advance in the realm of campaign politics in the past 20 years is a device that most people don't even know exists—the see-through TelePrompTer. This device deserves a lot of credit for Ronald Reagan's status as the "great communicator."

TelePrompTer is a trade name for a machine that projects written material onto a transparent screen. It enables a speaker to read while appearing to speak directly to an audience or to a TV camera. Television anchormen are big users of TelePrompTers. Studies show that news anchors who speak directly into the camera, in essence making eye contact with each and every viewer, evoke more trust in their audience. So a politician who wanted to improve his or her credibility with an audience, without changing what he or she said, could benefit from the TelePrompTer.

President Reagan's acting experience enabled him to use this new technology in a particularly effective way. Like an anchorman, he made eye contact with viewers when he used the version of the device mounted on the TV camera. And when he spoke before a large audience—say, in his State of the Union message to Congress—he got the same effect by using a model that involves transparent mirrors to his right and left. Audiences were invariably impressed by the smooth manner in which the President seemed to be speaking without the aid of notes, turning his head from side to side in continuous eye contact right through the see-through glass. Here was a President who didn't even have to read his speech—he was speaking straight from the heart!

I was always mystified that even people who disagreed sharply with Ronald Reagan said they liked him. Even when the content of his speech was aggressively negative, he got high marks for warmth and friendliness. The fact is, there was no personal bond between Reagan and the American voter. There was just a TelePrompTer, in a political environment that increasingly resembles a made-for-TV movie.

From now on, take a close look at your television when you see a candidate or office-holder speaking to a crowd. See-through panels in front of him will signal you whether his heart is speaking—or his script.

THE MIND MACHINES

The computer is an even greater technological boon for politicians. It has dramatically improved fund-raising abilities by exploiting direct-mail lists. Thousands, or millions, of letters can be computer-printed, carrying different messages to different audiences. Women on one mailing list might receive a letter about the importance of day-care centers and quality education, while Hispanic-Americans might receive a letter discussing immigration reform. There's nothing less personal than these computerized letters with a "personal" touch.

During the 1988 Iowa caucus race, 38,000 Republican women in the state each received a "hand-written letter" from Mrs. Jack Kemp, enclosed in a personalized envelope. They must have admired the stamina of the candidate's wife. Without the closest scrutiny of the letter, they couldn't have known—unless they read a *Wall Street Journal* story weeks later—that the entire mailing came straight from a computer and laser printer, right down to the signature in blue ink.

Computers can also replace humans in get-out-the-vote efforts, controlling automatic telephone-dialers and tape recorders in an effort to contact potential voters at home. Maybe you've answered the phone at dinnertime some night and heard the recorded voice of a national politician urging you to cast your ballot. *U.S. News and World Report* recounted a malfunction in which a computer repeatedly dialed an intensive-care ward at a Dallas hospital, only days before the 1986 election, and played recordings saying, "Hello, this is Ronald Reagan, and I need your help." The patients weren't too happy.

But computers are used for even more insidious purposes. For years, advertising agencies and manufacturers have used computers along with polling to determine a "model" of the population. In the 1960s, Ford Motor Company did a study recording 200 20-minute conversations with average people, talking about their cars. A consultant on the project told me how the words people used were then cross-programmed by computer against a thesaurus, looking for patterns. With the computer's help Ford was able to determine exactly what words people liked to use about their cars, and what words brought negative reactions. (Apparently, the word "hot" went over well with teenage boys.) New ads using the findings helped sales tremendously.

Politicians today use the same computerized methods to sell themselves. Political consultants have refined the art of polling so well that the models of the population drawn by the computer are about as accurate as the vote on election day. They may be even more important than the real vote, since the candidate uses the model to shape his campaign. Politicians now plot assaults on the voter's mind, scheming to design slogans and speeches that say only what people want to hear—nothing more.

Richard Wirthlin, who was Ronald Reagan's polling consultant in California and Washington, operates the most highly sophisticated computerized system known in American politics. His organization, Decision Making Information (DMI), has proven extremely successful in applying new technologies to campaigns. Have you ever had one of those dinnertime phone calls from somebody wanting to "take just a few moments of your time" to ask you a lot of questions about politics, issues and candidates? That's how DMI and outfits like it work, and they're plugging your answers directly into computer terminals.

Weaving together the responses of tens of thousands of Americans to hundreds of different questions, DMI's computer banks can develop a snapshot of the American electorate far more accurate than the old-time politician's "gut feelings." The model they develop then allows a candidate and his staff to write speeches, and even think up one-liner jokes, that will strike a chord in the television audience—oops, I mean the electorate. Basically, DMI provides Nielsen ratings for politicians.

Wirthlin's models proved immensely successful for Ronald Reagan, and Wirthlin was even named "Adman of the Year" in 1981 by an advertising association for successfully selling his candidate. Instead of considering the award a perverted joke on the American political system, Wirthlin proudly accepted his plaque.

Just because Republicans may be better at these tactics doesn't mean you'll hear Democrats condemning them. They want to make use of them in their own campaigns. Democratic Party mover-and-shaker Norman Lear, who has extensive experience in television as producer of "All in the Family" and other top shows, told *The New Republic* in 1988 that the Democrats needed to field a candidate with a more telegenic image: "I wish somewhere there was a little less cool and a little more personal passion." So you see Democrats following computer-recommended strategies to capture votes.

Straight from the Heart

Michael Dukakis, in the hectic weeks before the 1988 Iowa caucuses, brought on board a "media consultant" who told reporters that he was hired because "I think the mistake in the past was that the Dukakis campaign was more concerned about specific programs instead of Mike's feelings." And soon Dukakis began to radiate what the news stories called "passion."

Many voters are sophisticated enough to ignore the media hype of electronic candidacies, and they try to decide on issues. But the quest for election and reelection influences issues in ways not always apparent to the electorate. Policies of all kinds are manipulated by mayors, governors, legislators and Presidents, all of whom share the same interest: holding office against all challengers. Lost in the shuffle somewhere is the voter, you and me. We have become pawns in a chess game we can't even see.

The situation may not be hopeless. For all his expertise and computers, Richard Wirthlin wasn't able to manipulate enough votes for his 1988 client, Bob Dole. But the fact that so many of us don't even bother to vote is a clear enough indication of how removed politicians have become from the electorate.

Now that we've seen some of the conniving ways political candidates can campaign for our votes, let's look at what they do once they win.

C H A P T E R   7

★

The Price We Pay
for Lifetime Politicians

You probably receive a newsletter from your Representative every couple of months or so. On first glance, it seems to be a commendable effort, informing you of what goes on in Washington and enabling you to keep tabs on what your Representative is doing. A good use of your tax dollar? Look at that newsletter again.

Far from providing impartial news, it displays glossy photos of the Representative "holding an important meeting," "voting on a crucial bill." The newsletter carries no criticism, presents no competing views, and amounts to little more than a reelection campaign brochure at taxpayer expense. If you were paying to receive a magazine like that at home, wouldn't you cancel your subscription? Well, you are paying for it.

THE PERKS OF INCUMBENCY

There are many perquisites office-holders can exploit for continual victory at the polls. Our Representatives and Senators tap taxpayers' money for a whole laundry list of campaign necessities. Your tax dollars pay for:

- Communications and public relations aimed at constituents, such as newsletters, "questionnaires," all the stationery they need plus the congressional "frank"—meaning free postage.

In 1986, members of Congress sent out more than 750 million pieces of mail (letters, books, brochures and pamphlets)—this in a country of only 240 million people. The cost to the taxpayer? Almost $100 million a year.

- Travel between Washington and their home district (invaluable for election years).

- Telephone expenses, both in Washington and in the district offices; rent, supplies and furnishings for all these offices—very expensive, and very handy in campaigns.

- Most essential of all, each Member of Congress has a staff, both in Washington and in his or her home district, paid for by you and me. A Senator's office gets between $900,000 and $1.5 million (depending on the size of the state) for staff pay each year, while Representatives get around $400,000 each.

Members of Congress are legally bound not to use those resources for campaign purposes, but in fact incumbents become expert at channeling them into their reelection drives. All told, those perks can be worth at least $2 million a year. That kind of advantage translated into campaign terms can decide whether an incumbent will face a tough challenger or be a shoo-in for reelection.

CONGRESS'S "STAFF" INFECTION

Members of Congress have at their disposal huge staffs, a resource unavailable to a challenger. It's common for staff members in a Senator's office to double as reelection campaign workers, even though it's illegal under Federal Election Commission rules.

Before World War II, a Representative had to make do with only a secretary and a clerk, while a Senator enjoyed an office staff of four. It was hard to get into too much trouble with so few staffers (maybe not too hard). There weren't more than 1,500 total Congressional staffers before 1941.

Boy, how times change. The total number of employees in the House of Representatives at the beginning of 1988 was approximately 12,800. That number includes elevator operators and the like, but the overwhelming majority are political support staff—press secretaries, legislative assistants, personal schedulers, mail-answerers and so on, both in Washington and in the home-district offices. That works out to an average of almost 30 staffers per Representative. On the Senate side, the figures are more striking: 7,914 full- or part-time staff for 100 Senators.

When you add in the staffs for each congressional committee, plus the various congressional branch organizations like the Congressional Research Service (which has 850 workers and is a valuable tool for the campaigning incumbent), you get a grand total of 39,600 people working for Congress. That's an average of over 74 staff members for each member of the House and Senate!

Oh, I know why there are so many staffers on the Hill. First, the incumbent needs workers to ferret out new, trendy social causes to legislate—rock-and-roll lyrics, yogurt flavorings, bills naming the national insect—much like Hollywood celebrities are forever finding more exotic diseases for telethons. Second, the amount of paper that needs to be pushed is tremendous. Just the administrative and research functions of the various congressional committees and subcommittees represent a huge bonanza of make-work on which Capitol Hill thrives.

Where would we be without the Senate-House Joint Committee on the Library of Congress, or the House Subcommittee on Tobacco and Peanuts? Once a Speaker of the House punished a political enemy by appointing him to the Committee on Ventilation and Acoustics. Here's a table showing the committee breakdown:

Table 2—The Complex Of Committees
House Committees: 22   Senate Committees: 16 Sub-committees: 140   Sub-committees: 89 Joint House-Senate Committees: 4 Sub-committees: 8 "Select committees": 11 Sub-committees: 7 "Congressional task forces": 7
Total: 304

Let's face it, Senators and Representatives aren't able to keep up with the administrative work of 300 committees. They become what Senator Dan Evans (of Washington state) has called "Bumblebee Senators, flitting among committee meetings, staying just long enough to be counted present." So staffers are allowed to run the committees, and for that they're paid very well. In fact, in 1988 they even got a pay raise. Those at the top of the Congressional staff ladder get $88,000.

That's a lot of money, and people like you and me might want to have a say about whether those staffers are worth that much pay, since it comes straight from our pockets. But, as usual, we don't have a say. The Lifetime Politicians pulled another fast one with that staff raise, sneaking it by in 1987 in a late-night secret vote on their own pay raise. Ralph Nader, the old consumer advocate and Congressional nemesis, brought the situation to light and argued, "Congress is part and parcel of the horrendous deficit, and then they turn around and increase the salaries of the staff." Nader obviously feels that staffers didn't deserve a raise and steamed that "if it had been done openly, it would have been blown out of the water." And if we didn't have lifers, we wouldn't have this lunacy.

What do the Lifetime Politicians get in return for showering their staffs with taxpayer dollars? Help in reelection, of course. Using congressional or other governmental staff people for campaign purposes is an old trick. Now, with so many committees, there are so many more staffers for the incumbents to use. In my home state, California, the longtime leader of the State Assembly, the late Jesse Unruh, was a master at this practice. Big Daddy was skilled at diverting staff members from legislative to campaign work for Democratic candidates. He shifted them from various state assembly members' offices, from committee staffs and from official state offices. Thus, workers on the state payroll—the so-called "public servants"—were transformed into campaign worker bees.

This practice is notorious in Presidential campaigns, when Senators and Representatives have their staffs often working side by side after hours. Everyone in Washington knows the FEC turns a blind eye to this scam because all the candidates do it. No one wants to break the unwritten code of not turning each other in.

The long and short of it is that our elected officials have available to them an elaborate benefits system that not only makes their lives comfortable but makes it very difficult for challengers to unseat them. My experience is limited to business, but I know that no efficient and successful company would allow this kind of flimflam. They couldn't afford it. But affordability is the last thing politicians think about. They're not paying the bills. We are.

GERRYMANDERING, OR "MAPS Я US"

Do politicians still "gerrymander" districts to get votes? You'd better believe it! Gerrymandering, or drawing district borders along weird and illogical lines to influence election results, is still as common as it was in the days of machine politics.

The origin of the word is amusing. In 1812, Governor Elbridge Gerry of Massachusetts ordered a secret redrawing of a district in his state. The new boundaries were clearly designed with politics as the compass. The drafters disregarded existing city, town and county borders in order to construct a safe seat. One opponent claimed the district now looked more like a salamander than a district, whereupon the press and public seized upon the name "gerrymander."

Congressional and state legislative districts all over the United States have been touched by gerrymandering. In California, we have an absurd apportionment of districts. In the 1982 congressional elections, for example, there was a sizable discrepancy between the total votes received by Democratic candidates (51.6 percent) and the proportion of seats won by Democrats (62.2 percent). Those in the know attribute the results to gerrymandering conducted by the Democratic-controlled state legislature after the 1980 census.

The most insidious aspect of gerrymandering by state legislatures is that incumbents have begun to see it as a bipartisan effort. The party that holds the upper hand is usually willing to cut a deal with the minority party, carving out safe seats for all the incumbents just to ensure that the redistricting legislation passes. Districts become noncompetitive, and incumbents on both sides keep ever-tighter grips on their seats. Our California incumbent protection plan secured victory for every incumbent state legislator who ran for reelection in 1986. Gerrymandering is just another of the games Lifetime Politicians play at our expense to ensure their long tenure.

SITTING BULL: ALL CHIEFS AND NO INDIANS

When I make my argument against career politicians, I am often asked: aren't the experience and acquired expertise of incumbents valuable government assets? My unequivocal answer is no. The expertise they gain comes at great costs to good government.

We've seen the lengths to which politicians will go to secure their reelection. They manipulate their images and personalities, they change their views on issues in exchange for votes, and they raise huge amounts of money through practices that amount to little more than legal extortion.

We're going to see later how Lifetime Politicians have put our economy and foreign policy at risk with their fouled-up priorities. Few of them make the sacrifices needed to solve the country's problems. They're more concerned that they look like a big chief come election day back on the reservation.

A gold-medal lifer himself, former House Speaker Tip O'Neill tells in his autobiography, *Man of the House,* that he tried to talk Ted Kennedy out of running against President Carter in 1980. "You can't beat an incumbent President," he told the Senator. "He's got a hundred billion dollars at his disposal to distribute back to local governments, and he can send that money wherever he wants. Everybody from Alabama to Alaska files for projects, and the administration decides which ones to approve. In an election year, they go where the votes are." If that is how crucial economic decisions are being made by Washington incumbents, then I want no part of it.

BOTH OF THEM ARE "GRAND OLD PARTIES"

So many of these jokers have been around for just too darned long. Mississippi's Senator John Stennis decided to retire in 1988; he was 86 years old. He first entered the Senate in 1947 and will have served 41 years, almost breaking the record of Carl Hayden, who served nearly 42 years earlier this century. Barry Goldwater of Arizona just retired after serving 35 years in the Senate.

Congress is nothing if not a comfortable life—and most incumbents will go to almost any lengths to stay in office. Claude Pepper is the oldest member of Congress, 87 years old in 1988. He served in the Senate from 1936 to 1951, and then in the House from 1962 on. (His new House seat was created—you guessed it—when Democrats in the Florida state legislature gerrymandered the districts after the 1960 census.) He's been in Washington for quite a while.

Pepper's wife seems to see things a bit more clearly than her husband does, at least on the subject of Lifetime Politicians. She once said, "The mistake a lot of politicians make is in forgetting they've been appointed and thinking they've been anointed." I wonder what the pillow-talk was like that night.

The seniority system in Congress contributes to these difficulties, because it promotes individuals to leadership not by expertise or performance, but by their hold on safe seats. Seniority will grant increasing prestige and power to the permanent incumbent as long as he or she lives—whether senile or not. Back in 1971, doctors at Bethesda Naval Hospital judged Representative John Dowdy of Texas "neither physically nor mentally capable of standing trial" on charges of bribery and conspiracy. Why is that remarkable? Because his colleagues allowed him to keep on chairing his subcommittee anyway!

State and local politics also develop their cadres of Lifetime Politicians who use incumbency to prolong their tenures indefinitely. They often emulate their big brothers in Congress, never acknowledging that it's time to admit that age or scandal has left them totally ineffective. Edwin Edwards served three terms as Governor of Louisiana but couldn't let go. In 1987 he ran for a fourth term even though he had been indicted on 16 different corruption charges during one of the most scandal-ridden state administrations in recent American history.

Edwards lost, and yet true-to-form he refused to concede the election even when the results were clear. That's understandable in a man who once boasted that the only thing that could defeat him was to be found in bed "with a live boy or a dead girl."

The Long Goodbye

Some lifers go to pathetic extremes in their attempts to hold power indefinitely. "Big Jim" Folsom of Alabama, who first ran for public office in 1936, never knew when to quit. He first served as Governor in 1943, and went on to serve a number of terms. He wasn't really a bad state leader, but the people of Alabama finally felt he had outstayed his welcome. A card-carrying Lifetime Politician, Folsom refused to give up. Comeback attempts came in 1962 and 1966, both unsuccessful. His last quest for political power came in 1982 in yet another race for the governorship, even though he was 74 years old, legally blind, and almost entirely deaf. He lost.

TRICKLE-DOWN REPRESENTATION

The public mostly responds to the scandal inside the Beltway by writing off politics. Apathy and resignation rule the day. People would rather watch some more TV than pursue what they see as a hopeless cause—the restoration of good government. Americans are saying, "Forget it, let's rent a video."

Our lack of commitment to our duties as citizens is alarming. You'd think that the only three things we owe to our country are to forget to vote, skip out on jury duty and evade taxes.

It isn't that people just don't care anymore about politics or about their duty to the country. We still care, but no one asks us to sacrifice for the common good. Instead, we are made to feel powerless. Our votes don't seem to count and nothing we could do seems capable of cutting through the Washington morass.

What we have is "trickle-down representation." The permanent elite concern themselves with serving the rich and the special interests, not the country or the greater good. They may not always state it boldly and will speak piously of compassion for the common man—but then they retreat behind the curtains of incumbency. When actor Hal Holbrook was preparing to play a Senator on TV, he spoke to a member of Congress to get a feel for the job. The *New York Times* reported that the politician admitted to Holbrook that he hated having to meet constituents:

> In come John Doe and Mary Doe and eight little Does expecting to see you. They're on vacation and he's in Bermuda shorts and the kids are tired and mad. When they lean back

on that sofa to rest and visit and you've got to make a speech that night and you're just not prepared and the mail is stacking up, you just can't imagine the feeling that comes over you. It's almost intolerable. But you've got to see them.

It may be too much to expect that a Representative will be able to spend time with each and every constituent. That would be impossible, although maybe the Representatives from Idaho or Nevada could manage it. But, after all, those few constituents who do trek all the way to Capitol Hill should be granted a little attention and respect.

When the most John Doe can expect from his Representative is a patronizing moment, and if he is lucky a smile and a pat on the back, it seems to me that the Representative has been in Washington too long. His attention is much more focused on the fund-raiser he's holding for corporate PACs later that afternoon, or on scheduling his "fact-finding" free junket to European capitals. The money people, the Representative's real constituents, get most of his attention; we ordinary folks get table scraps. Except, that is, at reelection time. Then he's everybody's friend.

As the days and years pass and the acceptance of the status quo grows, it gets harder and harder to replace trickle-down representation with effective accountability.

How do we escape the political vicious circle? There are only two hopes. We can hope for a miracle—that somehow, on their own initiative, the politicians will reject their sinful ways and lead us to the promised land. That is about as forlorn a hope as you can imagine.

Or we, the people, can take charge of our own lives. Later I'll tell you how we can shed our apathy and kick the bums out, making sure that their replacements know the meaning of the phrase "public servant." But before we get to our proposals for new leadership, we have to examine where our previous leaders have led us.

C H A P T E R   8

★

Send in the Clowns

When I sat down to write this chapter on leadership, I naturally began to think about the man in the Oval Office: Ronald Reagan, 78 years old, with his finger on the button. I have an uncle who's 78 and we don't even let him touch the remote control.

Why is there such a leadership void? In election-year surveys, people always say they're looking for a candidate "who can lead," even though we Americans like to think of ourselves as individualistic and independent. I remember that during World War II we would compare ourselves to the Germans and sneer at their "respect for authority." That, we thought, had allowed a nut like Hitler to take over.

Even so, I think that we want to be led as much as anyone. We like to elect somebody President every four years and then forget the whole thing. That's why one scholar back in 1898 called the Presidency "the elective kingship."

For that important task we expect leadership qualities, and we need to be looking for those qualities in our candidates. We must have a first-class mind at the top—how could anybody dispute that? Who would be so stupid as to elect a President, a *President*, who did not have a first-rate mind?

Well, that's exactly what we've done, over and over again. America has suffered six leadership crises since the last world war.

SIX CRISES IN POST-WAR LEADERSHIP

I borrowed the phrase, "six crises," from Richard Nixon's famous book, which he published in 1962 to convince California voters that he could provide tough leadership as our governor. He lost that race, telling the press after it was over, "You won't have Dick Nixon to kick around anymore." Do you remember Nixon's six crises?

Here's the list: the Alger Hiss case, Nixon's pet witch-hunt for the old House Un-American Activities Committee; the Checkers affair, a slush-fund scandal remembered only for the TV speech with the dog; Eisenhower's mild heart attack, after which Nixon chaired several cabinet meetings for two uneventful weeks; Nixon's visit to Venezuela, where he was chased back into his limo by a gang of students led by (I'm quoting) "cold-eyed Communist operatives"; "the Kitchen Debate," a shouting match with Khrushchev in Moscow over which country had more modern kitchen appliances (believe it or not); and the 1960 campaign, which he lost to John F. Kennedy.

The six crises I am interested in were far more important.

Ike: A War Hero Defeated by Politics

Many readers will not remember first-hand one of the darkest chapters in our history. There will always be politicians who will try to take advantage of the gullibility of the American people. Senator Joseph McCarthy of Wisconsin was a notorious example. He persuaded the public that the Soviet Union and international communism were immediate threats to national security, both externally and internally. Other authors have described the pain McCarthy brought into the lives of the individuals he accused and the harm he did to the nation. For several years his venom infected the entire social and political system.

A wise leader, with the sense to see McCarthy's extremist crusade for what it was and the courage to speak up, would have denounced him. Indeed, we should have expected even more of Dwight D. Eisenhower, who had a reputation as a moderate (both parties tried to get him to run for President in 1948), and who fostered the image of a tough, decisive military leader.

But when it came to McCarthy, Ike had no backbone. He badly needed the support of the conservative Robert Taft wing of the Republican party. Taft was a quiet but powerful McCarthy supporter, and he pulled Ike's string throughout the 1952 campaign on the issue of "creeping communist infiltration and subversion."

Possibly the most shameful incident occurred when McCarthy attacked as a "traitor" one of the greatest political-military statesmen this country has known since George Washington, George C. Marshall. Eisenhower told friends he was appalled that McCarthy would attack someone who was clearly no traitor, but he kept quiet in public. Speaking in Milwaukee during the campaign with McCarthy beside him on the platform, Eisenhower chickened out. His prepared speech had a section defending General Marshall (then Secretary of State) as a true patriot, but Ike wimped out under the beady eye of McCarthy and omitted the passage.

Why did Eisenhower let McCarthy tear down George Marshall? To win votes. Ike, who had retired as NATO commander in early 1952, had learned quickly the political truism "follow the noise." When it was apparent that McCarthy was striking a responsive chord in the public, Eisenhower chimed right in. By the end of the campaign he, too, was slandering his opponents, calling the Democratic platform "un-American."

A genuine leader ignores the cry of the mob and heeds the call of conscience. Political cowardice should have been beneath Eisenhower. He was not alone in succumbing to the fervor of the crusade; even Senator Hubert Humphrey, a staunch liberal, suggested that the American Communist party be outlawed and that concentration camps be set up to intern "unpatriotic" Americans in time of war. But in a crisis we expect more of the President. Our highest elected official should rise above the prevailing passion. Eisenhower failed this Presidential test. By allowing McCarthyism to spread he violated his own principles for political expedience.

The Old Nixon: Red-Baiter

Dick Nixon is someone you love or you hate. Well, I've never met anyone who claimed to love him, but I'll be darned if I don't still meet people who defend him after all these years. Many of them have been Nixon supporters since his earliest days in California politics. The history of Richard Nixon is a history of dirty politics and poor leadership, leadership that departed from principle or high-mindedness whenever a vote could be obtained or an opponent bloodied.

From his first congressional campaign in 1946 against Jerry Voorhis, Nixon saw the advantages of McCarthyist tactics. In *RN: The Memoirs of Richard Nixon*, he describes the 1946 race as a "high-risk campaign," although the only risk was that voters would have the common sense to see through such behavior. A debate with Voorhis taught Nixon how readily people would swallow guilt-by-association. Nixon writes that Voorhis protested that his accusations were untrue, "but I could tell from the audience's reaction that I had made my point."

Nixon bears a good deal of the blame for fostering the nationwide McCarthy fever. He brayed to the crowds about the Red menace in Washington. His anti-communist gusto worked, bringing him to the attention of party leaders and earning him a place on the 1952 ticket. During the 1952 campaign he slandered the Democratic candidate as "Adlai the Appeaser," and sneered that Stevenson had received a "Ph.D. from [Secretary of State] Dean Acheson's College of Cowardly Communist Containment."

As a Congressman and Vice President, Richard Nixon pandered to the same fears that McCarthy and Eisenhower did. And he was proud of this pandering. In his book, he writes: "If some of my rhetoric [in 1946] seems overstated now, it was nonetheless in keeping with the approach that seasoned Republican politicians were using that year." In other words, whatever the crowd wants, give it to them.

The American people turned thumbs down on Nixon's Presidential potential in 1960 based on that failure of leadership, but we weren't to see the last of him. A politician that willing to pander can't be kept down. The "old" Nixon foreshadowed the "new" Nixon.

Kennedy, Johnson and the Slippery Slope of Vietnam

John F. Kennedy served only a thousand days as President, but on many issues he showed good instincts for tough decision-making, and he grew into the office more than most chief executives. Lyndon Johnson might be remembered as a great leader in his own right, as JFK's Vice President and later as President, for his control of government legislation and his dynamic social programs. On one crucial issue, however, Kennedy's legacy to his successor and to the nation was a disaster. That issue, which ultimately brought LBJ down, was Vietnam.

Kennedy was an enthusiastic, willing subscriber to global containment of communism. His strategy was rooted in "flexible response," whereby the United States would not have to rely solely on nuclear weapons for deterrence but might respond to communist aggression with conventional forces. Kennedy's defense spending ate up more than half of the federal budget (more than today), and his thinking on international affairs came out of the Cold War.

Faced with an escalating guerrilla war in South Vietnam, Kennedy agonized over how to respond. First Kennedy and then Johnson allowed the country to be dragged deeper and deeper into that nightmare by the assurances of experts. Those assurances were far too pat, yet neither President ever analyzed the predicament from first principles. Each considered it more important to stand tall abroad for political reasons at home. Personal stubbornness also played a role.

The policy misconceptions were legion: Kennedy, Johnson and their advisers did not understand their enemy. They tended to over-Americanize the thinking of the Vietnamese, much as we do today with Iran. The Cabinet and chief foreign policy advisers all engaged in "GroupThink"; they were "yes men" rather than responsible counselors. And throughout the conflict our military followed misleading historical analogies, resulting in horrendous losses and an ignominious military failure.

Both Presidents placed more emphasis on being firm for the sake of political appearances than on questioning our ultimate ends and commitment. It was easier to lose soldiers in a war we could not win than to find the political courage to pull out. Kennedy was beginning to have second thoughts before he was assassinated. Johnson never did summon the will to admit the truth, for fear political opponents would savage him as "soft on communism." In the end, we failed to change the outcome of the conflict—we only prolonged it. Our national consensus on foreign policy was smashed and has never been recovered. Both Presidents failed an important test of Presidential leadership: putting the long-term good of the country before personal political welfare.

The New Nixon: Textbook Crook

From choosing Spiro Agnew for Vice President ("Looking for Mr. Nobody") to the enormous significance of the Watergate break-in and cover-up, the 1968-1974 vintage Nixon was a textbook case of the dangerous President. The question I have to ask is not, "Was he a crook?" but rather, "Why on earth didn't we see through him?"

Nixon's genius was in using the unscrupulous political tactics we discussed in early chapters to overcome the negative image most people held of him after his 1960 defeat. He was a modern-media Presidential candidate. Professional advertising men worked on his 1968 campaign to erase the taint of scandal that still tarred him from the 1950s. One ad man admitted to author Joe McGinniss (*The Selling of the Presidency 1968*): "The radicalness of this approach is in the fact of creating an image without actually saying anything." That was nothing new in commercial advertising, but in politics it gave us a different kind of President.

John Coyne, one of Nixon's White House speechwriters, admitted years later in his book *Fall in and Cheer* that he worked hard to create the illusion of a President with intelligence, integrity and even a pleasant personality. The writers used inflated rhetoric, catchy phrases, and "above all anecdotes, especially things we could invent that his mother might have said to him. These remarks would be written in the form of short paragraphs, Nixon would commit them to memory and deliver them without a text." Coyne says that Nixon "did this masterfully," and was so convincing that he won reelection by a landslide. The seamy underside of the White House could only stay hidden so long, though, and with Watergate the fiction crumbled.

Was that national nightmare avoidable? Absolutely. The word was out on Nixon long before 1968; most of us simply chose to ignore it. As early as 1959 a *Baltimore Sun* correspondent described Nixon as "the scientific pitchman of politics, who coldly tries to figure what will sell, packages his products neatly, and then goes out to peddle them."

Jimmy Carter and the Politics of Doubt

From a leadership standpoint, Jimmy Carter was a puzzling and disappointing President. My friend Gene Holley, who was a leader in the Georgia state legislature, tells me that Jimmy was the greatest one-on-one politician he has ever seen. I can attest to that, I guess. I was on a plane a few years after Carter had left the White House, and he happened to be on the same flight. I stood there and watched as the man, a former President who might be expected to want a little privacy, went up and down the aisles, shaking every single hand and exchanging small talk with all the passengers. Quite a performance for a guy who's not running for anything, I thought.

But then one last woman sitting by a window was engrossed in a paperback novel and didn't notice Carter when he stood by her, waiting to get her attention. Rather than tapping her on the shoulder, or even better just moving on, Carter stood there, waiting and waiting for her to look up. I kept thinking, "Boy, this is embarrassing"—a man who was once President of the United States reduced to waiting for what seemed like ages for someone to look up, just so he could shake her hand. Something strange about that.

I think Carter was a great campaigner, but unsuccessful as an administrator and decision-maker. This point is crucial, for it strikes to the very core of the dichotomy between the campaigner and the man who governs. Carter was a self-righteous man whose self-confidence helped make him a master at asking people for their support and their votes. But his self-righteousness made it exceedingly difficult for him to admit that on some issues he needed help. He never digested the great truth, that a large part of smart leadership is delegating work and responsibility.

According to one Georgia politician who knew Carter well, he was a know-it-all who alienated the state legislature by botching a major governmental reorganization. That rings true, because Carter was to face the same problem in his relations with Congress. While Carter was very good with people on the campaign trail, when you really had to work with him, his preachy egoism could be very trying. A true leader does not find it excruciatingly hard to admit he is wrong.

Often Carter recognized problems but misjudged America's capacity to deal with them, underestimating the American character. He felt Americans were too bound by the "post-Vietnam" syndrome to follow an assertive foreign policy, but he was unaware of the growing tide of patriotism later tapped by

Reagan. He identified, and perhaps sponsored, a sense of national malaise and an era of limits, unaware that one cause was a lack of confidence in his leadership. Also, Carter was too submerged in the process of decision-making to make the tough choices. George Marshall used to say, "Don't fight a problem, decide it." Carter too often tried to fight problems.

When problems and the pressures of the 1980 campaign began to overwhelm him, Carter adopted the Nixon stonewall approach, instituting a "Rose Garden strategy," which basically meant hiding out in the White House only to appear in carefully staged photo opportunities in the Rose Garden as he escorted visitors in and out. Ted Kennedy became so frustrated in his race against Carter for the Democratic nomination in 1980 that he began using a tape recorder as a Carter stand-in. Kennedy would appear on a platform with the tape recorder sitting on an empty chair, and would play a few sentences of a Carter speech—and then respond, as if it were an actual debate. Voters were given little opportunity to see their own President. Carter became more and more isolated, losing the confidence of the public. No wonder Reagan swept in on a landslide.

Elder Statesmen

I will say one thing for Jimmy Carter. He has proven to be our best ex-President. Every summer, he travels to an inner-city slum and works for Habitat for Humanity, a ministry that builds housing projects for the poor. Seeing the news photos of Carter, hammer in hand, always brings to my mind a contrast with Jerry Ford. Here's a fellow who was a Lifetime Politician himself, serving out 25 years in the House of Representatives. Then, he lucks out like a madman, gets appointed Vice President by Richard Nixon, and the rest is history. What has Ford done in his ex-presidency? Hired himself an agent and gone on the road. And while Jerry Ford skis in Vail and parties in Palm Springs, Jimmy Carter carries his hammer to Harlem.

Ronald Reagan: Symbol of Our Times

I am not writing this book as a diatribe against Ronald Reagan, who, in many ways, provided valuable leadership for our nation in a troubled time. It is difficult to look back to the fall of 1980 and remember without some pain our national mood of despair.

Ronald Reagan put forward a clear vision and, if you will, an "image" of an America that did not walk with its head bowed or accept inevitable economic decline.

Unfortunately, he gave us only that: an impressionistic facsimile of what America should look like. In the crunch, President Reagan failed the crucial test of providing the policies to translate those visions into reality. He also failed the test of Presidential leadership by not asserting himself as the Ultimate Decider, the Ultimate Doer, able to confront real problems, appraise their dangers and consequences and fashion decisive policies to combat them. As a person, he always has been a great fellow, but as a politician Reagan represented the final triumph of style over substance, the victory of the modern politician.

I judge Reagan harshly not because he was the worst of the Lifetime Politicians and all they represent, but because he became the most conspicuous. His administration is open to criticism not because he caused the problems but because he passively accepted them. He was a status quo politician, full of ineffectual "solutions" reflecting an inappropriate ideology. I consider myself a conservative in many ways (not all), but more often than not the policies Reagan espoused undercut his rhetoric of conservatism and prosperity. They brought to life the starkest fantasies of his antigovernment dreams: a federal government in ruins, unable to finance itself but hostile to the stern measures needed to revive it, and reliant on its vision of military supremacy and external threat.

As with Nixon, we should have known all this would happen. To a degree we did. But we chose the symbol over the reality. The perversions of the electoral process I described in the previous chapters made it easier for us to do so, but they didn't make it inevitable. We chose to close our eyes to unpleasant truths, to the threatened consequences, and we voted for Reagan. We got what we deserved.

I remember that when Reagan was Governor of California, he tried to bring his antiwelfare crusade to Sacramento but was unable to thwart the liberal California legislature. During his eight years in office, all of California's central trends contradicted his stated purposes and convictions. Reagan had run for Governor as a strong conservative, especially on economic matters; "I'll cut taxes and spending," he promised, castigating his Democratic predecessor for profligate spending.

Sound familiar? Well, so will the results. Many of Reagan's far-right backers felt betrayed when, instead of declining, state spending went from $4.6 billion a year to $10.2 billion under Governor Reagan. Taxes increased from $6.64 to $7.62 per $100 of personal income. In 1976, President Ford's campaign committee tagged Reagan as "the biggest taxer and spender" in California's history.

Part of the explanation lies in Reagan's personality. He was, of course, an actor, and he was good in the part of a tough, no-nonsense, rock-ribbed conservative on the campaign trail. Yet when it came down to the hard choices on policy issues—deciding where spending cuts are to be made, for example—Reagan preferred to let others do the work for him, finally making yes-or-no decisions on the options laid before him.

That kind of leadership is no leadership at all. From my experience in business, I know that if an executive delegates too much authority over the steps leading to decision-making, the options he will finally have are likely to be much inferior to those he might have had with a more concerted hands-on effort. In a leadership position, you have to go after what you want and make it clear to everyone concerned that you will expend the necessary effort to get it.

Reagan was almost harmless as long as he had strong and well-intentioned aides. But when allowed to run free, he tended to spew ideological nonsense. During the 1980 campaign, his aides dealt with his tendency to shoot from the hip by shielding him from probing questions. When his press aide Lyn Nofziger left the campaign due to a conflict with campaign manager John Sears, he noted that Reagan wanted so much to be President that he wasn't saying what he really believed in, for fear of making himself unelectable. "They have him so intimidated, so convinced he shouldn't speak out for what he believes, that he's not Ronald Reagan," Nofziger said. But when Nofziger rejoined the Reagan campaign, a reporter asked him if there would be time to question Reagan. Nofziger replied, "Not if I can help it."

Reagan's leadership consisted of ignoring real problems and using a fairy-tale vision of the world and the American character to gloss over issues, avoid conflict and ensure his popularity. He left it for aides to deal with the real world. His 1976 and 1980 campaign manager, John Sears, admitted to the press during Reagan's first term that "his decisions rarely originate with him. He is an endorser...[often] he simply looks to someone to tell him what to do."

How well did his aides guide him? How did Reagan like to get his information and make his decisions? David Stockman, Reagan's first director of the Office of Management and Budget (OMB), recalls a particularly horrifying example in his book *The Triumph of Politics* (Harper & Row). Secretary of Defense Caspar Weinberger was presenting a Pentagon budget plan:

> Weinberger ...had brought with him a blown-up cartoon. It showed three soldiers. One was a pygmy who carried no rifle. He represented the Carter budget. The second was a four-eyed wimp who looked like Woody Allen, carrying a tiny rifle. That was...the OMB budget. Finally, there was G.I. Joe himself, 190 pounds of fighting man, all decked out in helmet and flakjacket and pointing an M-60 machine gun menacingly at me....

Of course G.I. Joe was Weinberger's proposed budget. Stockman notes that the ploy was very effective with Reagan.

Why on earth would a President of the United States need cartoons and yes/no options to understand his job and make decisions? This namby-pamby approach was also in evidence after the "meltdown Monday" stock market crash on October 19, 1987. One of the President's senior aides said Reagan was not really worried because he has a "generally Pollyannaish attitude toward most things." Reagan's rose-colored glasses blinded him to the real world. He simply followed a script: "It's Morning Again in America."

Reagan didn't worry about budget deficits or debt crises, or anything else technical and unpleasant. He let his advisors manage those issues. So when things went wrong, he could pass the buck(s). His foreign policy often seemed out of control, lurching from crisis to avoidable crisis. How could the President sell arms to the Iranians, the very people responsible for the Beirut bombing of our Marines? The answer came in the Iran-*contra* hearings when Admiral Poindexter, Reagan's cipher of a National Security Adviser, told the United States Congress, "The buck stops with me." Not with the President, whom we elected to lead this nation, but with somebody named John Poindexter.

This sixth crisis of poor leadership derived from a President who stressed *form* over *substance*. He bragged about "standing tall" against terrorists while he sold arms to Khomeni. He preached against big government while presiding over an unprecedented expansion of federal spending. He talked about the evil federal government but headed an administration in which more than 125 officials (including some of the President's closest friends) were accused of various crimes, felonies, misconduct and ethical lapses. What would the Founding Fathers say?

Reagan's reaction to the crisis of government in his administration was to rely on his personal Teflon to see him through, with a smile and a wink. No wonder that his appointees tried to do the same thing when accused of misconduct. R. Leonard Vance, the director of health standards at the Occupational Safety and Health Administration was under investigation for possible misconduct in 1984. He told a House subcommittee that the documents it sought had been destroyed when his dog threw up on them.

You can't help but retain a lingering affection for Ronald Reagan. I know I do. But I also realize what a disastrous President he was. He was the logical result of a political process that has become increasingly removed from public involvement and control.

WHAT IS TRUE LEADERSHIP?

In our history, a small number of politicians have, by luck, by fate, by hook or crook, found themselves at the top of the greased pole—in the Oval Office. In no way, though, does the Presidency invest them with wisdom or greatness. There are a lot of great men and women out there who never will be President.

I think it's a big mistake when the American people treat the occupant of the White House as a god. The office deserves respect, but the occupant doesn't deserve anything—unless he or she is doing a good job, thereby earning our respect for performing creditably.

Presidents should be judged by their ability, and more importantly, their performance. If Presidents screw up, then they deserve to be pilloried. The man (or woman) has to earn our esteem. Even to use the term "reverence for the Presidency" and the name "Richard Nixon" in the same breath almost makes me nauseous.

John Mueller, a professor at the University of Rochester, has written that there are citizens who, "whatever their partisan or ideological predilections, are inclined to rally to the support of the President no matter what he does...the President's strength in this area seems to derive from the majesty of the office and from his singular position as head of state....For them, the President is the country." So it's no wonder that we, the people of America, can be held in awe of the Presidency while the President himself is a mediocrity.

Blind hero-worship has given us too many false leaders. We do need an aggressive and strong leader who is not afraid to confront the issues. However, aggressiveness has played a troubling role in our recent Presidential choices: "War-Hero" Eisenhower verasus "Egghead" Stevenson; the Nixon-McGovern race of 1972, in the midst of protest at home against war abroad; and of course "Gunslinger" Reagan versus "The Wimp Brothers"— Carter and Mondale.

There is the constant danger that this image of aggressiveness becomes machoism for its own sake. What is the result of all this tough talk? In very crude terms, we can look at how many U.S. soldiers were killed under Carter's Presidency and Reagan's. Carter (who served only four years to Reagan's eight) lost only eight men, who died in the desert of Iran trying to free American hostages. Under Reagan, 241 Marines were killed in Lebanon, two airmen in the Libya raid, 29 in Grenada, at least 40 in attacks on the Persian Gulf naval forces...and for what?

Instead of swooning for tough-guy characters, we should be looking for a President with the wisdom to identify and attack problems as well as an understanding of the national character. The people cannot lead themselves, not because we're too stupid but because, as I have said, we are not a pure democracy in the classical sense. The average person like me doesn't know what is going on until he has read it in the media, and the media often rely too heavily on government propaganda. Also the media tend to report rather than to analyze, and the analysis they do offer often comes from government officials or government reports.

Our elected leader has to show prospective leadership, intelligently looking toward the future. That takes wisdom and dedication and vision. And yet we nominate and elect our leaders almost off-handedly. We judge on superficialities, on whether a candidate "looks" Presidential or not. In the next chapter I'll discuss the job requirements for the Presidency. First, though, let's look at another vital aspect of White House leadership: the other people in a President's administration.

POWERS BEHIND THE THRONE

To be successful, a President must have an administrative team of the highest quality. As Tip O'Neill said about Jimmy Carter, "With his intelligence and energy, and his tremendous moral strength, he could have been a great leader. But talent isn't enough, and raw power won't do it either. As Carter found out the hard way, even the President of the United States needs all the help he can get."

So the President's staff must be the best and most talented available. You'd think choosing these people would be a rigorous process, accepting only the most intelligent, qualified and honorable people. Yet such care seems the exception rather than the rule. Cabinet, White House and ambassadorial positions tend to be filled not by qualified and experienced people but contributors and close personal or political friends of the President. That's nothing new, but that doesn't make it right.

Why is it wrong for a President to choose from among his closest circle? Once again, we see the dirty hand of Reelection Fever at work. Usually these cronies were campaign workers or prominent supporters who are given high-level jobs as rewards. In the campaign, their job was to sell a political image and to protect the candidate. Once in the administration, they should be concerned with providing the best possible government, instead of protecting and shielding their leader.

William Casey was a brilliant man with many good qualities. But Reagan's CIA chief, who got the administration into so much trouble in the Iran-*contra* deal, had been Reagan's campaign chairman in 1980. In fact, he had been responsible for "acquiring" Jimmy Carter's briefing book in the famous debate scandal of the 1980 campaign. As a campaign manager, Casey proved to be a tenaciously loyal supporter of his candidate. But does that quality make a good CIA head? Of course not. The director of Central Intelligence has to be an impartial professional who can provide expert and nonpolitical advice. Otherwise, disaster is inevitable.

Picking the best aides may be against a President's political instincts, but it is undeniably better for the administration and for the country as a whole. I think the smarter Presidents are, the more likely they will be to choose good staff people. A good staff person is not necessarily a person who will always agree with you; I've seen too many business people who never learn that lesson.

It is understandable that a President would feel more comfortable with staffers who share the same way of thinking. Yet a President could learn so much more and make much better decisions with advice from different perspectives. Perhaps we need an institutionalized way to get outside, unfiltered counsel to a President.

But that would be pie in the sky. Modern Presidents have almost always appointed friends and political partners to positions that should have been held by professionals. Nixon appointed Haldeman, Ehrlichman and Mitchell to White House staff or Cabinet positions. Carter had Jordan, Lance and Caddell join his staff. Reagan gave Baker, Meese and Casey high governmental offices. All were campaign types, with few qualifications for their White House positions. You might note that almost all these appointees got into some kind of trouble and some went to jail. We can't blame the President for poor decisions if we haven't objected to his poor choices for the Presidential team.

One other obstacle to top-quality Presidential staffing is the hierarchical "one-dominant-adviser," a President's chief of staff who assumes the power to control the information flow and access to the President. Jimmy Carter began his term with a "wheel" organization, as opposed to a hierarchy. This organization allowed multiple channels of access to the President, different spokes of the wheel representing a wide spectrum of Cabinet officials, military and intelligence officials. He didn't even appoint a Chief of Staff for a year.

This decentralization forces the President to make the tough decisions on his own, and to make them cleanly and clearly. But Carter simply wasn't up to that task because he didn't deal well with the flow of conflicting opinions. He was too indecisive to make the system succeed. He ended up appointing Hamilton Jordan Chief of Staff, who centralized the flow in the traditional pattern.

The wheel system can work, however. One President, the supremely self-confident FDR, used it with great success. He had experience in the Washington bureaucracy and as Governor of New York. He was intelligent, well-educated and smart enough to know what he didn't know and needed advice on. He was capable of making swift decisions. More recently, JFK was also very self-assured. He liked having smart people around him, but he always reminded them that the final decision was his.

Reagan, by comparison, never felt competent to make his own decisions on most issues. In Sacramento and again in Washington, he preferred to be left out of the loop and to let a strong Chief of Staff—James Baker, Don Regan, Howard Baker—guide most of his decisions. A member of Reagan's California cabinet confided to me that the Governor wanted all memos boiled down to one page—and only met the full cabinet once a year.

So there are two ways to deal with decision-making, the true leader's way and the "check-yes-or-no memo" way. It should be possible to look at the experience of Presidential candidates to see whether they will be strong, decision-oriented national leaders, or whether they will prefer to sit at the top of a pyramid, unaware of what goes on below. Delegation can work, as many executives in the private sector know, but only as long as the top officer knows what is going on. If a President is ill-informed or if the information filtering system is faulty, then the President loses control. Poor policy and bad decisions are then inevitable.

A President with strong ideological predispositions is at an automatic disadvantage when it comes to delegating because that President will choose people to serve on the basis of their ideology rather than their competence. As I noted in Chapter 2, an ideologue with an ingrained mindset is likely to ignore unpleasant facts and go with his beliefs.

Perhaps the role of Congress should include hearings on a wide spectrum of Presidential appointees, much like those for Supreme Court justices and top Cabinet members. In light of recent experience, it seems a good idea to give a President's choices for National Security Adviser and White House Chief of Staff the same scrutiny. That might provide better oversight of people who end up advising our leaders. Getting a more balanced cross section of ideas and approaches could not fail to improve the decisions made in the White House.

NEXT: ANSWERS

These ideas only scratch the surface of the changes we need to make in our political system if we are to overcome the blight of Lifetime Politicians. It is time to examine fundamental reforms for the fundamental problems we have seen in these first chapters. Up to now in Part I, I've talked only about "Leadership Lost." Now, finally, it's time to discuss "Leadership Found."

CHAPTER 9

★

New Choices

Some fellow with no political background ran for Governor of Louisiana in 1979. He didn't have much money to spend, and most of his campaign was unorthodox, but he did make a TV commercial for the primary. It featured clips from other commercials run by his opponents, to which he added this rejoinder: "Are you tired of the same old political bull?" Well, voters may have been tired (I know I am), but not tired enough. The guy finished last.

Sometimes it seems as if things never change for the better, they only get worse. I don't think that way. Our political system is far from hopeless, no matter how bad I and others make things sound. So think of this chapter as a compass, pointing out the direction we should follow to improve the way we govern our country.

In our democratic system, pressure for reform rises from a growing recognition of problems coupled with a realistic view of their seriousness. Many in the elite know about the problems but refuse to deal honestly with them for the political reasons we've noted.

But I don't care about the elite. This book addresses you, the public. I want to raise the general public's awareness of the problems we face. I think that real people can change things by putting a bit more thought and responsibility into political decisions this year and every year.

FORM VERSUS SUBSTANCE

Everything you've read so far in this book must make it clear that modern politics awards success to those who excel in form alone—"image"—and often penalizes those who concentrate on the substance, meaning an intellectual and a gut-level understanding of the issues. The average voter, like me, needs to keep that in mind to evade the political, psychological and media traps that have been laid for us. We must break away from the idea that the candidate who looks or sounds "Presidential" is the one for whom we should vote. We need to elevate substance over form.

Form Means a Good Speaker

In this day of the TelePrompTer and the speechwriter, we need to ask ourselves if a prepared speech is a meaningful form of campaign communication. Compare Ronald Reagan delivering a masterful speech, with witty allusions, serious analysis, excellent phraseology and polished organization, to Ronald Reagan ducking or fumbling reporters' questions at a news conference or on his way to the helicopter. In contrast to that polished delivery of the prepackaged, rehearsed speech, his answers are halting, he is distracted, he forgets what he's talking about and he often gets his facts wrong. By which performance should he be judged?

Form Means Good-Looking

John F. Kennedy had a built-in television advantage over Richard Nixon: he was handsome. Many media "experts" have attached the label "Presidential looking" to candidates in the past, and that was a factor in 1988, with pretty-boy candidates like Jack Kemp and Albert Gore, and Jesse Jackson dressed in Wall Street garb. They may not have won but they made the semifinals. John Connally, in his 1980 campaign, used to say he looked "like a President ought to." That quality would be fine for an actor playing a President in a movie, but it should never be the reason for a single vote. When a President is alone in the Oval Office wrestling with a tough decision, it doesn't matter if he (or she) is the ugliest person earth.

Unfortunately, TV cameras love to focus on the good-looking candidate, and so do magazine covers. Before running for the

Democratic nomination for President in 1976, the late Henry "Scoop" Jackson underwent plastic surgery—he had his eyelids "lifted." (It didn't work, though. Even after he hired speech coaches, Scoop was too boring for most listeners to bear, and he lost in the primaries to Jimmy Carter.)

What we need are fewer handsome candidates and more qualified ones. And the qualified men and women who hesitate to run because of their looks, or who are told by political consultants that they have to change their style and appearance, should remember what Dick Yates, running on Lincoln's coattails in 1860 for Governor of Illinois, said about Abe: "Well, if all the ugly men in the United States vote for him, he will surely be elected!"

Form Means "Puffing" One's Past

At least two examples of this despicable practice emerged in the 1988 campaign. First, Joe Biden tried to portray himself as an award-winning college student and distinguished law-school graduate, when in fact he hadn't won the awards he claimed, was almost expelled from law school for plagiarizing a term paper, and scraped through near the bottom of his class. His supporters criticized media focus on his past, but let's face it, without this attention he might have been able to lie his way into the White House.

Then Pat Robertson provided another example of this kind of hyperbole. Former Congressman Pete McCloskey, who used to represent my district in California, was in Robertson's Marine unit in Korea, and charged that Robertson bragged of using the considerable influence of his father, a U.S. Senator, to get himself transferred from the front. Robertson started the Presidential campaign saying he had served "in combat"; later he had to drop that claim when the truth came out.

Of course, all these guys were doing is taking a page from the book (easy for Joe Biden) of Ronald Reagan, who once told Israeli Prime Minister Yitzhak Shamir that he had served in Europe with the Army and had visited Nazi concentration camps, when, in fact, he spent the war years in a "Hollywood unit" narrating training films and starring in musical comedies.

Why can't these guys just tell the truth? The embellishment of your record should be an automatic disqualification. A lot of people do things strictly for a resume, in contrast to those who actually do things because they mean something. Lord knows I've seen the difference in the business world.

Politics has its own share of resume-stuffers. George Bush has a very impressive one: Congressman, chairman of the Republican party, ambassador to China, director of the CIA, Vice President. He held some very important posts—but what did he accomplish? He seems to have more on-the-record experience but less to show for it than any recent candidate for the Presidency and more willingness to talk about what he has been than what he has done.

I think that as voters we have to start calling the bluffs of these resume-builders. We need to see whether they have any concrete achievements as hole cards. I'm talking real accomplishments. Otherwise, we will continue to be saddled with smooth talkers totally incapable of coping with our problems.

For incumbents in Congress seeking reelection, a good test would be: have they steered any important pieces of legislation into law? Forget about the flashy TV hearings. Let's see what they have done to help us.

Substance Means Integrity

We all remember the well-publicized collapse of the Presidential campaigns of Gary Hart and the rise and fall of Douglas Ginsburg, who withdrew as a Reagan nominee to the Supreme Court after admitting he had once smoked pot. Many people criticized the media for paying too much attention to such peccadillos. They said that under that kind of scrutiny, anybody would look bad.

Maybe so. Unquestionably some of our great Presidents had human failings. But that doesn't make failing a virtue, and it doesn't mean that we should not look for decent candidates with high moral standards. In the world I know best, business, there are few Ivan Boeskys. But too many of the people in politics today are Boesky types, and we need to weed them out.

What can the average citizen do? Cultivate a healthy skepticism toward those who take a moral high ground in their words but not in their actions. They are the worst hypocrites. Oliver North came across beautifully on television. He stated his case earnestly and tied his actions to patriotism. What he did, though, was lie to Congress, lie to his superiors, lie to the Justice Department, subvert the Constitution—and then agree to tell us what happened *only* after being granted immunity from prosecution based on his testimony. Keep that in mind when Ollie North goes out on the lecture circuit.

Substance Means a Good Thinker

It's strange that the American public rarely seems to take intelligence into account when electing Presidents. We even make fun of some candidates—like Adlai Stevenson running against Eisenhower—for being "eggheads." It is time we got our priorities straight and realized that the job of running the country demands more than just a friendly smile and a good staff. Businesses are not likely to keep promoting somebody who isn't smart, and we shouldn't do it in government.

I've never heard anybody propose IQ testing for candidates, but it might not be a bad idea—I'm sure we'd get some interesting results. Of course formal education isn't the only measure of intelligence. There are different kinds of smarts. We need politicians who use common sense—at least enough to know that trees don't cause pollution. We need to reward the politicians we recognize as instinctively bright, who have shown the ability to propose innovative solutions to difficult problems. In short, what we need in the top echelons of government are people with "smarts," like canny baseball team managers.

Too Smart for the Job?

Thomas Jefferson was a genius—a brilliant architect, musician, writer, philosopher—and he proved to be a wise and effective President. Would he get elected today, or would his opponents make fun of his cultured speech and high-brow tastes? We need the best thinkers, not the best position-paper memorizers and speech-readers.

Substance Means a Good Debater

And I mean in real debates, not the kind of wimpy performances we've had in past Presidential campaigns. The Ford-Carter and Reagan-Carter debates in 1976 and 1980 were jokes, with each candidate trying to appear more "Presidential" and fielding mostly softball questions. The candidates had their answers memorized, especially Reagan in 1980. (His staff had stolen Carter's briefing book, so all he had to do was memorize a script.) The 1984 Reagan-Mondale debates were even more pathetic, with Mondale making snide allusions to Reagan's age, and Reagan forgetting his lines and rambling aimlessly.

We need debates with the candidates in a no-nonsense environment—heck, just have them sit down together and go at it. In other words, force them to think for themselves in a real intellectual trial by fire, with each candidate allowed to question the other and without the predictable dumb questions from journalists: "What do you see as the future of our nation?"

Substance Means Hard Work

We cannot afford another loafer in the White House. Ronald Reagan's staff acknowledged that his "work" habits were pretty lax: a six-hour day at best, Wednesday afternoons off, leaving "early" on Fridays for long Camp David weekends. If you added up the time he and Nancy spent at their ranch in Santa Barbara during his two terms, it would come to more than a year. All that time "clearing brush," far away from the crises in Washington.

If Ronald Reagan had been a corporate executive, he would have been fired long ago. I know for sure that I would have fired him.

We should question candidates very closely on their management styles. And we should explore how informed they are on issues. That should be a major focus of the press; it deserves more attention than their sex lives. The problems we face are complex, and it's important to have a leader who is willing to make the effort to study their roots. An incoming President doesn't have to be an expert on every national issue, but he has to be ready to spend the long hours needed to review them once in office. Study, thought, deliberation—that's the only way to reach solutions.

Even more, a good chief executive must become a real student of the Presidency, as Harry Truman was, by reading the writings of his predecessors, examining the sources of their failures and successes, and gaining an appreciation for the weight of the office.

It's simple: we need a smart, hard-working President, not someone who is lusting after the applause, snappy salutes and ego-gratification of great power.

ONE STAGGERS HOME

When it comes to politics, you are the boss and you want to hire the best possible person for the future good of us all. But the way we've let campaigns become horse-races, we end up with the last nag to stagger home. The nomination process is now self-selection for the tiny circle of people who end up on our primary ballots, and then a media circus until one guy emerges unscathed. Was Dukakis the Democrats' first choice—or the last choice left?

We have to consider each election as a stake in the country's future, not just as a one-shot deal. The primary system can work, but only if enough citizens are willing to get involved early in the process—before we are left with only dwarfs. If you keep settling for the "lesser of two evils" after failing to police the process in the early stages, you ensure that your choices will be worse and worse, year after year.

CONSIDERING THE UNELECTABLES

I shouldn't have to make the obvious point that the most attractive and magnetic personalities do not automatically make the best leaders. There are politicians who might make great leaders but who either don't have the attributes that sell in the media age or don't have the stomach for the hijinks of modern campaigning. I call them the "unelectables." They don't have slick game-show host looks, they don't posture for the TV cameras, they refuse to play the games of modern politics. They are often recognized by party moguls as effective and intelligent. But they are ruled out as not charismatic enough to run for the White House.

There are many well-qualified Presidential men and women around the country. Some are in Congress, some have chosen to remain in local politics. Some aren't in politics at all. Two prominent "unelectables" who have caught my eye as Presidential timber are Sam Nunn of Georgia and Daniel Evans of Washington. One is Democrat, one Republican. Both are superb leaders who will probably never make the run for the White House—to our loss.

Sam Nunn: Unelectable?

The inside-the-Beltway line on Senator Sam Nunn of Georgia has been that he might make a plausible Vice Presidential nominee, but few Washingtonians give him much chance as a Presidential candidate. In 1988 he decided not to run for the Presidency after considerable media focus on his "unelectability."

I know Sam slightly—we've played together in pro-am golf tournaments and he has been a guest at my house a few times. I know he is extremely intelligent. Georgia voters think so, too. In his last race, he swamped his opponent by capturing 80 percent of the vote. But he shouldn't be satisfied with Senate incumbency—he's so good he should try for a promotion.

Many politicians who serve with Sam in the U.S. Senate urged him to run in 1988, especially after front-runner Gary Hart dropped out in mid-1987. Two factors made him say no. First, he doesn't have a burning ambition to sit in the Oval Office. As chairman of the Armed Services Committee, he is the top authority in the Senate on arms control and defense issues, and he appreciates the importance of that role. He is smart, studious, knowledgable on public issues, and he takes the business of governing seriously. In declining to run, he cited his wish to concentrate on the Senate debate over ratification of the U.S.-Soviet nuclear arms treaty, an issue important to all of us.

But there is a second and more disturbing reason for his refusal. Nunn is a workhorse, not a showhorse. He focuses on getting the job done. Those are not qualities that help you get elected President in our media-dominated campaign process. You need to be a showhorse. You have to spend at least two years campaigning for the early primaries. You have to present a flashy, colorful image that will intrigue the media. You have to raise a lot of money.

Nunn was not having any of that. He doesn't have the most dynamic speaking style around (but neither did Harry Truman). He is not a slick-looking JFK clone. And when he was considering whether to run, media commentators declared that Senator Nunn was just too boring, too devoid of charisma, to win. Moreover, they pointed out, he is from Georgia and would remind people too much of Jimmy Carter, who spoke with the same soft Georgian drawl. For those media-centered reasons, party professionals like Robert Strauss advised Nunn that he was unelectable and shouldn't run.

Dan Evans: Unelectable?

Daniel Evans decided to retire from politics in 1988 after five years in the U.S. Senate. (Already he's looking good in my book.) A Seattle native, he has an interesting past that is not typical of his colleagues in the Senate.

Evans is a civil engineer by training (not a lawyer), and after becoming involved in politics he served for a dozen years (1965 to 1977) as Governor of the state of Washington. Although effective and popular, he then quit politics to become president of Evergreen College, not the career move of a typical politician. But Evans is not your typical politician.

In 1983, when Scoop Jackson died, Washington's Republican governor appointed Evans to the vacant seat in the U.S. Senate. Evans later won a special election to finish out Jackson's term.

In the Senate Evans demonstrated independence and common sense. The fact that he is a Republican did not keep him from opposing Ronald Reagan on the issues of aid to the Nicaraguan *contras* and Star Wars. Serving on the Senate Foreign Relations Committee, he consistently used an independent mind to decide his vote on key issues. In the debate over the U.S.-Soviet INF treaty, Evans took exception to the zealotry of right-wing colleagues like Jesse Helms. During the hearings Evans criticized his fellow Republican Helms for bringing up "red herrings...no, worse—crimson whales."

In the fall of 1987 Evans announced he would not run for reelection in 1988. What—a Senator serving just one term? Impossible, you say? In an article in the *New York Times* Magazine, Evans explained his decision this way:

> I came to Washington with a slightly romantic notion of the Senate—perhaps natural for a former Governor and civil engineer whose hobby is the study of history—and I looked forward to the duel of debate, the exchange of ideas. What I found was a legislative body that had lost its focus and was in danger of losing its soul.
>
> In the United States Senate, debate has come to consist of set speeches read before a largely empty chamber.... I have lived through five years of bickering and protracted paralysis. Five years is enough. I just can't face another six years of frustrating gridlock.

Evans' remarks show that we are losing precisely the kind of values and leadership we desperately need. Our political system has deteriorated so much that honest, independent people like Dan Evans don't even want to make the effort to change it. As he said in one of his parting shots, the only thing Senators do is "read yesterday's headlines so that we can write today's amendments so that we can garner tomorrow's headlines."

That's the kind of honesty we need in a President—someone who is more interested in the truth than in a political career. But it's not the campaign approach that gets you to the Oval Office. No one mentions Evans as a Presidential candidate, even though he served as a Governor for longer than Jimmy Carter, Ronald Reagan or Michael Dukakis.

Maybe Nunn and Evans wouldn't make great leaders after all. But it's a crime that we're not given the chance—the choice—to find out. We have to take the reins and transform the system, so that we can step back from the dizzying hype of primary campaigns and consider the names of people who don't run the media race—like an Evans, a Nunn, a _____?

That transformation is possible. In the next chapter, I'll propose specific reforms to address some of the problems we've seen in Congress, the Presidency and our political system in general. Remember, I'm an amateur. But after the damage done by the professional politicians, maybe amateurs are precisely what we need.

CHAPTER 10

★

Euthanasia for the Lifetime Politician

This book is my opportunity to attack the politicians who refuse to search for genuine solutions and lack the political guts to acknowledge the scope and severity of our problems. It's only fair for you to hold me to the same standards, so I am proposing specific remedies for the ailments I have documented. In this chapter you'll discover new ways to recapture government.

"MR. SMITH LEAVES WASHINGTON"

Reformers have shown up in Washington from time to time. But so many of them become frustrated with the inertia of Washington's ways that their impact is small. In 1988 we saw four reform-minded U.S. Senators decide not to run for reelection because they had simply been worn down by the effort of fighting a losing battle. Senators Dan Evans (Washington), Lawton Chiles (Florida), Paul Trible (Virginia) and William Proxmire (Wisconsin) may have differed in the way they defined Congress's problems, but they were all sensible men who left Washington disheartened at the possibility of change.

Many Representatives and Senators go to Capitol Hill bright-eyed and idealistic. That's one reason they get our votes. But the stagnation wears them down. Our longtime Congressman from San Jose, Representative Don Edwards, told me how he went to Washington full of optimism but learned the difficult realities of government:

> It's a risky business the way we run it, but I don't know how to cure it....It's too, too tough. I've tried that. Lyndon Johnson had me carry the ball [on a specific reform], but we couldn't get the members to go for it, even when he put it in one of his State of the Union messages.

We're going to have to provide answers from the bottom up, instead of waiting for the elite at the top to produce them.

Reducing the Workload in Congress

Here's the first of two quick ideas on how to make the House and Senate work more effectively. We have to refocus the work of Congress back on the important issues of government and away from the mind-numbing list of nonsense that masquerades as legislation today.

In the very first Congress (which convened in 1789 and lasted for two years), 167 bills were introduced in the House and Senate; 117 were passed into law. The federal government is much larger today and is involved in many more issues, so it's only natural that Congress would be passing more laws. The 99th Congress, which began in January 1985, passed 664 bills into law.

That's an acceptable number. But that was out of a mind-boggling 7,522 bills actually introduced! We have to stop the flood of idiotic measures being brought to the floor of the House and Senate. Most of these are a result of the bloated committee system we described in Chapter 7. As a result, very little is ever done in the open, on the floor of the Senate or House where the public can monitor what transpires.

We need fewer bills introduced in Congress and a drastic reduction in the number of committees and subcommittees that are choking Capitol Hill and wasting the time and energy of members.

Members of congress should serve on no more than two committees or subcommittees. Period. Any business that falls through the cracks is business that doesn't deserve attention at that level of government anyway. Members of Congress will have fewer televised committee hearings to publicize, and fewer cosmetic bills to brag about in their newsletters, but that's all to our benefit.

Give C-Span Viewers the Full Picture of Congress

I want to make our politicians TV stars—but on our terms, not theirs.

When Tip O'Neill first permitted live televised coverage of the House of Representatives, he made sure that the cameras only focused on the person actually standing at the microphone, and not on the chamber as a whole. That way, the public wouldn't see that the chamber is practically empty almost all the time, that the few members who are present are dozing or goofing off, and that nobody pays any attention to the debate that is supposedly the whole point of the exercise. Tip argued in his autobiography (*Man of the House*): "Why should the greatest legislative body in the world allow itself to be demeaned and humiliated before millions of people?"

Yeah, right. If it was such a great body, there would be no question of it demeaning itself. In fact, such secrecy and self-censorship mean members of Congress rarely show up in the chamber except to run in and cast their votes—and some have even sent aides to do that! One of my "unelectables," Dan Evans, told the truth to a *New York Times* reporter: "There almost never is a mind changed by debate on the floor of the Senate because, for the most part, no one is ever listening....We need to debate the issues again, and in a full, not an empty, chamber."

One quick and easy way to enforce attendance is to take away control of the cameras from Congress. The C-Span channel, an independent, nonprofit organization that broadcasts live and taped sessions of the House and Senate, is currently hostage to the Speaker of the House. The Speaker's office, not C-Span, decides what will be shown and what will be censored. As O'Neill tells it, the only time he directed the cameramen towards the chamber was when he wanted to embarass a Republican legislator who was speaking to an empty room.

Let's give C-Span some independence from the political bosses and the freedom to show the two chambers exactly as they are. Let's have some bipartisan honesty on a regular basis. Shine the spotlight of public attention on what really goes on in the House and Senate, and you'll see how quickly debates become meaningful, articulate and well attended. Who knows, we may even wake up a few of the back row codgers!

BREAKING THE LIFETIME CHAIN

Those two reforms only scratch at the surface of the central problem I've been concerned with in this book—Lifetime Politicians. We have to go to the source. We must remember that our *system* is not failing; the humans who are charged with running it are. Those who say the Constitution is faulty and needs amending—and stop there—are absolving individual leaders of their responsibility.

Our political process has been twisted into a mechanism to keep politicians in office and we need to change it back to its original plan as part of a government of laws, not of men.

Limiting Congressional Terms

The most direct way to curtail the power of incumbency, but also the most difficult to accomplish, is to amend the Constitution's Article I, which sets out the rules on service in the House and Senate. Right now a Representative can be elected to any number of two-year terms, and a Senator likewise to six-year terms. I propose that we limit the number of consecutive terms a Representative and Senator may serve and lengthen the House term from two years to four. These changes will remove (or at least reduce) the driving impulse for reelection.

A reasonable change would be to place a two-term limit for House members (making eight years total) and for Senators (which would span 12 years). These limits would not negate the rationale behind different terms for the two bodies, making Representatives more subject to changing popular sentiment and keeping the Senate as a more deliberative body less subject to a fickle electorate.

To those negative thinkers who say we could never get this passed, there are precedents: the 17th and the 22nd Amendments to the Constitution. The 17th Amendment was ratified in 1913, changing the way U.S. Senators are elected. It took the power of election away from state legislatures and gave it to the people by popular vote. The change was controversial, and it required a lot of Senators to vote against their own interests. But popular pressure succeeded.

The 22nd Amendment was passed after FDR died during his fourth term as President. It limits Presidents to two terms. Of course, that was one branch of the government placing limits on another, in the spirit of checks and balances. With my proposal, Congress would have to restrict itself, and the odds of individual members of Congress "voting themselves out of office" are not too good. The old catch-22, you might say.

There is an answer to that political hurdle. Members of Congress, being the self-interested creatures they are, would be more willing to vote for such an amendment if it exempted current incumbents from the new limits. Such a formula has been used before, to get congressional support for campaign contribution reform and other measures that have directly hit a politician's interest. It would saddle us with the current crop of losers for a while, but we could rest assured that the next class of cronies would not be able to wreak their havoc for so long.

Why would a limit on the number of terms be good? As we pointed out in the first chapter, the main evil in politics today is the permanent politician. The perpetual incumbent, who wants to stay in office because of the perks, prestige and power it offers, makes decisions—or avoids them—based on job security, not the public interest. We never get meaningful action on the federal deficit because politicians are afraid to raise taxes or cut the pork-barrel spending that gets them votes. Hard decisions are postponed or ignored if they are seen as politically unpopular.

When we permit political office to become a lifetime job for a few, we bar from office all those others who might have fresh ideas and approaches to our problems. Congress has become an inbred body, an old boys club where the chummy deals and tradeoffs are the rule. Citizens don't have any real input because they've almost lost their most potent threat: to throw the bums out.

THE MYTH OF EXPERIENCE

While some people might argue that limits on terms would inevitably end up kicking some good legislators out of office, there's no reason why that should be so. After all, the competent Representative would not have to leave politics completely at the expiration of the second term. He or she could run for the Senate, or even the Presidency.

The Best Training for the Oval Office

Most people are shocked when I remind them of Abraham Lincoln's own career. Many of us have the impression that Lincoln was an experienced national leader before he was elected President. In fact, his only experience in Washington was a single two-year term in the House of Representatives. And that was from 1846 to 1848; for twelve years after, Lincoln held no political office until he became President!

Even Abraham Lincoln had to bear a limit on terms—a one-term "rotation principle" imposed by the Illinois Whig party to keep fresh blood flowing into Congress. After serving his term, Lincoln settled back into his life as a circuit lawyer. He did make two runs for the U.S. Senate, including the famous 1858 campaign featuring the Lincoln-Douglas debates, but he lost both times.

I can hear dubious Representatives and Senators asking: "How did Lincoln reach the White House without a long career on Capitol Hill?" They should hear the answer loud and clear: "he was qualified!" Lincoln didn't need a resume of years in Washington, he needed to have leadership qualities. And the country needed someone who could lead.

Even with the terms I propose, a wise politician like Lincoln who proves effective and responsible can have a career of eight years in the House of Representatives, twelve years in the Senate, and perhaps a resume-capping eight years in the White House. All in all, that would total 28 years at the top levels of federal government, which should be enough for any one person. Also, there are many appointive jobs of high responsibility, or elective positions at local and state levels, all open to good politicians. Experience will not be going to waste!

BLOOD FROM A STONE: GETTING REAL REFORM

It will be difficult to persuade Congress to enact these changes. It might be necessary to use the back-up provisions the Founding Fathers put into the Constitution for cases like this, when members of Congress thwart good ideas. If the required two-thirds of the House and Senate cannot be persuaded to pass such an amendment, a constitutional convention could be convened by a majority vote in 33 state legislatures.

Such a convention could pass the amendment, which would then have to be ratified by three-fourths of the state legislatures. The odds of passing the amendment are good because armies of state legislators are dying to move up and replace their big brothers as members of Congress. Term limits would be their best key to Washington.

In any case, the best way to get limits on terms is to appeal to the self-interest of the politicians who will vote on them. As I indicated, that could be done to some extent by exempting current members from the limits. Most of all, though, the answer has to come from the people.

In their book, *Congress: Two Decades of Analysis*, Ralph Huitt and Robert Peabody argue that to get a "productive burst of congressional energy" like the one that gave birth to the New Deal, Congress has to feel the "hot breath of the country." This is where the power of the people comes into play. It must be made clear to incumbents that they had better pass the reforms, or they're gone at the next election.

In other words, if public opinion can be sufficiently aroused on the issue of limiting terms, then the smart Representative and Senator will take the best offer available—an exemption for him- or herself —and vote for the limits.

We're not doomed to the tyranny of the incumbents just because these reforms may take a while. There are a number of less radical reforms we can enact right now (without constitutional amendments) that would restrict the power of the permanent politicians and infuse vitality and intelligence into our political process. They also center on the crucial need for more turnover in Congress.

Campaign Finance Reform

One critical area that cries for action is reforming the way candidates finance their campaigns. It has received some attention in the academic community, but members of Congress have succeeded in thwarting reform for years. In the spring of 1988 a group of Senators mounted the first round-the-clock filibuster in ten years, blocking a proposal to limit campaign spending and PAC contributions.

One change I strongly recommend is introducing limited public financing for congressional races.

I like public financing because it makes it easier for challengers to take on entrenched incumbents. As I showed in earlier chapters, incumbents maintain their grip by using their legislative clout to raise huge sums for their reelection races. Potential challengers need help to combat the advantages held by the incumbent. Evening the playing field is in everybody's interest—everybody except the Lifetime Politician.

The idea of federal financing of campaigns is an old one. President Teddy Roosevelt advocated it back in 1907. And we have been financing Presidential races since 1971. You know that little check-off box at the top of your IRS 1040 Form every year? That pays for those Presidential TV ads you see in the fall and for the campaign trips and speeches by the nominees.

The time has come to extend public financing to congressional races. The question is not whether we should have it but how to make it work. We could follow the Presidential campaign financing model, which uses equal ceilings for each candidate. The Republican and the Democrat each receive the same amount of money (the level rises a little for every election) to spend during the campaign, even if one is an incumbent in the Oval Office.

Each can spend only that much, and can't raise any outside money above that ceiling. The problem is, even that ostensibly even-handed split gives an advantage to the incumbent, who on top of the money has the priceless value of the office.

Why Should I Pay for a Politician's Campaign?

The honest answer is, you already do. You the taxpayer are picking up the tab for the incumbent, by paying for every European junket taken and all the public relations trips back to the home district from Washington. You foot the bill for every ton of "constituent newsletter" propaganda mailed, and for the staff members diverted to campaign purposes. You and I are suckers for allowing our pockets to be picked so cleanly.

The best proposal so far for congressional campaign financing calls for floors, not ceilings. Floors would give each candidate a base amount, and let them raise additional money above that. The best approach might be to give *only* the challenger a floor amount—say $100,000, a pittance by modern campaign standards—and then give the challenger funds to match whatever the incumbent raises. In this way the incumbent would always be behind the challenger, losing the built-in advantages of holding office. Best of all, the incumbent would have no incentive to raise more and more money because the challenger would always be keeping up with him, stride for stride.

A side-by-side measure should limit the amount PACs can give to any one candidate, reducing the current $5,000 cap to $1,000, as called for in the Senate bill that was filibustered to death in 1988 by incumbents. We should also have a federal law requiring that at least half of a candidate's funds be raised inside his or her district (or state, for a Senator). That measure has been proposed as a referendum question in California. I believe it would keep candidates tied closer to their constituents at home than to their money-bagged friends in Washington.

The overall effect of this plan should be to reduce the role of special interest groups and PACs in bankrolling incumbents. It should also reduce overall campaign spending.

This reform may not come any time soon. As Dr. Larry Sabato pointed out in his excellent book, *PAC Power*, incumbent Representatives and Senators are not likely to "do any favors for their opponents by enacting public-funding floors that favor challengers rather than ceilings that favor themselves."

But then, it was considered unlikely that all the original 1974 campaign finance reforms would pass—reforms that outlawed direct corporate giving and mandated complete disclosure of all political contributions.

I repeat, it is possible to pass good laws as long as the "hot breath of the people" is felt on the neck of each legislator. Grassroots pressure from the people who read this book can impress upon incumbents the wisdom of supporting campaign reforms. And voters should reward the growing number of upright challengers who refuse PAC money in their campaigns (at the Presidential level, Bruce Babbitt and Gary Hart both refused to accept PAC dollars in their 1988 campaigns). Representative "Buddy" Roemer of Louisiana defeated incumbent Governor Edwin Edwards in a tight gubernatorial race in 1987, and later said he won "because in the end I did what I said I would do. I ran a campaign that took no big checks, took no PAC money. What I am telling you is that the people knew before the politicians what was wrong with Louisiana politics—money."

One final suggestion on money in politics. A conscientious leader would beef up the enforcement staff and penalty provisions of the Federal Election Commission to deal with the wanton disregard of spending laws by some campaigners. As things stand now, some violations aren't penalized until long after Election Day, when the candidate is sitting in office. A cardinal reform would be to speed up the enforcement process so that campaigners could be fined before they've stolen the election.

How could we do this? One of my researchers found an obscure passage in the FEC's campaign laws (Title 2, Section 437g, paragraph 4, subparagraphs A and B, in case you're interested) that actually prevents the commission from timely enforcement. It says that if the commission knows a violation has been or is about to be committed, it has to:

> ...attempt, for a period of at least 30 days [and up to 90 days], to correct or prevent such violation by informal methods of conference, conciliation and persuasion, and to enter into conciliation agreement with any person involved....[No such action] may be made public by the Commission without the written consent of the respondent.

All that before any enforcement action can be taken! Let's get serious with the politicians who try to skirt the law. If the FEC has information ("probable cause," the law calls it) about campaign cheating, let the public know. And let's stop all this namby-pambiness about informal conciliation talks. If a campaigner overspends, slap the penalty on.

Punt the Perks

We have to hit incumbents where they live, dismantling the tools they use to maintain their safe positions. An end to congressional franking would be a tremendous advance since the taxpayer would no longer be subsidizing the Lifetime Politician's free propaganda machine, which blankets his constituency with "newsletters" plastered with his picture and name. That sort of free political advertising has to end. Here in California we have had state ballot initiatives that would eliminate public funding for incumbents' newsletters in the state legislature. We need pressure for the same thing at the federal level.

At the very least, we can rewrite the law that allows incumbents to include in their newsletters "a biography or autobiography of the member...or the spouse or other members of the family," as well as "a picture, sketch or other likeness of the Member." Enough of ego boosts for the Lifetime Politicians. Delete those sections of Title 39, Chapter 32 of the Federal Code, and we won't be getting propaganda sheets anymore.

Similarly, limits on congressional staffs should be imposed, and I'm talking about real cutbacks. As we discussed earlier, most of the thousands upon thousands of staffers are not engaged in constituency service but in work aimed ultimately at promoting the reelection prospects of the incumbent. With limits on terms, incumbents will no longer be so focused on reelection and will not need hordes of political flunkies doing campaign work at public expense.

Today, it is not uncommon for a congressional office to have thirty staffers on the payroll. A sensible limit would be seven staffers per office: three legislative assistants, a press secretary, a scheduler and two secretaries. The rest of the workload can either be cut out or handled by volunteers from the home state who would welcome experience on Capitol Hill.

An End To Gerrymandering

We have to reverse the process of carving our geographical and cultural communities into illogical districts just to ensure safe seats. How can we end such "incumbent protection plans" when we know the old boys will never surrender voluntarily?

To end the back-room scandals, we need to create a better reapportionment system with a nonpartisan organization designated to create genuinely competitive districts. We have to get the responsibility for redistricting out of the hands of the state legislature and into another branch of government—the judiciary.

In the few cases where the courts have been charged with redistricting, they have usually drawn fair lines based on geographical and demographic criteria rather than partisan politics. Sometimes the courts have become involved because of the Voting Rights Act and desegregation, as in North Carolina where elections now produce close results in almost every district.

More predictably, the courts step in when a legislature and Governor can't agree on a plan. In California, we had exactly that in the early 1970s when a Democratic legislature fought Governor Ronald Reagan to a deadlock over new districting. The state supreme court finally stepped in to draw the lines, producing a rational map with some genuinely competitive seats.

WHITE HOUSE REFORMS

I see some neccesary changes we can employ to make the President work harder and perform better. In the last chapter we discussed reforms of the way we choose our President—to make sure we get the best man or woman in the first place.

But we've seen a major problem with the Presidency. The occupant of the Oval Office is accountable to no one but the people and to them only every four years. Short of impeachment, there is nothing a President has to fear from any outside agency.

As I said in my discussion of Ronald Reagan's Presidency, if a President wants to hide from the people and the Congress when his policies are exposed as failed or fraudulent, there is nothing to stop him. All the outside world ever gets are statements from his press secretary saying everything is fine. And Reagan's longtime press secretary, Larry Speakes, even admitted making up supposed quotes from the President to feed to the media, writing in his autobiography *Speaking Out* that he wanted to "spruce up the President's image by taking a bit of liberty with my PR man's license."

I have three suggestions to make on Presidential accountability. All three are inspired by looking at the parliamentary system of government. The dean of Presidential historians, Arthur Schlesinger, Jr., argues in his book *The Cycles of American History* that there is little to be gained by borrowing from the British system. I disagree, and propose some limited adaptations that would improve accountability while retaining all the essentials of the American system.

President's Question Time

One way to end the isolation of the President from the media and the people is to adopt a version of the parliamentary "Question Time."

Every two weeks, Prime Minister Margaret Thatcher has to stand before the House of Commons to face the questions (and sometimes taunts and insults) of members. Her own party members can ask questions, but primarily it's a time for members of the opposition to get tough with her on various current issues. It's something like a press conference, but harder on the Prime Minister because it is a regular event. The questioners know exactly what they are asking about. They can't be hoodwinked by grins and a softshoe. They are determined to get real answers, and the Prime Minister takes the procedure seriously.

The result? The Prime Minister, and her cabinet, must stay on top of every issue, every current policy area, on the chance that they will have to justify their actions or inaction before Parliament (and to the public, since sessions of Parliament are broadcast). Leadership is more responsible because it has to be more responsive. And very often government policies are exposed as folly while still in the development stage, or are altered to meet criticism or advice from the opposition. All in all, Question Time makes for better government.

What do we have to match this in the United States? Absolutely nothing. The only time a President has to appear before Congress is for the State of the Union address, a once-a-year affair that has become just another media event. The President stands before TV cameras and gives a sugar-coated message about how great things are going. There is no chance, of course, for members of Congress to ask questions. After hearing the address, they just stand and applaud while he walks back up the aisle, waving at the cameras. And then the President is gone.

That is the only time that a President has to appear in public. As we saw first with Carter in the Rose Garden during the hostage crisis, and with Reagan during the whole Iran-*contra* scandal, a President can hide from the media, the Congress and the public if he wants. All the White House staff has to do is send him out to read an occasional speech or cue card, just to show he's still alive. The press is reduced to yelling questions at him from across a fence in the Rose Garden.

Presidential Question Time would not require a constitutional amendment or even an act of Congress. All it would take is a new President with some political spine and the confidence in his own policies and administration to face up to the outside world. Each new President should pledge to make himself available to a joint session of Congress (or to the House or Senate on a rotating basis) periodically, for open and honest political questions and answers. The sessions would be televised, of course, so that the public could judge the President's performance.

The President would be obliged to know his stuff, to be on top of problems. No longer would we have a Reagan saying as the Iran-*contra* scandal bubbled, "I'm still waiting for somebody to tell me what happened." The President would have to take responsibility for his staff and policies.

Most importantly, a Question Time would lessen the hostility and deep suspicion that now exist between the executive and legislative branches, without compromising existing checks and balances. A President would be able to reopen the lines of communication with the House and Senate. The accountability of the administration, not only to the opposition party and Congress but to the public at large, would increase tremendously. Public opinion now holds government institutions in contempt for their lack of responsiveness to the crises of the day.

Arthur Schlesinger dismisses the idea of a Question Time for the United States, but only based on its practice in Great Britain and Canada. Naturally, its operation here would differ somewhat from those parliamentary systems. We already have a media-oriented Presidency. Ordinary people have less and less access to a real live President. A televised Question Time would at least give us a less formal, less manipulable media setting to view our leaders.

In fact, if it were taken seriously by the White House and the Congress, a regular Question Time could prevent policy disasters before they happened. Would Vietnam or "Irangate" have followed the same patterns if we had had a Question Time? In the case of Vietnam, Lyndon Johnson would have had to face congressional skepticism over the original Gulf of Tonkin incident. He would have had to justify the continued escalation of the war to an increasingly impatient and disapproving Congress. And the Iran-*contra* scandal might have been nipped in the bud. If the President had been answering all along for his policies toward Nicaragua and Iran, we wouldn't have had to go through the whole agonizing episode culminating in the TV hearings circus. The Watergate and Irangate coverups would have been much harder to sustain with Question Time.

Encourage Shadow Cabinets

One concrete move that could improve the quality of Presidential Cabinets and staffs would be the adoption of the Pell-Mathias amendment, which Arthur Schlesinger also endorses. That proposal would advance the inauguration of the new President from January to November, almost immediately after the election. (Schlesinger himself prefers the first of December.) Newly elected Presidents would have to be ready to make their appointments and develop their policies almost immediately. To do that, they would need to have already considered top appointments and staff assignments.

With such a change, we could emulate another element of the British system: the Shadow Cabinet, which publicly identifies prospective Cabinet members before elections. This pressure would certainly encourage a candidate to make the most qualified appointments possible. The Pell-Mathias proposal also could forestall the kind of farce we saw in 1980-1981, when Reagan spent millions on his glitzy circus inauguration.

Overall, the process of preparing for the next Question Time and anticipating the types of information members of Congress might request would spur Presidents to surround themselves with good lieutenants. We should encourage new Presidents to select Cabinet members and top staff for their expertise in appropriate areas and not for their personal political ties to the President. This would not only avoid appointees like Bill Casey or Ed Meese (under Reagan) and Bert Lance or Hamilton Jordan (under Carter), it also would improve the information flow to the President.

There is no way we can force the President to make good appointments. In the end we have to be able to expect that a President will do his or her best to make quality appointments. We can only hope that the Reagan administration will serve as a negative example to future Presidents.

A Reagan Staff Meeting

How could any President ignore the ugly and un-American spectacle that occurred on November 4, 1987? On that day, four former top Reagan officials showed up in the same federal court in Washington—on different cases! Mike Deaver, Ed Meese, Robert MacFarlane, and Ollie North all could have thrown a reunion party, if they hadn't been escorted by phalanxes of lawyers and TV cameras as they went before judges to tell their versions of the truth.

We might also encourage a new President-elect to spend time with his or her predecessor to get advice and tips on how to run the White House, deal with Congress and move the country forward. Presidents don't get enough information from the previous occupants of the Oval Office. When Eisenhower took over from Truman in 1953, the only contact between the two was in the limousine on the way to the Inauguration. They bickered for a few minutes, then spent the rest of the ride in silence.

We Need a King

I have one more idea, and hear me out before you think I'm crazy. One problem, particularly in the Reagan administration, has been that Presidents apparently find it hard to distinguish between the ceremonial aspects of the job and the real work of governing the nation. Ronald Reagan obviously enjoyed the pomp and ceremony but not the actual work. It's true that in this media age we place more and more demands on our Presidents to be TV father-figures, with ceremonies like the Statue of Liberty celebration, the Constitution's bicentennial, the 1984 Los Angeles Olympics and all the similar events that Reagan always seemed to find time to attend.

Even summit meetings with world leaders have a large element of pageantry and fluff that waste the time of a real working President. Most other countries in the world have a head of state and a separate head of government. Maybe the White House needs two occupants—one for form, one for substance.

Or maybe we need a king. Perhaps the only way we can get our Presidents to concentrate on the job to which we have elected them is to hand over the ceremonial and symbolic functions of the office—which people have come to expect—to an American King. After all, the popularity of *People* magazine shows that we are infatuated with the idea of royalty; we've practically elevated our Hollywood stars and sports figures to that level. Let's just be honest, admit that people yearn for a ceremonial figurehead, and elect His or Her Majesty.

All right, we don't have to call the position "King" or "Queen." We could have a "national cheerleader" to embody all the symbolic qualities people want in a leader: personal attractiveness, stage presence and an appealing TV voice. He or she would only be a figurehead with no political power and no authority over decisions. But that's how it works in England, where even the annual speech that the Queen makes to open Parliament (like our State of the Union address) is written by the Prime Minister. The Queen reads it word for word.

We could use "form criteria" to elect the monarch, and concentrate on "substance criteria" for Presidential campaigns. We might be lucky enough to end up with an "unelectable" in the Oval Office. And, best of all, we could still have had King Ronald Reagan right where we liked him—on TV, visiting our living rooms with a warm smile and a wink. Who else could read cue cards so well? Who else could be so reassuring about America's golden future? Who else could welcome home soldiers from war with such a smart salute? Remember what Tip O'Neill, in his autobiography, said of Reagan: "Let me give him his due: he would have made a hell of a king."

A JOURNEY OF A THOUSAND LEAGUES...

...begins with but one step. The first and most important of the ways we need to reform our political system is to GET THE PEOPLE TO CAST THEIR BALLOTS. We saw earlier how political incompetence and public apathy feed on each other. We need to break that connection, and to do that we need to start voting again!

A Motor-Voter Program

We know that only about half of the people who are eligible to vote in the United States are voting—even fewer in nonpresidential elections. But we also know that 85 percent to 90 percent of those people who are *registered* to vote actually turn out at the polls. So the non-voting problem, which is at the core of our political captivity, is primarily a matter of getting people registered.

Are you registered to vote? I know that a sizable number of people who read this are not. Do it. It's easy to register to vote. All you have to do is go down to the city hall and fill out one form—it's probably the easiest bureaucratic exercise our government has.

But it could be made easier. Voter registration drives have proven effective in the past. Jesse Jackson achieved much of his electoral success in 1984 and 1988 by getting unregistered citizens onto the voting rolls. Pat Robertson also built up his support by using fundamentalist churches for registration drives.

The federal government has been unable to come up with innovative programs designed to reach citizens who aren't already motivated to register. One state, however, has done so. Michigan has been in the forefront of voter-registration drives, using a great idea: the "Motor-Voter Program."

What is it that every American over 18 does? No, not that. Drive a car! So, since every American is going to have contact with a state department of motor vehicles at some point, why not have them begin their careers as active voters at the same time they begin their careers as drivers?

In a motor-voter program (there are several different versions or proposals now in different states), the idea is to take individuals who show up at the department of motor vehicles for their driver's license or auto registration, and simultaneously provide them with the opportunity to register to vote. The process has worked remarkably well in Detroit, where the numbers of registered voters are climbing.

This program can reach people who haven't registered when it would be convenient for them to do so, without a trip to another government office. For years civic activists have urged the adoption of programs like postcard registration, which wouldn't even require the person to leave the house.

But even if successful, these measures will only help us so far. We not only have to free ourselves from the clutches of Lifetime Politicians, we have to solve the problems they have been ignoring or exacerbating. So we must now go through a painful process, plumbing the depths of our mistakes in economics and foreign policy. If you have a weak heart, put this book down immediately.

PART II

--- ★ ---

ECONOMICS: THE SEARCH FOR PROSPERITY

CHAPTER 11

★

Reaganomics
and Other Bedtime Stories

I suspect that if in 1981 I had unfolded to Ronald Reagan a scenario that had him tripling the national debt, he would have told me I was crazy. What's crazy is the state of the American economy today.

We pay a heavy price for the irresponsibility of our politicians, but nowhere is it more obvious than in the national economy. Lifetime Politicians have been running us down the tubes as fast as they can, with the problems rumbling from administration to administration. They may not realize they are doing that; they may even be trying to solve the problems, in their blundering ways. Nevertheless, the end effect has been disastrous. Ronald Reagan, you remember, was elected President in 1980 with a mandate to plug the drain, and the policies he said would do the job came to be called Reaganomics.

Reaganomics is a set of economic beliefs based on two faulty principles. The first one states that reducing taxes will motivate businesses and individuals to work more and produce more. As a result, there will be more income to be taxed, and government revenues will go up even with a lower tax rate. Reagan originally claimed that the greater tax revenues could be used to pay for his defense buildup. This has proven to be wrong, dead wrong, although even in 1988 Reagan continued to stick to his (empty) guns, giving such simplistic explanations as "when taxes go down, revenues go up; when taxes go up, revenues go down." And black is white, and night is day....

We really loved the whole idea because it was painless, just like all fairy-tale solutions. While a massive infusion of foreign cash made it appear we were doing okay, we also had low taxes to make us feel good. Deficits were unseen or unrecognized. This was Reagan's economic "feel-goodism," which proved in the election years of 1980 and 1984 to be an enormously popular political program, even if it failed as economics.

WHEN IT RAINS IT TRICKLES

The second principle of Reaganomics is the so-called "trickle-down" theory, which states that by giving tax breaks to business and the rich, they will invest more and hire more workers so that the benefits of the tax breaks trickle down to middle-income earners and the poor. The amount that actually trickles down is puny compared to the sums diverted to business and the rich. This is a crucial consequence of Reaganomics: ordinary folks are screwed while the rich get richer.

Reagan was able to get away with this transfer of wealth to the rich by hiding behind a false populism of "getting government off people's backs." In reality, Reagan's changes simply got government off the backs of corporations by deregulating industries (airlines, banks), cutting down on consumer protection (the Federal Trade Commission) and reducing tax rates. There was no such diminution of government involvement in the life of the ordinary citizen.

Reagan's promises to cut spending were just that—promises. Let's remember (I do because I was there) that when Ronald Reagan was Governor of California, he more than doubled state spending. Another clue to what he would do in the White House was dropped immediately after he was elected President in 1980. He dipped into the taxpayers' pockets for more than $2 million to pay for "transition-team costs."

As Arthur Schlesinger, Jr., pointed out in his book, *The Cycles of American History*, this figure was far greater than had been spent by any previous incoming administration. Reagan was clearly setting up shop as the biggest overspender in the history of the country. In fact, Reagan's first budget director, David

Stockman, has admitted now that the "Reagan Revolution ended up as an unintended exercise in free lunch economics." How could our government seem so much like Alice in Wonderland?

In his book, *The Triumph of Politics*, Stockman lays much of the blame on the public relations background of the men in the White House, who were "fiscally illiterate" and refused to take economic problems seriously, preferring to talk about feel-good themes. Stockman writes, "They didn't realize that we were in a much tougher fiscal and political equation than they had previously assumed....[Reagan and his top advisers had no] conception of what the federal budget looked like or how it was calculated."

In fact, Stockman admits that when the crunch came, "the massive deficit inherent in the true supply-side fiscal equation was substantially covered up" by doctoring statistics on gross national product (GNP) growth and producing phony inflation forecasts. If you ran your household budget the way the politicians run the national budget, you'd wake up quivering every morning and wondering where you were going to borrow the money to cover the incoming bills. And then come April 15 you'd risk the wrath of the IRS by lying on your tax returns.

But the Reagan administration isn't solely to blame. Our friends the Lifetime Politicians bear much of the responsibility for massive mismanagement of the economy. But our politicians don't even confront the problems as they stand. One of the biggest reasons I decided to write this book was that I saw politicians refusing to give us the facts and figures on our troubles.

THE SINKHOLE

Enough is enough. I'm tired of the feeling I get when I sign my tax returns, that feeling of helplessness as I watch my money go down a sinkhole.

We're all members of the American household, and we're responsible in the end for the mistakes we let our government make. We have nothing to fear but the facts. So we're going to have to go over the financial books in the next few chapters, see the bad spots (and maybe a few good ones) and figure a way to balance our books (see Figure 3).

Figure 3—The government's balance sheet

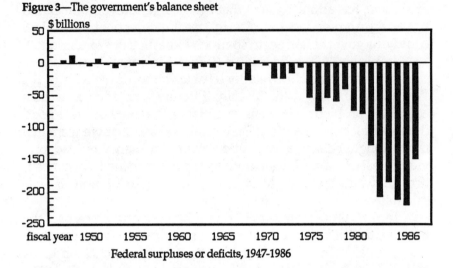

Federal surpluses or deficits, 1947-1986

Prescriptions to cure our economic ills are not new. We need to reduce government spending—and beef up the income side by increasing taxes. The trouble, of course, is that people tend to vote their pocketbooks and rarely take into account the long-term costs, which is how this mess was foisted on us in the first place. It's important for Americans to realize that we will pay in the long run. The way things are going (rapidly), we can't even leave the problem to our children—it will hit us sooner than that.

CHAPTER 1 2

*

The Government Giveth— and Taketh Away

Most of us moan about the money we have to pay to the tax collector. I don't think that's selfish. I suspect the griping goes on because we don't see fairness in the way taxes are collected. We see people who should be paying taxes but aren't.

Let me assure you very quickly that I am not another Nelson Bunker Hunt—one of the infamous Hunt brothers who allegedly tried to corner the silver market a few years ago. According to press reports, his 1986 tax returns claimed that he had earned only $6,000 in salary, yet he received a $3.4 million tax refund. Something seems just a little out of whack there! No, I had no such luck. I paid no less than $841,000 in federal taxes last year and $232,000 in California taxes.

Over a million dollars in personal income tax in one year. I realize that's not going to make a dent in the federal deficit, but it's still a lot of money to me. Like most Americans, I don't object to paying taxes if there is fairness in the collection system and if our tax monies are being used to help people who need help.

I'll bet most people don't realize that the first income tax, authorized under the Sixteenth Amendment in 1913, was sold to the public as a way to "soak the rich"; it only applied to people with an annual income of over $117,000. That was a heck of a lot of money in 1913 (only 347,000 people made that much then).

As the size of government increased, so did income taxes. Before long it wasn't only rich people who were hit. Individuals at all income levels now provide most of the revenues collected by the federal government, and their contributions, measured as a percent of the total, have been increasing.

While individuals are being socked, corporate taxes are notoriously too low. In 1956, corporate income taxes accounted for almost 25 percent of government revenues. This meant that government planners could count on corporations supplying one out of every four dollars needed by the federal government.

That assurance has gone by the boards, as government and big business have settled snugly into bed together. By 1976, that ratio of 25 percent had been cut almost in half to 13.8 percent. By 1987, after the Reagan "tax reforms," corporations were providing only 12.4 percent of all government revenue (see Figure 4).

ROBBING HOOD: THE REAGAN RECORD ON TAXES

The 1981 tax laws were infamous for the lower rates, shelters and loopholes they created and inevitably there was a massive loss in government revenue. Some estimates hold that lost tax revenues account for $700 billion of the $2 trillion added to the national debt under Reagan. The administration's rationale was that tax cuts would create jobs. As it turned out, very few jobs were created in the sectors that most benefited. Most of the new jobs were in services, like fast-food places. Service jobs, as you know, are the worst-paying jobs around.

An example in my business was large across-the-board reductions in the number of years buildings may be depreciated. Before 1981, it took from 33 to 50 years to get the full value of tax write-offs on most buildings. The Reagan bill accelerated that schedule to 15 years. And although the administration claimed the move would spur construction and create jobs, the law was also good for existing buildings, so it handed out windfalls to building owners.

While all individual taxpayers benefited from the cuts in the form of lower tax rates, rich individuals profited the most, and by a substantial amount. Before Reaganomics came to town, the top bracket had its earned income taxed at a rate of 50 percent. Unearned income such as dividends and interest was taxed at 70 percent. Now the top rate on all income is just 28 percent!

Figure 4—How does the government get our money? (1960 compared to 1987)

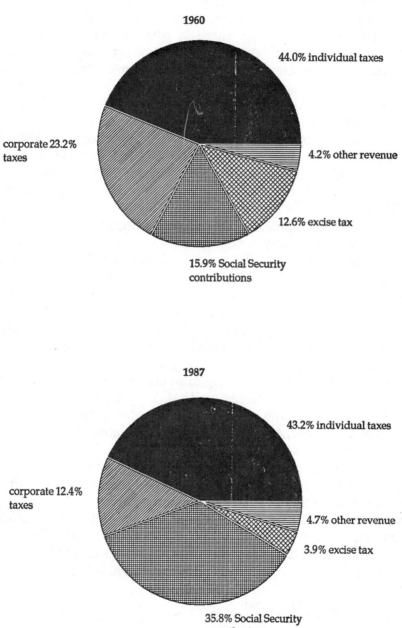

1960

44.0% individual taxes

corporate 23.2% taxes

4.2% other revenue

12.6% excise tax

15.9% Social Security contributions

1987

43.2% individual taxes

corporate 12.4% taxes

4.7% other revenue

3.9% excise tax

35.8% Social Security contributions

My own tax adviser is a contradiction in terms—an honest lawyer. I can remember him coming into my office dumbfounded back in 1981. "This is a Rich Man's tax law," he told me, shaking his head. The changes enabled the wealthy to shelter great amounts of money through what David Stockman admitted later was a "cornucopia of tax ornaments" pushed through the Congress by an administration-big business coalition. In the real estate business, you had to be stupid not to take advantage of the new depreciation schedules and other loopholes.

The Treasury Department's own figures show that just 4.4 percent of the taxpayers (those making over $50,000 a year) received 33 percent of the benefits from the 1981 changes. I was part of that 4.4 percent, and I can tell you, the rich got much richer.

At the same time, middle- and lower-income taxpayers suffered because the government squeezed them by increasing their Social Security taxes. The payroll tax for Social Security was raised continually through the 1980s, going from 6.13 percent to 7.51 percent of wages.

The bottom line is that the Reagan tax cuts redistributed wealth, taking from the poor and giving to the rich. Of course, that was in line with the thinking of wealthy members of Congress and administration officials, and even more with the wishes of the lobbyists and big campaign contributors who had such influence over Reagan policies. Everybody in the power elite went along with the White House, from the Chamber of Commerce to the AFL-CIO. Only three Senators voted against the tax cuts.

One argument of the Reagan brain trust was that if the rich were blessed in this way (by giving them more money), they would put it to good use in the economy. In fact, what we now know is they just funneled much of the windfall into the stock market, tax-free bonds and other paper investments. They are perceptive investors. They invest in good times and pull in their horns in bad times, just when their investment is most needed.

THE BILLIONAIRE BOOM

Forbes magazine has an annual issue identifying the 400 richest people in the country. It's the magazine's best seller. I read the list, too, but every year it gives me an uneasy feeling about the direction we're heading.

The 1987 issue revealed that the wealthiest 400 individuals were worth $220 billion—a giant leap upwards of 41 percent in one year. Did the economy grow at a 41-percent clip in 1987? Hardly. And the number of billionaires almost doubled, surging from 26 to 49.

Coincidentally, the October stock market crash, coming just after the *Forbes* issue hit the stands, deflated the paper value of some of those fortunes. But the party isn't over. In 1988 George Bush called for yet another big tax cut for the wealthy, proposing that the tax on capital gains be cut from 28 percent to 15 percent. Are most Americans earning profits on the sale of things like stock, real estate and art works—which is what capital gains are?

Believe me, I deal with this stuff every day. It's obvious who would benefit. The congressional Joint Committee on Taxation estimates that more than two-thirds of capital gains income goes to people making $200,000 a year or more. Those people don't make the decision to sell capital assets based primarily on the tax rate, anyway. They consider more long-term factors like their age, health and family considerations, depreciation factors, or a desire to replace one asset with something more valuable.

Caution: More Trouble in the Gulf

I may be upsetting a lot of the people in my tax bracket, but anyone with a conscience can see the widening gulf between rich and poor. In 1972, the richest one percent of American families held 27 percent of the nation's wealth. The figure has been rising steadily since then. By 1988, the top 1 percent held 36 percent of the wealth. That equals the record set just before everything came tumbling down in the great crash of 1929.

Redistribution of wealth is an inevitable result of weighting tax cuts toward the rich. A cut is easy to sell to anyone, rich or poor, but after all, if you cut everyone's tax rate by 10 percent, you are helping the big guy a lot more than the little guy. I'm no goody-goody, and I know throwing money at social problems doesn't work, but I sure as hell don't think the rich need to be subsidized, either. The rich can take care of themselves.

THE TAX DOLLARS WE NEVER SEE

Taxes are supposed to be levied on all kinds of income earners, but let's not kid ourselves. We lose a lot of money to tax evaders. One estimate, made by the Internal Revenue Service in 1983, found that the federal government was stiffed more than $100 billion—that was more than half the federal deficit—by under-reporting of income, overstated deductions and failure to file returns at all. That was on *legal* income. In some areas, such as capital gains, only a third of taxable income is reported to the IRS.

Then there's that shadowy area known as the "underground economy." No one knows how big it really is but everyone agrees it is huge. The amounts of money flowing in and out of private hands through organized crime, drug dealing, "off-the-books" work and bartering represent an enormous sector of financial activity that is not being counted in the GNP. It's not reported—and it's not taxed.

Just the figures on organized crime and drugs are staggering. The President's Commission on Organized Crime estimated that in 1986 organized crime generated as much as $300 billion of income—in one year! That was almost equal to the 1986 federal budget deficit and trade deficit combined! Of that total, more than a third (around $110 billion) was from drug trafficking.

The numbers for illegal gambling also run into the billions. A 1983 estimate of the total amount wagered illegally ran to almost $30 billion, with over $5 billion scooped off as profits, which are, of course, untaxed. Illegal prostitution probably represents another $8 billion in untaxed business.

According to a 1987 IRS estimate, if these shadow entrepreneurs had to check in with the IRS, the government would be able to raise another $80 to $100 billion a year in tax revenues. I'm not proposing here that we legalize all these businesses so that we can tax them. I am just appalled at the size and scope of the problem.

We soak middle-income earners and let the rich get away with murder. We give tax breaks to corporations. We have an enormous underground economy that mocks the government. Everyone looks for ways to get out of paying taxes. And then we go on such a spending spree that we have to borrow money to pay for everything we're buying. What a recipe for disaster!

GIVING AWAY THE RANCH

Since the revenues collected by the IRS don't come close to meeting the obligations we have taken on, the government borrows heavily to pay the bills. In the next chapter we'll see how we're drowning in interest payments by not balancing our books. But there's another sneaky way the feds try to mask the gaping deficit holes: massive giveaways.

Every year, when budget-making gets tight and the lifers are looking for bucks at the margins, you'll see news accounts reporting that "the proposed budget calls for raising an additional x billion dollars through the sale of government assets." What exactly does that mean—is Washington about to sell off the family jewels to raise a little cash?

You bet. In 1987, as part of such a fire sale, the Bureau of Land Management sold 82,000 acres of land in Colorado for $2.50 an acre. You may not be up to date on land values (the bureau obviously isn't), but that's like selling a parking lot full of brand new cars for $25 apiece. What happened after the land was sold to a wealthy family trust at that bargain-basement price? Why, the buyers turned right around and sold most of it to Shell Oil for $2,000 an acre! Their profit was a hefty $34 million (they only paid $205,000 to begin with).

Incredible! I'll say it again—incredible! How could such a thing happen? It all dates back to an obscure mining law passed in 1872, which allowed individuals or companies to stake claims to public lands. If they kept the claim for five years and invested at least $100 an acre in the property every year, they would then be able to purchase the land outright for $2.50 an acre.

That was the price set over a hundred years ago, when we were trying hard to encourage people to settle the West. But times have changed. We don't need such incentives for land buyers now. Much of the land is rich in shale oil, like the acreage that was sold to Shell. For some insane reason, neither Congress nor the executive branch has ever seen fit to update the law and its set prices.

So every few years a quiet scandal slips by when yet another claimant is able to buy up huge chunks of the American West for a pittance. Jay Hair, president of the National Wildlife Federation, points out that over 270,000 acres in Colorado, Utah and

Wyoming could potentially be sold in the near future unless this hole in the government's barn door is shut.

Why has Washington done nothing about the scandal? Maybe it's because the claimants to the remaining acres are powerful interests: oil companies mainly, including Exxon, Marathon and Union Oil of California. Meanwhile, the cost to the rest of us is incalculable. The oil royalties we could lose from selling off other resource-rich land could range anywhere from $30 billion to hundreds of billions. Those future revenues could go a long way towards reducing our budget deficits.

Remember, deficits can go on but you can only sell your country once. We are just passing through and should be playing the role of caretaker for America's future. This nation is not ours to sell lightly.

GET YOURS NOW

The rich aren't the only problem. The truth is that many groups in our society—farmers and homeowners, as well as corporate bosses and millionaires—have stakes in the current madness continuing. No one wants to give up his or her benefits, the "bennies" everybody craves. Just ask your neighbor if he would like to help balance the federal budget by giving up his mortgage interest deduction.

The message of Reaganomics was: "Get as much as you can, as quick as you can." It was a message that registered with a lot of the people in the country. It wasn't just the income side of the budget that suffered; never before has there been a raiding party on the Treasury as the past eight years have seen. Let's look next at federal spending, which can be defined in three little words: out of control.

CHAPTER 13

★

Government Spending: Out Of Control

Cause and effect. Simple little words, but they carry such different meanings. We all have a natural tendency to concentrate on the effects we see, rather than the causes that lie behind them.

Take the budget deficit. (Please.) Probably no two words were spoken more frequently during the 1988 Presidential primaries than "budget deficit." It was a great example of a focus on the effect. The cause of the budget deficit was usually ignored.

Why does the federal government spend more money than it takes in? From the discussion in Part I, we know that Lifetime Politicians focus on reelection rather than smart policy. That phenomenon is the primary cause of budget deficits. With their drive for perpetual power, it's not in the self-interest of Lifetime Politicians to pursue a rational budget policy.

It's even against their own interests to tell the American people the truth about government spending, since we might then exercise some common-sense oversight and fire those responsible for our budget problems. Lifetime Politicians and the entire political elite want to keep our eyes turned to the effect, not the cause. So we get a fog of disinformation from Washington, sprinkled liberally with confusing statistics and baffling numbers.

In this chapter I'd like to change all that. We'll look plainly at the budget—how much we spend, how much we have cut in the past, and why. But there is one thing we should keep in mind. If Lifetime Politicians are responsible for our budget crisis, then the ultimate responsibility lies with the rest of us, for we elect them. Their priorities are determined by our priorities.

Our priorities were made clear in a 1987 *New York Times*/CBS News national poll: by a 4-to-1 margin, Americans want government to "guarantee medical care for all people." By almost 3-to-1 Americans say the government ought to "see to it that everyone who wants a job has a job." By 2-to-1 we think that government should provide day care for all children. But the same poll also showed that, by a 2-to-1 margin, we are unwilling to pay more federal taxes for such programs and unwilling to see other social programs cut to pay for new ones. A magician couldn't balance a budget with such priorities; but we seem to want magicians, since the poll found that we favor a constitutional amendment requiring a balanced budget by more than 5-to-1.

No wonder we haven't had a balanced budget since 1969.

THE GIPPER MOVES THE GOALPOSTS

Far from cutting federal spending as he promised, Ronald Reagan presided over a large increase in the federal budget since he took over from Jimmy Carter. As a percentage of GNP, federal spending went from 20.6 percent when Carter left office to 23.8 percent in 1986. That jump means that the government is spending at a level *15 percent higher* than under Carter, whom Reagan blasted as a spendthrift.

In actual dollar amounts, spending went up by more than 23 percent during the Reagan era. That's calculated in constant 1982 dollars—in other words, it was a 23 percent jump *after* the inflation factor was eliminated. Defense spending, which Reagan did promise to increase, rose 48 percent. Nondefense spending grew by more than 15 percent (see Figure 5).

The Reagan tax cuts pushed up federal spending. They resulted in more borrowing, and we have to pay interest on the national debt. Interest payments on the debt went over the $100 billion mark for the first time ever in 1984.

The 1980s showed year after year of huge deficits in the government's balance sheet. After a while, if you're like me, the

Figure 5—Levels of federal spending during Reagan administration

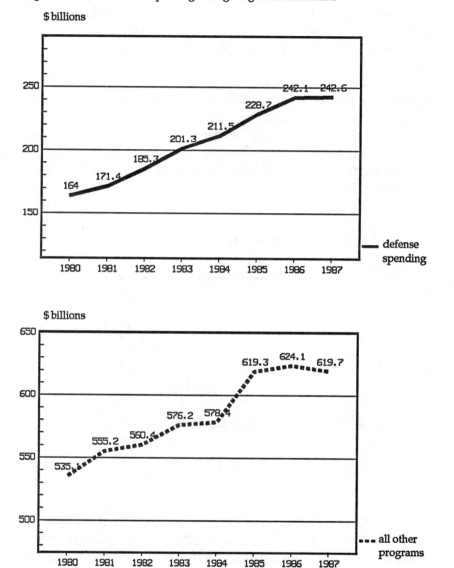

$ billions

defense spending

$ billions

all other programs

(Amounts are calculated in constant 1982 dollars)

numbers tend to produce a glaze over your eyes, but it should be clear to all of us by now that Ronald Reagan showed no ability to cut the big items in the budget. He wasn't even thrifty in the executive branch, where he had more control than other areas. People working in the executive branch increased in the Reagan years (1981-1987) from 2,829,423 to 3,010,895. That's a 7 percent increase, not a cut. Some of that growth was in the military, most was in various bureaucracies. That's a lot of people, all working for an administration that had pledged to get "government off our backs."

Of course that growth cannot be blamed only on Ronald Reagan. We all know from our own lives that once patterns become established, it's extremely difficult to undo them. The trend toward big government has been running for some time (see Figure 6). It has momentum. The important point to remember is that not even a Reagan was able to muster the political guts to make real cuts.

Figure 6—When did our big budget deficits start?

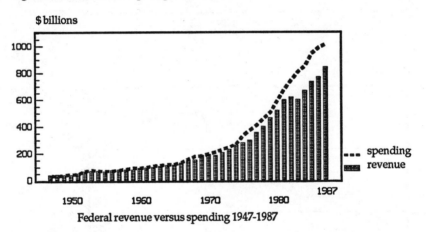

Federal revenue versus spending 1947-1987

"Mr. Cut Spending" and "Mr. Balance the Budget" entered the White House with a $958 billion debt—and he is leaving with a $2.8 trillion debt. This represents a tripling of the national debt. About half ($1 trillion) of the increase resulted from his tax cuts. The other half came from increased spending.

The arithmetic is simple. It's harder to cover the interest on $3 trillion in debt than on $1 trillion. But that's easier than $4 or $5 trillion, which is where we are heading if we don't do something.

WHERE DOES THE MONEY GO?

Out of every federal dollar we spend, 28 cents goes to the military, while 35 cents is spent on "entitlement programs," which entitle people by law to receive something—like Social Security, Medicare or food stamps, for example. And we have to spend 14 cents for interest on the national debt. What does that leave? Just 23 cents of the budget dollar for everything else the government has to do, the "discretionary" programs, all the way from the space shuttle to the strategic petroleum reserve to salaries for the Supreme Court (see Figure 7).

SOCIAL SECURITY

The Social Security program is the closest thing we have to a sacred cow in our budget. That is because the easiest way to get votes is to give money away. The program was slated to pay out $217 billion in 1988 to 38 million people, for hospitalization, disability and most of all retiree benefits.

Most people think of Social Security as an insurance plan. They pay in through payroll deductions for all those years, and then receive benefit checks from the money they've contributed. The notion of a "trust fund," building up year after year as payroll taxes go in, supports that view of Social Security. And by law that money can't be used for anything but Social Security payments.

But some funny things have been going on in the creative accounting department of the federal government. From the 1930s until the late 1960s, the Social Security trust fund was counted separately from the rest of the budget. But in 1967 and 1968, the Vietnam War and new "Great Society" social programs faced Lyndon Johnson with the prospect of huge federal deficits. Like most politicians, LBJ was afraid to raise taxes, so he and Congress devised an ingenious scheme to move the Social Security trust fund into the ledger of general federal revenues— even though it couldn't be spent on anything but Social Security. That way, the government seemed to be in fine fiscal health. We could spend more money, because we had all that money accumulating through the payroll tax. Deficit? What deficit?

Life is never that easy. In truth, Social Security is more like a welfare program. It pays for itself day-by-day, which means that

Figure 7—Have our budget spending priorities changed? (1980 compared to 1987)

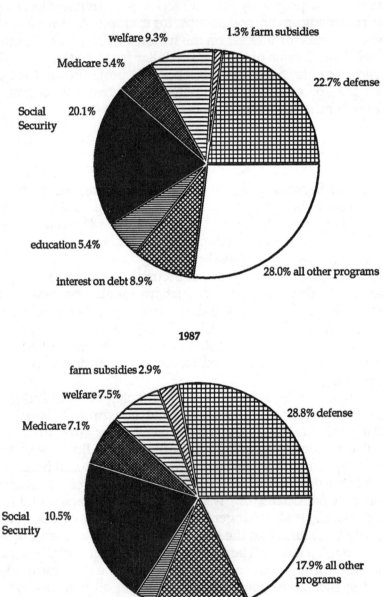

1980

welfare 9.3%

1.3% farm subsidies

Medicare 5.4%

22.7% defense

Social 20.1%
Security

education 5.4%

interest on debt 8.9%

28.0% all other programs

1987

farm subsidies 2.9%

welfare 7.5%

28.8% defense

Medicare 7.1%

Social 10.5%
Security

17.9% all other
programs

education 2.9%

13.5% interest on debt

each person's contributions are not saved for him or her until retirement, but are paid out as benefits to retired people right now. That's because most retirees now receive much more money than they paid in over their working years, even counting interest. So the Social Security trust fund is not a big heap of unused cash that can offset the annual budget deficit—it's money that we spend, every year, for benefit checks.

That was the reason behind the big Social Security scare in the first Reagan administration, leading to the 1983 Presidential commission that "saved" Social Security. It turned out that the payroll tax wasn't bringing in enough money to cover the yearly payment costs, so the tax had to be increased. Otherwise the trust fund would have been bankrupted in just one more year. With the payroll tax increased to 7.5 percent, and with Social Security taxes on self-employed people raised by a third, the trust fund started building up again.

We're actually letting another fast one slip by us. As the surpluses build up, year by year, between what Social Security taxes bring in and what the program pays out, that trust fund actually is becoming a large pile of cash. But budget planners in the White House and Congress are salivating after the money.

The *New York Times* is already reporting that there is a move to let the surplus "mask deep deficits in the government's other accounts....[that way] less has to be cut from the military budget and from domestic social spending," even though that money cannot be spent for anything except Social Security payments.

The Lifetime Politicians think they've found a painless way to keep running huge deficits without the public noticing. But that approach is a sham, because those hidden deficits still add to the national debt since the Social Security surplus can't be used to balance the budget. On paper, at least on a politician's piece of paper, our deficits look like they're decreasing. In the real world, we're losing more and more in interest payments on a ballooning national debt.

OTHER ENTITLEMENT PROGRAMS

The next largest entitlement program is Medicare, which pays out $75 billion a year to cover medical care for 30 million elderly and disabled people. The Medicare part that covers

Figure 8—Where does federal welfare spending go?

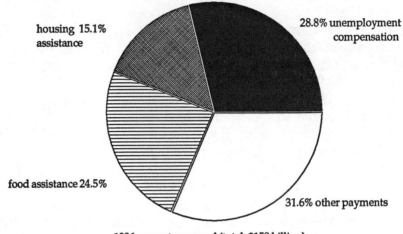

housing 15.1% assistance

28.8% unemployment compensation

food assistance 24.5%

31.6% other payments

1986 percentages used (total: $158 billion)

hospitalization is paid for with Social Security funds. Medicaid, which pays for medical care for the 25 million poorest Americans, costs $50 billion a year, but the federal government pays only half of that; the states pay the rest.

Overall, Medicare and Medicaid spending are 70 percent higher than in 1980 (after adjusting for inflation). That's not only because of rising hospital costs, though. Lifetime Politicians increase the benefits every now and then because that is a very popular move.

Unemployment insurance covers a little over two million people at a time and ate up $18 billion in 1987. If the economy goes into a recession, causing unemployment, these payments will go up. In 1983, at the end of the last recession, the federal government spent more than $30 billion on unemployment payments (see Figure 8).

The government spends $14 billion a year on pensions to needy vets and to those with service-related disabilities. The Veterans Administration (VA) as a whole, though, spends double that amount, with most of the rest going to medical care and the VA hospitals.

MILKING THE GOVERNMENT COW

One of the biggest of the government handout programs is agriculture. Farm subsidies are the third largest benefits program after Social Security and Medicare. Agriculture subsidies set a record in 1986, costing the federal government $26 billion. Subsidies from Washington now represent almost a *third* of all farm income.

Is this good or bad? Are you reading this in Manhattan or in Eau Claire, Wisconsin—dairy capital of the world? Actually, we can't let this issue become one of city versus country. That division benefits the Lifetime Politicians who play trade-off games among themselves while they ladle out the dollars. The real issue lies between rich and poor.

Here are some quick figures on agricultural subsidies. According to the Department of Agriculture, 30,000 farms gross more than $500,000 a year. These are not small family farms but rural big business enterprises. They make up only 1.3 percent of the total number of farms but receive 9 percent of the government handouts. These enterprises are not doing so badly. In many cases the rules are structured so that they get subsidies for *not* growing crops—to keep the price levels artificially high!

Meanwhile, the real family farms don't benefit in the same way from the Washington trough. Farmers earning under $40,000 a year are actually the vast majority of all American farmers, more than 72 percent of the total. But they get only 18 percent of the government subsidies.

Agricultural business leaders siphon a hefty amount straight from the federal budget. Syndicated newspaper columnist Jack Anderson reported on one particular scam that some farmers use to get around a $50,000 cap on the amount any one person can be paid by the government in subsidies. They break up their operations on paper, using "absentee investors" as recipients, and then *each* name collects the full $50,000.

In a recent example, two brothers owned a cotton farm in Louisiana and in 1985 each received the $50,000. So far, so good. But somehow, they weren't satisfied with that hundred grand of the taxpayers' money. So in 1986 they "reorganized" their farm and formed five "corporations"—one for each brother, one for a 50/50 "partnership" between them, and two more for 50/50 "partnerships" with their mother. The result: in 1986, that single farm received $235,000. Just a matter of style.

Why do these scams continue? Because farmers make up a big voting bloc. Presidents play the game, too. The first important caucus of the Presidential election year is held in Iowa. Who make up an important number of voters in Iowa? Farmers, of course. *Harper's Index* (which loves to point out striking figures like these) noted that the World Bank gave $2.9 billion in economic and food assistance to all African nations in 1986; the same year, the U.S. Congress gave $3.7 billion to Iowa farmers.

What's That You Stepped In, Pete?

We saw that farm subsidies are a mess, but Lifetime Politicians prefer to keep shoveling the money into their states, and especially into the hands of the big business farmers, who in turn contribute large sums of money as campaign contributions. Pete du Pont was the only 1988 Presidential candidate who was willing to say, flat out, that he'd cut farm subsidies. How did old Pete do out on the campaign trail?

Tony Coelho, a California congressmen, is the chairman of a House agricultural subcommittee and a chief architect of farm bill subsidies. I'd like to hear him explain a statistic pointed out by economist Warren Brookes in his syndicated column. Why has the number of American cotton farms fallen from 30,000 in 1978 to 20,000 today, while cotton-subsidy recipients have increased from 50,000 to 125,000—at a cost of a billion-and-a-half dollars? Could it have anything to do with the fact that there are 760 cotton farms in Coelho's district, half of which average more than $125,000 in subsidies?

WHO LEADS THE BUDGET CHARGE?

Let's get straight who actually spills the red ink we've been talking about. There's plenty of blame to go around. Until 1921, Congress had exclusive power over the budget, and would only present a finished budget to the executive branch for signing into law or for veto. Since then the President and the executive branch have taken a stronger grip on the process.

First, the President and the Office of Management and Budget come up with a proposed budget for the next fiscal year.

It is then presented to Congress. The President has the final word, by signing or vetoing the appropriations bills (although there is always the veto-override).

Both branches are guilty of overspending. As *Harper's Index* showed, from 1982 to 1987 Ronald Reagan requested from Congress $5.25 trillion in overall spending; Congress actually approved $5.35 trillion. The one-hundred-billion dollar markup is significant, but it's negligible in assigning blame for high spending.

Since 1981, Congress has passed its budget an average of two months late (only once in 12 years has it met a deadline). Because it's easier to tack on budget-busting amendments to one big bill, we end up every year with a fat "continuing resolution" instead of genuine appropriations bills. This omnibus disaster rolls to the floor of the House long overdue and with immense pressure to vote it through as is. Representatives and Senators pressure each other into approving it, and the President into signing it, by leaving the bill so late that defeat or a veto would "cause the entire federal government to shut down."

There is no real debate on what's hidden inside, because there's no time. The House of Representatives had only three hours to debate the 1988 budget, a 43-pound 2,000-page monster. A staff member reportedly told a Representative, "You can look at it if you want, but don't mess it up." Days go by before we even know exactly what our tax dollars buy—if we ever find out, that is.

MAMBO-JUMBO, OR THE POLITICAL DANCE

The two groups at the center of the budget controversy are both intensely political creatures. Congress and the White House play hypocritical games with the budget process, trying to deflect the political heat of spending off on each other. Each shares the responsibility for the deficits. The administration does not have the political will to submit a balanced budget to the Congress, and members of Congress have political reasons for adding even more to the budget once submitted. Neither side is above monkeying with the Constitution to serve its ends.

The budget process from the beginning of the Republic until the 1970s had Congress voting broad appropriations for general areas, leaving the President free to spend or "impound" the money. Impounding meant a President could refuse to spend money, thereby maintaining control over spending even when Congress was out of control. But the lifers on the Hill didn't like the idea of a President blocking pork-barrel funds they voted. In 1974 the Impoundment Control Act cancelled a President's ability to hold Congress in check. In response, the White House now argues that the President should have a line-item veto (which would require an amendment to the Constitution).

Beyond the Call of Duty

When nobody really wants to take responsibility, the budget process deteriorates into political game-playing. Did you know that in November 1987, when members of Congress were writing a bill that would raise taxes and cut spending to reduce the federal deficit, they actually included in the very same bill a 3-percent pay raise for themselves?

The result of this political dance is a budget process incomprehensible to outsiders. My researchers and I had a difficult time boiling down the mass of misinformation about government spending into this chapter, and it's no wonder that average citizens throw their hands up in disgust. Unfortunately, that just leaves the field open to the elite in Washington. It is perfectly obvious that they themselves are overwhelmed at the immensity of the problems. David Stockman confessed to his friend William Greider, "None of us really understands what's going on with these numbers."

PORKY'S REVENGE

A former director of the Congressional Budget Office, Alice Rivlin, has said: "The problem is that the budget process is too complicated. There are too many power centers." Translated, that means each member of Congress tries to channel federal dollars to those who support him or her, with their votes or campaign contributions. That process—pork-barreling—isn't as insidious as it sounds. After all, it is a fundamental tenet of American democracy that a community should be able to have its own representative in Washington to argue for its interests, and those interests include receiving a fair share of the federal purse.

That's fine in good times. But these aren't good times. These are bad times, even though you can't expect Lifetime Politicians to say that. Can we count on Senator John Stennis, who was first elected in 1947, to exercise some sanity in his role as chairman of the Senate Appropriations Committee? No, we can count on him to funnel $2 billion to his state for the Tombigbee Waterway, which has been called a classic example of federal pork-barrel politics. But wait, a ray of hope? Lifer Stennis was retiring in 1988. Maybe his successor in the appropriations chair, Senator Robert Byrd, will use his influence as a former Senate majority leader to restore some sense to the process. No chance. Byrd explained that he gave up the post as majority leader to take "that role which at this point in time will be best for West Virginia." A reporter asked the obvious question, whether Byrd meant he would use his appropriations chairmanship to fight for more big-dollar projects. He answered, "I will do my best to see that West Virginia receives the share for which it is eligible."

The voters play along with this farce. Our short-term interests are served when our own Representative or Senator racks up the seniority to pull down federal dollars for our districts, but our long-term interests are savaged by the cumulative result of *every* Lifetime Politician doing the same thing.

THE ELECTION YEAR SCAM

Lifetime Politicians keep us in the dark about the ultimate costs of the political mambo-jumbo. The numbers game is played with finesse and gusto by both sides in Washington. A study at Carnegie-Mellon University in 1987 found that Presidents "seemingly wish to appear fiscally prudent in the budget that is debated during the Presidential campaign," but then go on to inflate spending commitments for the next year, *after* the election.

One ludicrous example came during the 1980 campaign. According to Dr. Timothy Tregarthen, an economist at the University of Colorado, Jimmy Carter shaved $2 billion from his proposed 1981 budget by assuming that there wouldn't be any natural disasters such as floods or tornados during the year—therefore, no federal disaster funds. Once Reagan won and entered office the funds had to be restored.

The numbers game is bipartisan. During the 1988 campaign, the Reagan administration projected a 1989 deficit of $130 billion, down from 1988's $150 billion. But that budget projection was based on inflated sales of U.S. assets, as well as some patently phony predictions for interest rates and GNP growth. The Congressional Budget Office plugged some real-world numbers into the White House projections and instead of $130 billion came up with a $165 billion deficit. Hey, what's $35 billion among friends?

POLITICAL WILL—AND WON'T

Not everyone in Washington feels comfortable with a government out of control. Efforts have been made to reduce federal spending. In the fall of 1987, the stock market crash scared the White House and Capitol Hill into negotiations on deficit reduction. The result after four weeks of agonizing meetings? Three cents were pared from the budget dollar with a combination of taxes and spending cuts. Even that amount was criticized by *New Republic* columnist Michael Kinsley as "filled with gimmicks, like allowing cut-rate repayment of government loans now instead of paying them back in full later." Representative Charles Schumer of New York said afterwards that it was "about the best we can do when there is no real leadership."

Where could we cut if we had the political will? We know that only 23 cents of the budget dollar is left for "discretionary" spending after the military, entitlements, and interest on the national debt. But deficit spending each year is on the order of 15 to 20 cents of that dollar. So we have to look at those three big chunks for real cuts. Entitlements dollars are especially hard to cut from the budget, because people obviously feel they're entitled to them. Every interest group that draws from the government till fights to keep (or increase) its piece of the pie. For example, the American Association of Retired People, a powerful lobby against any cuts in Social Security payments, spent $8 million for "political education" in 1988.

It is also increasingly hard to cut the deficit because of the snowball effect of interest payments on the giant government debt. We are now paying interest of more than $100 billion a year. As the budget deficits roll on, the debt continues to mount (the government *never* pays off principal), and the interest payments get bigger and bigger. More than 14 percent of the federal budget now goes toward interest payments, but the way things are going, soon Washington might need the entire budget to pay the loan interest. Forget about the Pentagon, farm subsidies, Medicare, unemployment insurance—they could all go by the boards just so interest payments can be made. Otherwise, the Japanese might decide to stop lending us money, and then we'll really be in miso soup.

The truth is, there is only one real item in the budget that can sustain large enough cuts to make a significant dent in deficit spending: defense dollars. I'll make my case for that in Part III. But we also have to regain control of the entire budget process from the Lifetime Politicians, or else they'll swell their pork-barrel spending and erase whatever progress we make on other fronts.

THE TRUTH COULD SET US FREE

The biggest single reason it is so difficult to cut the deficit is that the electorate, the ultimate master of the government purse, is fed contrived numbers. I've made an effort in this chapter to unveil the dark side of government spending, but uncovering the truth is getting harder and harder.

As I noted above, lifers are already planning to use the future Social Security trust fund surpluses to disguise their true deficits. The Economic Studies Program at the Brookings Institution reveals that while Congress hopes to whittle down the deficit to "only" $139 billion by 1993, that's based on a $97 billion contribution from the Social Security surplus, thereby masking a real $236 billion deficit.

We need to stop the lifers before they strike again. Government spending is out of control, but we can regain control by using the government's biggest weapon—information—on our side. An informed citizenry is an outraged citizenry, and we can turn outrage into action. First, let's look at how the out-of-control atmosphere has infected our personal economic practices and our society's most trusted financial institutions.

CHAPTER 1 4

★

The Greeding of America

We have a new national pastime, and it's not that we've given up baseball. The new pastime is playing with Other People's Money, the great OPM. The government is the biggest player in this game, running up an obscene national debt, but everybody plays: banks, corporations, even Joe and Jane Citizen, when they get the chance. The object of the game is to be as deep in debt as you can, and to make someone else (like Uncle Sam) pay for it if things turn out badly.

The dictionary defines "greed" as a selfish desire for more than you need or deserve. We've all run up debt that we do not deserve, in the public and private sectors, in our own households—and some have no way of paying it off. I guess I am old-fashioned enough to feel that when I enjoy life, I should have the integrity to pay my own way. The height of selfishness would be to continue on our wayward path, knowing that we are jeopardizing our children's prosperity.

THE MONEY GAME

Everyone wants to be in on the action. We are bombarded daily with the media message that we should live the lifestyle of the rich and famous. Do we ever hear that to do so requires the workstyle of the poor and obscure? No, there's an easier way: use somebody else's money.

The movie industry, which I dabble in, is notorious for this practice. Movie people seldom put their own money into production, and creative bookkeeping is rampant. In real estate, my main business, we have "syndicators" who put together deals without using their own money. They sniff around for "money looking for a home," and simply buy into the projects of others using OPM for a free ride. They end up getting a piece of the action plus one commission when the property is bought, another when it's sold, and a management fee in between.

Now this wouldn't be so bad if the syndicators were actually developing the project, putting up buildings, laying in streets and utilities, filling the place with new owners. That would be meeting a need. But that's what *we*, the developers, do.

PAPER, PAPER EVERYWHERE

Exercises using OPM come in all shapes and forms: high-grade bonds, Treasury notes and bills, convertible bonds, commercial paper, junk bonds, home equity loans, lines of credit, leveraged buyouts, credit cards. The common element is an IOU. All these instruments are borrowing—they represent the exchange of money for paper.

When the day of reckoning comes for us, when we have to settle our accounts, it will be a long way down the debt mountain. Total public and private debt in the U.S. economy amounts to about $8 trillion, give or take a few billion. That's over $30,000 for each and every American; I'll bet you didn't realize what a high credit limit you have. Households, businesses and government have borrowed in roughly equal amounts. And that debt comes to 170 percent of our yearly gross national product, an unprecedented level in our history.

These figures have ballooned in recent years, up $3 trillion since 1981. In both 1985 and 1986, businesses and households each borrowed almost $300 billion more than they paid back, while the federal debt grew by $200 billion each year. States and cities also took on a load of new debt. When everyone is doing it, you get swept along. It's trendy.

THE NATIONAL DEBT

When President Reagan took office, the total national debt, the cumulative result of deficit spending, was $958 billion. After mounting budget deficits, the federal debt had doubled by 1986, by 1988 it was $2.5 trillion, and by the time Reagan leaves office, it will have tripled—to almost $3 trillion. His successor will be faced with a budget way out of balance, guaranteeing further big increases in the national debt (see Figure 9). When I was in school they used to say, "Don't worry about the national debt. We owe it to ourselves." This is no longer true of a large portion of the debt. We owe it to foreigners.

Figure 9—The tallest mountain in America!

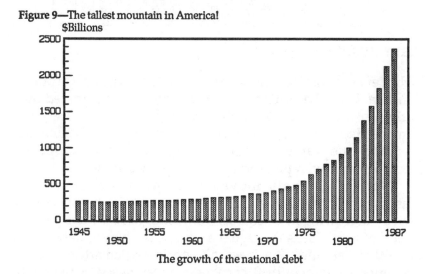

The growth of the national debt

Just looking at the record of the past decade is enough to persuade me that we're mortgaging ourselves to the hilt. In 1978, the national debt was 35.9 percent of GNP; by 1988, the Office of Management and Budget estimated that it had reached 54.6 percent of GNP. The debt/GNP ratio would be irrelevant if incomes were being more evenly taxed to gain higher revenues—to keep the annual deficits low. Instead, we are in a situation now where the debt is still growing very fast, and there's no end in sight to big deficits—but we're cutting our tax rates (see Figure 10).

That's not fiscal sanity, it is "voodoo economics." We cannot continue this nightmare plunge into arrears, where every year we borrow more and more to finance another deficit.

Figure 10—How big is the budget deficit as a percentage of GNP?

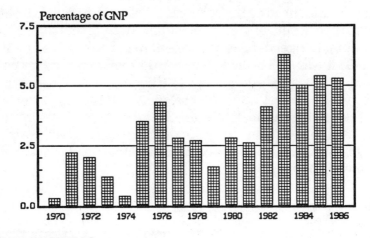

RISKY BUSINESS

Debt fever caught on nowhere so furiously as in corporate America. Until the 1970s, most large corporations operated on a fairly conservative theory of financial management. If the company needed additional money to run its affairs or to expand, the tried and true way to raise that money was to issue corporate stock, or "equity," representing the company's value.

But OPM mania moved into the boardroom from Washington in the 1970s and 1980s. Companies began raising cash by borrowing it. Of course, companies have always had the option of using loans through the issuance of bonds, debentures and other liabilities. But it wasn't considered smart to put the firm out on a limb. In 1960, corporate money raised by debt only amounted to half of the money raised through equity. The 1980s saw debt financing's share double, almost triple, until debt was outpacing stock issues by 25 percent.

What happened? The go-go atmosphere of the Reagan years pushed corporate leaders into more aggressive growth, more adventurous ways to expand rapidly. The Ivan Boesky mentality of "greed is good" began to take hold in top corporate offices. To achieve fast growth, corporations developed risky new ways to extend their debt, to underwrite further expansion or to finance takeover efforts against other companies. Two new mechanisms to exploit corporate debt for companies were "junk bonds" and leveraged buyouts.

I take my hat off to anybody who can have faith in something called junk. Junk bonds are the riskiest way to borrow money. They represent high risk and high returns. Despite the warnings of some experts, junk bond issues exploded from $3 billion in 1982 to $160 billion by 1988.

The other significant avenue of debt was the leveraged buyout, where a company's executives—or outsiders looking for a quick buck—arrange a huge amount of debt to finance their own takeover of the corporation *without putting up any money of their own.* They use the collateral of the company to secure the loans; it is a little like destroying a village to save it.

Fortune magazine noted in December 1987 how critics were pointing out that "these deals serve little economic purpose beyond enriching management, underwriters and lenders, [but] the companies have become so prodigiously leveraged with debt that they could not withstand a financial storm." There are personal fortunes to be made by the executives and financial planners involved in structuring such deals. When businesses are pushed out on a debt limb, executives jump from the branches with their golden parachutes intact.

Heavy corporate borrowing naturally drove up interest payments, leaving some corporations highly vulnerable to a recession. Those of you who work for a large corporation may just want to check on your own company's debt situation.

CONSUMER DEBT

It's easy to criticize the federal government for financial mismanagement, but we're not doing too well in our own households either.

In 1987, after-tax individual income of Americans inched up 0.8 percent, but consumer expenditures rose 2.2 percent. So we increased our spending almost three times faster than we increased our income. That's not a good sign of long-term planning. Total consumer debt at the end of 1987 stood at $612 billion, up 6 percent over the year before. We have been living beyond our means, and paying for a higher standard of living with credit that's easily extended to us.

For households, more than 60 percent of their debt derived from home mortgages (the value of the house was securing the loan), another 10 percent or more from auto loans, and 5 percent (that's almost $150 billion, remember) flowed from simple consumer installment credit. A lot of people who've seen the value of their houses soar over the last 15 years have taken out home equity loans that are sometimes bigger than their original mortgages to get extra cash to spend, spend, spend.

Why do we ignore the advice of our elders—spend only what you have? The advertising culture of America pushes us to consume extravagantly. American advertisers spend $100 billion a year telling us that we need to buy what they're selling. I saw an ad in *Fortune* magazine only a month after the 1987 stock market crash. Spread across two pages was a lavish photograph in gold tones of an expensively decorated living room, complete with grand piano. The caption read: "No sooner have you achieved your goals than new ones need to be set—the American Express Gold Card." I could just picture all the out-of-work yuppie stockbrokers, setting new goals.

DOWN ON THE FARM

We heard many horror stories about farm debt in 1985 and 1986, as farmers with loans owed to the government defaulted left and right. The Farmers Home Administration (FHA), the chief issuer of those loans, has a loan portfolio of $26 billion, owed by 242,000 farm borrowers. But $10 billion of those loans are delinquent, and many are not going to be paid back. Those bad farm debts make up a third of all the $32 billion in delinquent loans that Americans owe to government agencies, not including the IRS (see Figure 11).

PLAYING HOOKY

The federal Guaranteed Student Loan (GSL) program for college students, like everything else the government guarantees, is in trouble. This program provides about $10 billion a year in loans to students, and about $43 billion is outstanding. Total defaults are at $1.6 billion, and there is another $4.4 billion in "overdue" loans. Because the government fully guarantees student loans, Washington has to repay the individual banks that loaned the money now in default.

Figure 11—Who gets federal loans? (1960 compared to 1987)

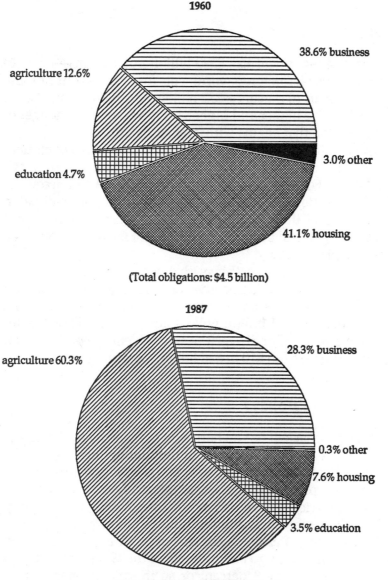

1960

38.6% business

agriculture 12.6%

3.0% other

education 4.7%

41.1% housing

(Total obligations: $4.5 billion)

1987

agriculture 60.3%

28.3% business

0.3% other

7.6% housing

3.5% education

(Total obligations: $34.9 billion)

By 1990 Uncle Sam will have swallowed $2 billion worth of defaulted loans. Putting the problem in a nutshell, Deputy Under Secretary of Education Bruce Carnes told *U.S. News and World Report:* "The fundamental problem is people ripping off the federal government. People do not take seriously their obligation."

THE POLITICS OF DEBT

The federal government has $290 billion out in loans—loans to students, farmers, foreign governments and others. But of these loans, more than 10 percent—$32 billion—are delinquent. As the debt levels move higher and higher, there's always the danger of a chain reaction that begins with a major default.

The inability of lifers in Washington to say no to constituent demands makes it hard to restore sense to the government's credit books. For example, the Farmers Home Administration, which carries most bad farm loans, had an ambitious campaign in 1987 to offset the debts by snatching government crop subsidies that might still be going to delinquent farms. That seems a reasonable plan to me.

Congress didn't see things that way. Instead, new farm credit legislation was passed that ordered the agency to stop blocking farm subsidies and to be more lenient on bad debts. The result: more than $2.1 billion will be added to the list of delinquent loans in 1988, and over the next several years bad farm loans will double from $10 to $20 billion, according to the FHA.

WHAT—ME SAVE MONEY?

A country so whacked out on borrowing obviously isn't going to concentrate very hard on saving for the future, since it is spending so lavishly today. Both privately and publicly, we're showing the effects of pitiful savings rates, especially when compared with the countries we see passing us in economic productivity. Traditionally Americans have been able to put away about 7 to 9 percent of their after-tax income, not high as industrialized countries go. In the go-go environment of the 1980s, however, we dropped to a pathetic 3 percent or so in savings, even less at times.

A postwar low of just over 2 percent was reached in the fall of 1987. The far-sighted Japanese are saving about 18 percent and the Germans more than 12 percent of their after-tax incomes.

The federal government sets a bad example for us. Twenty years ago, we spent 2.3 percent of our GNP to upgrade and expand infrastructure—investing in our future by building roads, bridges, communications and ports. In the 1980s, the Lifetime Politicians making the decisions on where the money goes have shown no long-term vision whatsoever, devoting only 0.4 percent of GNP to infrastructure. Instead, they put the money into bad loans, defense spending or farm subsidies—and gave us deficits to boot.

OPM ON AN INTERNATIONAL SCALE

Our country's decline to the subordinate status of a debtor nation is the OPM mania on an international scale. The central piece of the story is that for a few years we've borrowed more than is available at home to finance our budget deficits. Therefore, a good chunk of money had to come from overseas. We have been borrowing abroad about $130 billion annually just to prop up our budget. The result? Foreigners now own $500 billion of our debt, and that number will swell to $1 trillion within five years. That is one trillion dollars—equal to the entire 1988 federal budget—that we will owe to foreigners.

We have to pay interest on this debt, so in 1988 we shipped $28 billion overseas. What are the Japanese and the others doing with all those dollars? Why, they're using it to buy up parts of the United States. Japanese interests now own about $50 billion of U.S. stocks and bonds and about $11.5 billion worth of American real estate. In relative terms, those numbers aren't yet overwhelming. "Foreigners" aren't about to take our country away from us. But the numbers are growing, and current trends will have consequences in the near future—as we'll see in the next chapter.

THE HUMAN DUST CLOTHS

The debt we're saddled with could become a classic Broadway ticker-tape parade, with the paper IOUs raining down on a confused people. And in such dire times the only people who make out all right are the "Human Dust Cloths."

The Human Dust Cloths are the parasites of our economy. They don't create any wealth or jobs. They just move money around through the manipulation of paper. The huge boom in "financial services" since the late 1970s has opened up new vistas of glory for the Human Dust Cloths, better known as investment bankers, lawyers, accountants, financial planners and stock-brokers.

The long-term effects of this trend are not yet clear, but many people envision a weakening of American power. It's possible to live on other people's money for just so long. Eventually the lending window is closed, and the creditors come around to collect. They may even ask for a bigger say in domestic policy. Can we rely on our financial institutions to remain steady? I hope so, but I'm not too optimistic. Let's examine how the Human Dust Cloths have infiltrated our financial institutions.

CHAPTER 15

★

Institutions Gone Haywire

To many of us, the Crash of '87 was no real surprise. I had been thinking during that summer that the stock market was headed for a swift trip down, and I called a few broker acquaintances to discuss a strategy of "selling it short and riding it down." The prediction was not a hard one to make because of the research we were doing on this book. But I'm a real estate developer, not a stock market professional, and so I did not give selling short a high priority.

As September turned into October, the evidence pointing to a crash increased. On October 14 I called Jack Struble of E.F. Hutton in San Mateo and Rich Braugh of Hutton's San Jose office (my company shares the top floor of a San Jose high-rise building with "E.F. Hunch"). We scheduled a golf game away from the office to put my strategy into effect.

I make it a point not to invest in paper of any kind—land, bricks and mortar are my game. To me, the great bull market looked like crass speculation resulting in ridiculous stock prices. The indicators I saw were all bad, even in my business—the whole country was overbuilt, with the possible exception of single-family housing.

I felt compelled to talk to these brokers about a strategy for the bust. Well, the golf game was set for Tuesday, October 20. On the Thursday and Friday before that, the market dropped 200 points. On Meltdown Monday, the 19th, came the fierce 508-point collapse—the day *before* our fateful golf game.

We still had our game (the Hunch boys said they needed to get out of the office), but events had overtaken us. While the brokers said that I had made the greatest call they had seen in their combined 54 years in the market, I knew it wasn't because I am the brightest guy in town, or had ESP about market behavior. Heck, if I knew so much I would be telling you how great my timing was, not how lousy.

The point is that an outsider like me, with only an intuition for the way the business and economy of America were heading, could see this coming.

Our free capitalist system is built on a foundation of rich and essentially uncontrolled institutions. In the best of times it isn't easy to make those institutions serve us, instead of the other way around. The trouble is, those institutions have gotten out of hand, and that brings on the instability that worries me.

I'm a booster of the capitalist, free-market system, but I am critical of our leaders' inability to exercise proper oversight of that system. In this chapter I'd like to look at the two institutional foundations of the American economy: Wall Street and our banking system.

THE CASINO ON WALL STREET

Wall Street has always been a place for players who deal with paper. Unfortunately, they have become disconnected from the values that lie behind the paper.

The game has gotten bigger in the 1980s. Junk bonds and mergers are just exotic examples. This segment of the economy has become the plaything for those who run nothing—they take the money and run. Wall Street is not a place for small players. Most of those have been scared out, or driven out by losses.

All of this shows up on the nightly news, where the Dow Jones Index is supposed to reflect how we are doing in general. All it really reflects is how well the big boys are manipulating the market.

Is there anybody who still thinks that the stock market is a solid institution that facilitates the long-term health and financing of American industry? What we have is an unstable crapshoot and a risky location for investments.

The panic of Meltdown Monday was merely a glimpse of the worst that can happen when the culture of Wall Street becomes a get-rich-quick gamble in which any advantage is taken, legal or not. The small investor was at the mercy of computers on that day, as trading programs kicked into action and spat out sell orders by the millisecond.

In a crash, the average citizen can get trampled as program traders move blocks of hundreds of thousands of shares. If and when another meltdown occurs, don't think you'll be able to get out easily. Traders may not even take your calls. In the wake of October 19, one portfolio manager for the insurance industry (which dumped billions of dollars that day) even proposed new legislation to ensure that their selling orders be executed ahead of all others. Do you want to be in the market when another tumble occurs?

THE BIG BAIL-OUT: YOU DIDN'T KNOW YOU DID IT

After seeing just how close we really came to a complete collapse of the trading system on that day, I don't place much faith in the market's ability to weather another storm. The central problem is one of cash. There wasn't enough of it to buy all the stock the computers wanted to sell. Billions of dollars worth of shares were dumped on Monday and Tuesday, as the mechanisms intended to keep trading orderly simply fell apart.

Wall Street has so-called specialist firms, brokers who are supposed to "make a market" for a volatile stock by buying it up when others only want to sell, thus keeping the stock exchange running smoothly. The specialist firms didn't live up to their name. They were overwhelmed by the panic selling, and some decided to step back from the fray to cut their own losses. The Presidential Task Force on Market Mechanisms, appointed by President Reagan to examine the crash, reported that "market makers on the major stock exchanges appear to have largely abandoned serious attempts to stem the downward movement in prices." Some specialist firms lost their franchises in the furor over their behavior.

Why should one more example of self-interested incompetence concern the average person? Well, guess who ended up paying for the system's failure? Good guess. Only the intervention of the Federal Reserve Board, with promises of a massive infusion of public money, your money, "saved the markets from total meltdown," as the *Wall Street Journal* put it.

THE FED COUGHED UP THE DOUGH

One month after the crash, the *Wall Street Journal* uncovered the frightening story of how major U.S. banks refused to back up the specialist firms, afraid to commit their funds to support the stock market even though it appeared near collapse. At the height of the panic on Tuesday (October 20), it took direct pressure from the Federal Reserve Board to get the banks to cough up cash. Chairman Alan Greenspan rushed to Washington from Dallas and released what the *Journal* called an "extraordinary statement," vowing the Fed's "readiness to serve as a source of liquidity to support the economic and financial system." In New York, the chairman of the New York Fed personally telephoned top bankers to stress the urgency of the situation.

I feel uneasy about the state of Wall Street when I read the behind-the-scenes stories of what it took to sustain the market. Panicky phone conversations passed between the Securities and Exchange Commission and top brokerage firms about closing down the market; between top bankers and the Federal Reserve Board; and between the head of the New York Stock Exchange and White House Chief of Staff Howard Baker. Frantic phone conversations also buzzed between top investment bankers and chief executives of Fortune 500 companies, prompting stock consultant Stanley Abel to remark to a reporter that "it looks like there's almost a get-together on the part of corporate America to prop up the market."

Pressure on the banks was not enough. The Fed actually had to commit cash to save the stock market. One banker told the *Journal* that the Fed's message was, "Whatever you need, we'll give to you." In the end, the Fed committed more than $10 billion. The money was promised to large New York banks, which underwrote the brokers, who stabilized the stock market. The $10 billion was never publicly acknowledged by the government and was only revealed in informal remarks by the head of the Presidential task force months later in the *Wall Street Journal*.

The story behind the October market crash is a disturbing one. The innocent bystander, the taxpayer, wound up paying for the excesses of others. How could we have let our economic institutions slip so far?

DON'T BANK ON IT

A major danger sign in our current economic condition is the alarming condition of our most crucial financial institutions: the banks. The set of circumstances most likely to spark a depression would be massive bank and savings and loan failures, with a resultant confidence crisis. If there's any institution whose basic operating mode is using OPM, it's a bank.

A banker's product is money, the easiest commodity in the world to sell. He takes it from someone else, paying as little as possible for it, and lends it out at the highest rates possible. The difference is profit. The simplicity of the process is absurdly elementary.

The only way a bank can lose is if it makes bad loans. Banks, being a low-capitalization business, are not set up to take large losses.

We are always suspicious of people who make money off of money. That is even reflected in the body of most religious law.

My companies used to bank at Bank of America, the San Francisco Bay Area's homegrown financial giant founded by the greatest banker of all time, A.P. Giannini. At one point in the 1970s, we had 87 different accounts with B of A, with millions of dollars going in and out. But something changed at the bank. The officers we used to deal with had seemed professional, sensitive to our needs, and they were not above personal contact with their clients. These were *bankers*, back when the word implied something more than just a low-paid clerk.

A change came over B of A in the late 1970s and early 1980s. It was obvious in their dealings with my company, and it soon became obvious in their balance sheets. The bank lost much of its middle management. Many of their replacements were new to banking, and there was a lot of turnover. We never knew from one month to the next who "our" banker would be.

These comparatively inexperienced people were not allowed to make decisions. When responses did come down from above, through a long and convoluted process, the answers were indecisive, reflecting the problems at the top.

The top management of B of A stressed short-term paper profits over long-term investment value. They stopped loaning money to long-time clients with high liquidity and net worth to pursue huge loans to foreign countries and companies with little or no liquidity and no proven track record. Why would a bank do that? Because it looked like easy money. The loans we asked for were in the millions of dollars. Third World countries asked for billions. The bank could show big paper profits on its books with much less paperwork, even if the foreigners never paid back a dime.

Pathetically, the banks fooled themselves as well as their shareholders. They believed the lie! I asked them at the time, "How are you going to collect from Ecuador?"

It didn't take my partners and me long to look elsewhere for responsive banking. And we weren't the only ones. By coincidence, I found myself in a meeting with two other local landowners. When the talk got around to banking, I found that one had left B of A after 62 years and one after 41 years. With my 25 years, this added up to 128 years of solid banking relationships lost by Bank of America. What would A.P. Giannini, who nurtured many a farmer and small businessman, have thought of this?

Bank of America went on to bad times. From a 1980 profit of $643 million the bank fell to a 1986 loss of $518 million.

What happened at B of A happened elsewhere in our banking system, mirroring the go-go attitude in the economy. I saw an advertisement in *Fortune* magazine that epitomized the go-go attitude: it was by General Electric Credit Corporation promoting their financial offerings. They bragged that a client—an auto dealer—came to GECC asking for a $20 million credit line:

> "We ended up offering him not the $20 million credit line he requested, but an unprecedented $250 million instead....We can't promise to advance every business 12 times the financing it's looking for. But we *can* promise to look at your company's financial situation from a different point of view."

I'll say.

GOOD BANKS, BAD BANKS

There are about 14,000 banks in the United States. Although most are healthy institutions, more than 10 percent are in trouble. The Federal Deposit Insurance Corporation (FDIC) had almost 1,600 banks on its "problem list" in 1988, according to Director William Seidman.

Does the public know which banks are in trouble? No, the list isn't published. The first inkling we get about bad banks is when we hear or read that another one has been closed by the FDIC—essentially, when the bank is bankrupt. From 1945 until 1980, the United States averaged about ten bank failures a year.

The numbers have been climbing ever since, as Figure 12

Figure 12—How many U. S. banks have gone bust?

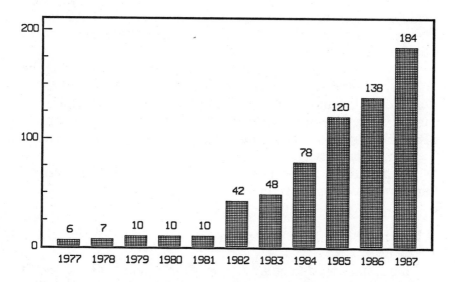

shows, from 10 in President Reagan's first year in office to around 200 in his last. On December 3, 1987, federal regulators closed nine banks, setting a record for the most shuttered on a single day. In the first 40 days of 1988, 20 banks failed.

The situation is bad across the financial spectrum. The Federal Savings and Loan Insurance Corporation (FSLIC) estimates that about 500 of 3,200 savings and loans in the country have a negative net worth (i.e., are bankrupt in all but name), while another 600 have less capital on their books than regulations actually require. 28 savings and loans were closed in 1987, and the FSLIC was preparing to shut over 50 in 1988.

Officials from the FDIC usually give three reasons why banks fail: "times are tough," and banks reflect the general economy, especially in currently depressed areas like Texas and Oklahoma; out-and-out fraud; and deregulation. I look at all three as facets of the same phenomenon: short-term thinking.

Arguing that a bank fails because times are tough is another way of saying that loans were made in good times without a realistic appraisal of what might happen in the future. Sure, the economy in Texas was booming back in the late 1970s when oil prices were sky-high and the TV show "Dallas" topped the ratings. But that atmosphere brought on an unrealistic expectation that good times would last forever, and loans were made on that assumption. I subscribe to the "get-rich-slow" theory. I've always thought that get-rich-quick schemes can also help you to get poor quickly, and banking is not immune to that basic law of the business world.

A lot of the banks which got into trouble were ignoring the needs of their own communities. Continental Illinois went to the oilfields of Oklahoma, and Bank of America went to Brazil.

Hardly anyone around advocates hard money anymore. Republicans used to be the hard-money party. They were always advocates of conservative financial policies. Now, they too have slipped into the easy-money game they used to warn against, and are shoveling the money out the door.

THE GOVERNMENT LENDS A HAND

Citing fraud and deregulation to explain recent bank failures is valid, but we need to look behind the visible symptoms to find their hidden causes. Behind the decline of our banking institutions lies the fact that bankers and politicians are in bed together, plain and simple.

I'm not just talking about out-and-out corruption, although you can find some of that. It is common knowledge that banks wield enormous political power at the local, state and national levels, and politicians cater to that power. Southern politics have been particularly entwined with banking, with Governors regarding bank charters and state contracts as "valuable gifts" to be bestowed on friends. R.E. Gormley, vice president of the Georgia Savings Bank and Trust, said thirty years ago: "The person or organization who controls the credit facilities of a state or nation will be able to not only control the economic life but also the political and social welfare....Money or credit is the most powerful dictator and the hand that controls its power may or may not use it wisely." In the thirty years since, those basic truths haven't changed.

In 1966, Chase Manhattan Bank and other New York banks gave big campaign contributions to liberal Democratic Senator John Sparkman of Alabama. The New York banks were interested in an Alabama Senate race because incumbent Sparkman was in line to become chairman of the Senate Banking Committee. When he did in 1967, bankers expected their financial investment to pay off.

The current chairman of the House Banking Committee, Fernand St. Germain (a Democrat from Rhode Island), has been under a long-term investigation by the Justice Department's criminal division for his close ties to the banking industry. Lobbyists for the American Bankers Association, the Securities Industry Association, and the United States League of Savings Institutions, an umbrella group for savings and loan associations, have admitted picking up the tab for extensive "entertainment" of Representative St. Germain. The *New York Times* even reported allegations that St. Germain would call up lobbyists demanding to be taken out to dinner at high-priced Washington restaurants, and at times personally signed the American Express card bill of at least one League of Savings Institutions lobbyist.

CUTTING RED TAPE, CREATING RED INK

Besides the level of out-and-out corruption, cozy relationships led to quid pro quos in lax supervision of the banking industry. According to *In Banks We Trust*, by investigative reporter Penny Lernoux, "Many bank regulators come from and return to the industry they are supposed to discipline." Conflicts of interest abound.

Because Americans have always been suspicious of bankers, these financial institutions have always been closely regulated, on federal and state levels. That's why we have so many of them.

We didn't allow banks to operate across state borders, and many states restricted them to specific localities in the state. Some states, notably Illinois and Colorado, went to the extreme step of prohibiting banks from operating more than one office. The rationale for that restriction was wonderfully explained in 1980 by James P. Thomas, a Colorado banker, who said: "The populists who framed the state constitution in 1877 wanted to make sure you could look your banker in the eye."

Well, that era is drawing to a close. You are not going to be able to look Citibank in the eye. Interstate banking is descending upon us. Banks—the big ones anyway—have pushed hard for deregulation. And they have been pushing with their wallets.

Representative Jim Leach of Iowa said: "A lot of money flowed between the institutions, their lobbyists and legislators." Encouraged by massive contributions from the American Bankers Association PAC, Congress obliged with the Depository Institutions Deregulation and Monetary Control Act of 1980. What a mouthful! I've never read that bill and probably you haven't either, but we both have been paying for it ever since.

Give and Ye Shall Receive

The American Bankers Association PAC gives over a million dollars every election year to candidates for the House and Senate. Most of that money goes to incumbents, but BANKPAC specializes in donations for "campaign debt retirement," *after* the election. The PAC even waits until congressional committee assignments are made— so it can make sure to give to members of the banking oversight committees.

Deregulation was designed to bring free enterprise competition into the banking industry. The new law changed the rules on how interest rates are set and other rules on bank operations. Previously, maximum interest rates on bank deposits were set by the Federal Reserve under Regulation Q. Savings deposits paid 5 percent interest, checking accounts paid no interest at all. In those days, banks were not good places to park your money— hence the rapid rise in the 1970s of money-market mutual funds not tied down by Regulation Q.

The 1980 bill abolished Regulation Q. Freed from interest rate controls, banks began to compete to attract deposits from each other, from the money-market mutual funds, and from the savings and loans, which under deregulation began to look more and more like commercial banks.

Competing for deposits is just the first part of the game. Then you have to attract borrowers. In the hell-bent era of deregulation, the banks found it easy to make a lot of bad loans—on the farm, in the city, around the world. Savings and loan associations were allowed to make consumer loans and offer credit cards for the first time, and the line between banks and S&L's was blurred.

The regulatory controls over the individuals allowed to open banks and savings and loans associations were softpedaled. Congress wanted to make banks and S&L's more competitive, so they clouded the lines of government supervision. The theme of deregulation was, "let the banks run wild, and only the strong will survive."

Watchdog responsibility for banks and savings and loans is divided among the Federal Reserve Board, the FDIC and FSLIC, the Office of the Comptroller of the Currency, the Department of Justice, and 50 state agencies. These huge bureaucracies have overlapping lines of authority and a lot of gray areas were intentionally written into the law. According to Congressman Leach, "Congress gave every incentive to federal regulators to be weak." They were following the rosy free-enterprise picture of a leaner banking world painted by ABA lobbyists, and in one way they were right. Competition did mean that more banks would go under.

GETTING GREED ON OUR BACKS

The go-go atmosphere sucked a lot of healthy institutions into trouble, too. The removal of interest rate ceilings left no limit to how high a competitor could go. Troubled savings associations began offering higher and higher rates with the acquiescence of the Fed, because they needed to bring in deposits. In 1988, one of the highest savings rates in the country was being offered by Beverly Hills Savings—even though it was actually insolvent and on the brink of being shut down. The FSLIC estimated in 1988 that the savings and loan industry was losing at least $1 billion a year because healthy S&L's had to raise rates to compete with the sick.

Given the predictable result of the interest-rate deregulation, it was senseless for Congress to break up the regulatory supervision of the industry. As a Brookings Institution study has pointed out, "Problems arise when two or more agencies share responsibility for safety and soundness....Gaps in regulation can occur if none of the agencies involved asserts sufficient control." Instead of a tough federal watchdog to fear, financial institutions only faced bureaucratic watchpuppies.

I've seen bank charters go to people who should have never been on the inside of a teller's window. Deregulation opened the door to go-go S&L executives to lend with ingenuity under the guise of being a more "entrepreneurial" lending institution.

Hollywood in Texas

Deregulation recently hit me in a strange way. A while back, my film production company gave our latest movie, *This Time for Me*, to a Hollywood distributor. Just recently, the distributor filed for protection under the bankruptcy laws. It turned out their lender was a Texas savings and loan association. Can you believe it, a Texas S&L can't find enough trouble in Texas and gets into the biggest crapshoot of them all, movie production and distribution? So the S&L took over the bankrupt distributor, and now we're in the unenviable position of having our movie distributed by Texas loan officers.

Numerous scandals have revealed that after deregulation, bank overseers routinely approved charter applications, failing to check the applicants' backgrounds. Since no one body has real authority, none of the various bodies will take responsibility.

The FDIC and FSLIC have done a pretty good job of gluing the failing institutions together. I only wish the politicians could learn their lesson the hard way. Dan Walker, once Governor of Illinois, is now serving a stretch in a federal prison for bank fraud and perjury. The savings and loan he left politics to start went bankrupt because of his own greed. Some of the money he took from the vault paid for an 80-foot yacht.

We're going to be paying for these mistakes for a long, long time.

FOREIGN LOANS: WHY DIDN'T THEY JUST SAY NO?

If there is any area of the banking crisis I find hardest to comprehend, it's the reasoning that went into loaning hundreds of billions of dollars to foreign countries. Did U.S. banks suddenly take leave of their senses only to wake up a few years later and find themselves faced with a debt bomb?

Since 1975 U.S. banks have lent a total of $100 billion to Latin American debtor countries and perhaps another $30 billion to other Third World states. Another $300 billion was lent to the Third World by foreign banks, governments, international agencies like the World Bank and the International Monetary Fund, and some exporting companies who sold their goods on credit. Brazil is the Third World's largest debtor country, owing $113 billion ($28 billion to American banks), while Mexico owes $105 billion ($30 billion to U.S. banks).

Will we ever see that money again? Loans to the Third World have become the worst kind of debt—in which the borrower holds the upper hand. Most of these debtor countries have economies that are weak, not to say falling apart. A lot of the money we extended went into white-elephant projects, or simply into the pockets of the Third World's elite. R.T. Naylor's 1987 book, *Hot Money and the Politics of Debt*, described how half of all the money from foreign loans to the Third World (up to $200 billion) may have gone into secret bank accounts held by those countries' own Lifetime Politicians.

A number of countries have already stopped paying interest on their loans. Brazil stopped paying its interest two years ago and told the World Bank that it would default on its debt unless the bank kept lending new money. American banks and the World Bank are in a sense the victims of continuing extortion. They can't foreclose on the debts because the borrowers are foreign countries, but the borrowers refuse to repay unless they keep getting new loans.

The pit has deepened as bankers eagerly throw more and more money into bulging Third World accounts. As the *New York Times* editorialized back in 1982, "Too many bankers think that there is no such thing as a bad loan to a government." Walter Wriston, longtime chairman of Citicorp, set the tone when he said there was no reason to worry—sovereign nations never die, they just reschedule their debts. In other words, a Third World country could never actually go bankrupt, and would keep on paying interest on their loans indefinitely, so banks would look profitable—on paper.

A former chairman of the board of BankAmerica Corporation told my researchers, "We used to talk about risk, where are the risks, and so on, but you know that optimism is the key to growth and success....Maybe if it hadn't gone on as long and aggressively as it did, it could have worked out." That's classic short-term thinking.

The biggest temptation Third World countries have is simply to stop paying and refuse to do so unless banks fork over even more money. In short, economists in the capital cities of developing nations realized that the nearsighted American bankers had created the perfect money machine. Countries could cloak their perilous financial conditions by borrowing more money while overall debt ballooned. Today's Latin politicos have a perfect political pitch: they tell us, "We didn't borrow the money, our predecessors did," and they tell their own people, "Let the gringos sweat."

Where was our government while all this was going on? Egging on the banks. In many cases, Uncle Sam pushed banks to make loans to countries for political reasons: "strategic American allies" seemed to get more and more money from U.S. banks even when their economies went sour. Sometimes the line between national interest and personal interest is very shadowy. The *New York Times* reported in 1988 that National Security Council (NSC) officials had approached the Overseas Private Investment Corporation (OPIC), a quasi-public agency, and used White House clout to get OPIC federally backed loan guarantees for an Iraqi pipeline project. Why would the NSC get involved? Because the project had the attention of Attorney General Edwin Meese.

Colonel Oliver North even got into the act when he was with the NSC, promising Panama's dictator Colonel Noriega that the American government would arrange U.S. loans to Panama in exchange for Noriega's support for the Nicaraguan *contras*. Most of the time, government pressure didn't have to be so blatant, and bankers got the message that loans to the Third World were in the national interest. Most of all, bankers fell back on their strongest safety net: if the house of cards collapses, Uncle Sam will bail us out.

BANKERS AND POLITICIANS SHARE ONE THING: YOUR WALLET

Even the World Bank is joining the raid on the U.S. Treasury to cover negligent lending practices. According to Harvard scholar Nicholas Eberstadt, the World Bank has lent nearly all of its current $125 billion in loans to Third World countries, but at least seven countries have stopped paying their loans back, and many of the rest will only pay with money from new loans. That's a lot of money down a rat hole.

But the U.S. Treasury is legally obliged to cover much of the World Bank's losses. The United States originally set up the bank (to help postwar reconstruction in Europe), and we've been underwriting it ever since. So now that the World Bank managers are feeling the heat from the mistakes they made, they're knocking at Uncle Sam's door for more cash to cover the bad loans.

How much could that cost? In 1988, the World Bank asked Congress for $15 billion as a "general capital increase." It's a farce to think our deficit-soaked budget can afford such new expenses, especially when the money is destined for new bad loans to disguise the old ones.

THE PORTRAIT OF DORIAN GRAY

When I was a kid, I saw the eerie movie based on Oscar Wilde's story about Dorian Gray, a guy whose face never aged. His friends wondered how he was able to appear so young and vibrant while they matured and passed away. Little did they know that a secret painting of him hidden in his attic was aging day by day. Only when he died was the secret revealed, and his corpse instantly took on the wrinkles and blemishes he had escaped for so long.

Our financial institutions are deeply troubled, but the regulators in Washington are gluing them together to keep Dorian Gray's portrait looking respectable.

I don't think our banking system is going to collapse, but only for one reason. The government won't let it. We may have to bail out the big banks the way we did Continental Illinois in 1984, because we can't afford to have them go under.

We're at a point where a lightning strike in the wrong place could bring our economic system tumbling down. In 1984, when Continental Illinois closed its doors, there was a brief panic as foreign investors moved their funds out of the U.S. financial system. The situation today is worse. You and Uncle Sam are going to take a pretty big hit. The question is, how big?

The 200 banks that fail in 1988 will all be taken over by the Federal Deposit Insurance Corporation (FDIC) at a tremendous cost, just as they bailed out Continental Illinois to the tune of $1.7 billion. The FDIC is obligated to cover all deposits up to $100,000 in member banks, but in reality the agency has admitted that when large banks fail, they cover deposits over that amount as well—to "maintain confidence" in the system.

Obviously, not every U.S. bank is going to fail, so the FDIC won't have to cover the total of $2 trillion deposited in all banks. The $18 billion in FDIC reserves would cover less than a penny on the dollar for those deposits. Up to now, the FDIC hasn't had to hit up Uncle Sam for additional cash. The money they receive in insurance fees from member banks has kept that $18 billion pretty steady.

But a recession, or any set of circumstances that greases the skids under the nation's troubled banks, could turn that situation around. In 1988, when First City Bancorp of Texas (the state's fourth-largest bank) went under, the FDIC had to pump in almost $1 billion to rescue depositors. The more failed banks the FDIC has to take over, the sooner they'll turn to Congress for backup appropriations.

In 1982, Congress passed a resolution extending "the full faith and credit" of the United States government to back the commitments of the FDIC and FSLIC. Before this, only the assets of those institutions themselves were at legal risk. Why the change? Again, Uncle Sam is the patsy of last resort.

S & L—SQUANDER AND LOSE

The situation in the savings and loan industry is much worse. The financial health of the FSLIC is much weaker than that of its sister institution, the FDIC. The cost to bail out depositors in today's 500 troubled associations would be at least $30 billion, and the figure keeps climbing.

Does the FSLIC have that much money? Well...not quite. In fact, the agency doesn't really have any money. Unlike the banks' FDIC, the savings and loans' FSLIC went under water a number of times, and Congress had to appropriate more money to keep it afloat as more and more associations went bust.

Just How Deep Are the Public Pockets?

At the beginning of 1987, the liabilities of the FSLIC exceeded its assets by $6.3 billion. By 1988, the liabilities outstripped assets by more than $13.7 billion—the debt more than doubled in a year. The 1987 "rescue" package that Congress voted in an emergency $10 billion budget appropriation was supposed to last until 1990, but already it isn't enough. The FSLIC is today "insolvent," in the words of its director.

The FSLIC doesn't like to admit just how deep the red ink flows. In its 1988 annual report, you had to read a footnote to learn that as many as 500 savings and loans are insolvent by generally accepted accounting principles, amounting to $21.8 billion in debt that the agency will eventually have to cover. The FSLIC doesn't want to shut them immediately because it doesn't have the funds. So, until Congress votes even more billions to prop it up, the FSLIC keeps those insolvent associations open. But they're losing money, money that we'll eventually have to cover. Incredibly, some of the larger successful S&L's are trying to leave FSLIC to get under the FDIC umbrella.

The FSLIC will probably see another $10 billion in losses piling up in 1988. It cost over $1.14 billion alone to bail out a single S&L, American Diversified, in June 1988. Was that in depressed Texas or Oklahoma? No, that was in rich, booming Orange County, California. More associations around the country head towards bankruptcy every day, as their profligate lending practices come home to roost.

The ultimate cost to the taxpayer may be in the stratospheric realm of $75 billion. Ask your Representative if there's that much money lying idle in the federal budget, looking for a home.

WHAT IF THE PRESSES RUN DRY?

We've seen that the taxpayers will bear the ultimate burden for paying off the massive debts our financial system has amassed. According to *Beyond Our Means*, by Alfred Malabre, Jr., economics editor of the *Wall Street Journal*, there is a better than even chance that the taxpayer bailouts will lead to massive government involvement in the economy. "All banks, indeed all thrift institutions, could wind up being nationalized....Wages and prices would largely be set by people in Washington." All because we refuse to act responsibly now.

To sum it all up, the Lifetime Politicians and their cronies in the financial elite have been handed the largest blank check in the history of the world. They have drawn heavily on that check, with all their subsidies, the giveaways, the bad loans, the guarantees, the incomprehensible overspending, the lack of oversight of our institutions—and it all leads back to Uncle Sam. And that means it leads back to me, and to you, and to the janitor down the street.

You've heard it a thousand times: Uncle Sam can't go bankrupt. When you own the printing presses, I guess you can't. But no other institution in the world would be able to get away with that. Overdrawing on a blank check has consequences, and will have more dramatic ones in the future, unless we call a halt to the party.

It has happened before. At the turn of the century, Argentina was one of the 10 richest countries in the world. Then in the 1940s it got its own feel-good politicians, led by Juan Peron. Peron was the ultimate Lifetime Politician, a dictator who relied on a populist strategy of government giveaways to stay in power. Argentina's economy paid the price. The grain and beef that had made the country rich declined, industry became lazy and inefficient, and no leader emerged to set things right.

The economy collapsed, workers went on strike constantly, and eventually things became so chaotic that the military took over and began a reign of terror, torturing and killing thousands of people. Decades passed before Argentina could again travel the road to democracy.

It is a sad story of what can happen when me-first politics sends rational action out the window. We *must* keep anything like that from happening here.

C H A P T E R   1 6

★

A New Path to Prosperity

The OPM mania sapped our economic strength and built a mountain of debt for all of us. So how do we turn things around? I was at a party in Palm Springs not long ago, talking politics, when a very rich oil man from Oklahoma said to the gathering, "Hell, we could take care of this national debt in no time, you and me and all of y'all...all the wealthy people would just give a certain amount and wipe it out."

I thought of that later when I read that in 1985 at least 17,000 Americans made over $1 million a year. A *year*. And the Federal Reserve estimates that there are 1.3 million millionaires in the United States. The wheels started turning, and I came up with an idea to pay off the national debt with contributions from rich Americans.

I got a little excited at the prospect of what the magic of compound interest could do to a big pool of money over a period of years and thought it would make a great national campaign. F.U.N.D. would be a neat slogan: Finish Up the National Debt.

With a well-publicized account in a Washington bank, and a reasonable rate of compound interest for a number of years, it seemed that Americans might be able to rescue their country from the crushing debt burden—if not for us or our children, then for our children's children.

A few minutes with the calculator sobered me up. I know that compound interest is a great savings device, but it turns out that $3 trillion of debt really is a colossal pile of money. Even if you assumed a healthy 6.75 percent return compounded annually for 50 years, the amount we would have to raise up front would be $114,479,300,000. More than a hundred billion dollars, just to start a pot that would grow for half a century.

I never imagined the starting nut would be anything like that. I don't think there are enough millionaires in all the world.

Realizing the enormity of our problems can be depressing. With all the bad paper, horrendous debt and economic disease we've allowed to accumulate, you'll hear some people argue that we ought to have another depression, just to shake out the ills in the economy and start over.

In some ways I see the logic of their thinking. We have been so prone to government by crisis that it might take a catastrophic collapse to wake up Wall Street and Washington and everyone in between.

But in a depression our deficits would explode to pay for the increase in unemployment. The government wouldn't be able to spend its way out of the slump and the price in human suffering would be costly. We can't really be in such sad shape that the doctor's only solution for the cancerous patient is a massive injection of arsenic.

We can return our economy to decent shape, but it won't be easy. The debt fetish extends into almost every area of our economic lives. The key to any successful plan is to set priorities at the outset. My plan to put the American economy back on the right road sets two chief priorities: one, reduce the government deficit by taking in more and spending less; and two, restore order to our financial institutions.

I'm proposing logical reforms we must take to reach this twin destination. It's important to see that nothing can be accomplished piecemeal. If you've heard it once, you've heard it a thousand times: everything is connected to everything else. Our economy is not a bunch of separate little pieces called the budget, trade, industrial production and so on. What happens in one area directly affects every other area.

BRINGING IN MORE MONEY

Whether we're talking about a household or a country, the best way to balance a budget is to bring in more money. The more we bring in, the less we have to worry about cutting our spending. You know as well as I that the best way to increase government revenues is to raise taxes. We lowered them too much, across the board. There, I said it. Most of the mealy-mouthed politicians who campaign for office never will.

Yes, the American people may have to be put through a little test. Let's see if we can handle a lower standard of living, with taxes taking more of the paycheck, a little tighter credit and some savings. I believe thinking people would rather pay some more in taxes and have a little austerity than face a depression. Sure, we'd like the party to continue with high consumption, high debt and low taxes. But it can't, and anyone who tells you it can is either a politician or a damn fool, or both.

It will be tough, but you can count on this: the longer we put off solutions, the worse trouble we will be in. First let's look for an honest tax policy, one that won't choke off business.

Introduce A Wealth Tax

The Reagan tax cuts have gone disproportionately to the wealthy, so that's a good place to tap more money.

I don't mind paying higher taxes, as long as I know that others are paying their fair share, in a national effort to put our country back on the right track. I know that there are wealthy men and women—I play golf with them all the time—who bitch endlessly about the sorry state of national affairs and then call their accountants to check on new loopholes and shelters.

By pushing the top rate for personal income tax back to the 1987 level of 38 percent (from the 1988 rate of 28 percent), we could raise revenues by $22 billion each year, according to economist Robert Kuttner. The supply-siders may still whine that higher taxes will decrease revenues, but the truth about Reaganomics speaks louder than their protests. The Japanese levy a 60-percent tax on the top income bracket.

Capital gains (profits on the sale of stocks and real estate) may still be taxed at 28 percent, but calls to lower that rate to 15 percent are irresponsible.

Raise Consumption Taxes

Most ideas for a sales or consumption tax would hurt people who earn lower incomes the worst, since they spend a bigger slice of their paycheck every week on consumer items. But there are three products I wouldn't mind taxing at a higher level: alcohol, tobacco and gasoline.

A friend who owns a California winery tells me that taxes on beer and wine have stayed at the same level since 1951, thanks to the efforts of the industry's lobbyists. Meanwhile, the social problems caused by alcoholism have been getting more and more costly. According to the congressional Joint Committee on Taxation, we could raise anywhere from $5 billion to $12 billion in revenue each year by hiking taxes on liquor, beer and wine. We could also raise $3 billion a year by raising the tax on tobacco. Likewise, we could kill two birds with one stone by raising the fee per barrel on imported oil. Not only will we raise government revenues, but we'll begin to cut our dependence on foreign oil and shrink our trade deficit, too. We might also consider increasing the tax on gas at the pump, which could raise a full $10 billion for every dime we add to a gallon.

Compete To Win In The Global Marketplace

The word "competitiveness" has become another election-year buzzword. But all it means is that we have to make better products that can sell in the global marketplace. If we can reorient manufacturing into a lean-mean-competing machine, we will be able to put a dent into our foreign debt and reduce our interest payments. Then we'll have more money to devote to things that really matter.

The politicians have been taking the wrong approach on trade, looking for easy answers. We have to stop blaming others for our failure to sell the goods we make.

The reason the Japanese have succeeded is their complete dedication to creating global marketplaces for their goods. As the Japanese management consultant Kenichi Ohmae wrote in the *Washington Post*, "We learn how to do business in the United States—when in Rome, learn the Roman way." Most American corporations have had the exact opposite approach: if the rest of the world wants the product, they can come and get it. Instead of concentrating on the slow, careful process of building a presence in foreign markets, many American corporations focus on short-term profits and quarterly earnings. Not only have we let foreign producers thrust into the domestic American market, now we're about to let them dominate the vast new markets opening up in China and the Soviet Union.

We may have lost the first battles in the drive for global markets, but we haven't lost the war. At least 85 percent of U.S. exports are produced by only 250 firms. The Government Accounting Office estimates that 11,000 additional U.S. firms could export but don't. They should. One on one, an American salesman is the most sophisticated salesman in the world.

Congress can play a role here by thinning the jungle of export restrictions on high-tech products. I've seen companies here in Silicon Valley develop great computer software, rivaling anything from Japan, but go bankrupt waiting for an export license from the Commerce and Defense departments. A National Academy of Sciences report estimated that the U.S. high-tech industry has lost nearly $9 billion in sales and 200,000 jobs because of the bureaucratic quagmire that keeps a company waiting up to three years for an export license. I'm not talking about national security items, just commercial computer technologies. If we decide we really want to compete, American creativity and our innovative thinking can outpace foreign rivals.

SPENDING LESS

No matter how much we raise in fairer taxes, no matter how much money we earn abroad with more competitive industries, we still have to adjust the other side of the fiscal equation. We cannot keep borrowing and spending as if there's no tomorrow. It is tomorrow, and our credit cards have been revoked. David Stockman's book about the failure of the Reagan Revolution was titled, *The Triumph of Politics.* His message was that the politicians in Congress and in the White House found it impossible to do what was politically unpopular—cut spending.

The biggest step we can take to halt our deficit spending is to toss out the Lifetime Politicians who can't say no to new federal expenditures. The political reforms in Chapter 10 addressed that approach. I also feel that dramatic budget cuts can be made in military spending with a strategy of waging peace instead of war. We'll go into that plan in Part III of this book.

Stop Congress's Money Hemorrhage

The congressional budget process encourages promiscuous spending. Omnibus spending bills have plenty of fat but the President finds it difficult to veto them because it might shut the government down. We need a safe-spending process that would work the way the Founding Fathers intended it to work—with separate spending bills proposed and passed for various government activities.

My unelectable hero, Senator Dan Evans, introduced an amendment to the 1988 budget bill that would have split the budget into its 13 component parts so that the President could have considered each separately and exercise some control over spending. But Congress didn't want oversight, it wanted pork, and Evans lost his battle. If Congress goes back to enacting 13 separate appropriations bills, the rest of us can easily judge the spending record: "last year they spent so much on agriculture, this year they're proposing so much more."

Trim The Fat From Farm Subsidies

We can't abruptly end the price-support subsidies we pay to farmers. Too many people rely on the program, and the shock to the economy would be highly inflationary. But we have to start phasing them out, so let's use common sense. Remove subsidy payments to farmers who have gross incomes above $100,000 a year. That money amounts to $8 billion a year in the federal budget. Cut it.

We also need to stop farmers from dividing their enterprises into separate, artificial entities to collect more subsidy checks. One farm, one check.

Take Social Security Out Of The Budget

Representative Claude Pepper used the rallying cry, "Don't touch Social Security," to lead the lobbying effort against cutting Social Security benefits. We don't need to cut benefits (except for the millionaires getting checks in the mail) since the program now runs a surplus, but we could use that slogan to keep the Lifetime Politicians' hands off the growing Social Security trust fund.

This year the program will collect $40 billion more than it pays out; in five years that annual surplus will be $80 billion, and by the year 2000 it will be close to $200 billion. We have to keep accumulating that money for the baby boomers who retire in the next century, when the ratio of worker-bees to taker-bees will be worse.

By law we can't spend it on anything else in the budget. But we must stop lifers from playing funny-numbers games with the cash surplus. Congress has to remove the Social Security surplus from the positive side of the budget. That just disguises the true deficit.

REBUILDING OUR INSTITUTIONS

I have a simple philosophy on financial oversight. If you want to be a big enough fool to give someone else carte blanche to handle your money without certain controls and assurances, well, I say go for it. I've seen a lot of good people lose their money this way. But I don't think we should allow our major financial institutions—banks, savings and loans, Wall Street investment firms—to engage in a free-for-all that threatens the savings of ordinary citizens.

The old phrase, "you can bank on it," should actually mean something once again. If there is one thing that would bring our entire economy crashing down, it is a collapse of the banking industry. We must prevent that from happening—or you can start boning up on the lifestyles of the 1930s.

Reregulate The Banks

We need to rethink the colossal mistake we made in 1980 by deregulating the financial sector. Obviously, good thought and planning didn't play as big a role in the changes as lobbyists did. When government got off these guys' backs, the greed monkey got on.

We should move to stop deregulation's blurring of the distinction between banks and savings associations. Responsible caps also have to be reimposed on the interest rates that banks and savings and loans offer to stop the reckless competition that sprang up. Just as risk and return are synonymous in banking, savings and safety should be, too.

Bank and savings and loan charters do not belong to daredevils and con men. Don't get me wrong, there's nothing wrong with a bank executive wanting the bank's stock value to go up. Motivation is the essence of our capitalist system. But we have to plant government firmly on the backs of those in banking. The lines of supervisory authority and regulatory control should be simple and uncompromising.

Emergency warning: one immediate issue we need to resolve involves the Glass-Steagall Act of 1933, the New Deal law that responded to Great Depression bank failures by separating commercial banks from the securities industry. That law prohibits banks from underwriting corporate debt and equity securities. In other words, it insulates the banks from the Wall Street casino. Glass-Steagall kept a lot of money safe for a lot of years. In this era of massive corporate debt and wild fluctuations in the stock exchanges, when more than 100 banks or savings and loans are under federal investigation for illegal trading in commodities futures, does it make any sense to talk about killing Glass-Steagall? Of course not.

But that's exactly what the greedy OPM lords of the American Bankers Association (ABA) want to do. The ABA and the Reagan administration spearheaded a drive in the Senate to gut Glass-Steagall and let banks into the casino, where they'll be gambling with your money. Even worse, they want to allow Wall Street firms to own and operate commercial banks. Have they gone crazy? Didn't we just see the brokerage firms fall off a cliff on Meltdown Monday? Aren't some banks hanging over the cliff? Do we want the cliff to give way?

There is no way we can allow the Boesky mentality of Wall Street to infect commercial banks, which are guaranteed by public funds. Leave Glass-Steagall alone. Franklin Roosevelt must be spinning in his grave.

Stop The Debt Madness

It's no mystery to me why eight of the ten largest banks in the world (measured by assets in dollars) are now Japanese. Their financial officers still consider the term "banker" to be a badge of honor and respect. Their lending policies are conservative and smart. As the *Wall Street Journal* reported in January 1988, Tokyo's banks "rarely indulge in 'creative finance' or other razzmatazz." American banks should follow their example.

Our banks have to kick their bad habits. To handle the massive Third World loan crisis, banks should be increasing the reserves they set aside in case the loans are never paid back—a distinct possibility in many cases. Currently, most banks only have reserves equivalent to about 25 percent of their problem loans, which is too low to survive a real crunch. In December 1987, the Bank of Boston set up a reserve of $430 million against $800 million in loans to troubled Latin American countries, representing about 50 percent of the total.

Most banks should be following suit. They don't because it would eat into quarterly earnings, and anyway they figure Uncle Sam will pick up the tab eventually.

Most importantly, American banks should be very tough on extending further credit to Third World countries, particularly large-scale loans for big governmental projects that are destined to fail. Let the Japanese banks, which are beginning to dominate the industry, commit their own resources to Third World needs. The Japanese will probably do a better job.

Closer to home, banks need to be stricter on student-loan defaults, which are rampant. *U.S. News and World Report* pointed out that since Uncle Sam guarantees student loans, banks "have little incentive to take suitable precautions before loans are approved or to track down defaulters when loans go bad."

Pull In The Chips From Wall Street's Casino

Stay off Wall Street...until it cleans up its act. Well into 1988, brokerage firms complained that daily activity was down sharply from 1987, ever since the October crash. They were moaning because daily trading was hovering at around 150 million shares, the break-even level for their commissions.

I don't feel sorry for the brokers. The stock exchanges have a role to play, but that role has been lost in the financial two-step. The Ivan Boesky case uncovered what federal prosecutors called "rampant criminal conduct" in various brokerage houses and investment banking firms, which is not surprising given the greedy atmosphere on Wall Street. According to the mayor of New York's office, the average Wall Street salary before the October crash was $65,000 a year—and that included secretaries and clerks. Are the Human Dust Cloths, most of whom let computers make their decisions, worth that much money?

When the stock market turns away from its casino atmosphere, in which people *play* with stocks instead of investing in companies based on their value, then you can expect long-range investors to return.

Until then, beware of "experts" who see another booming bull market. On Wall Street they called analyst Henry Prechter the "Bull Market Guru"—until the October crash. Two weeks before, he had predicted that the Dow Jones Average would climb from 2300 points to over 3600. He advised investors to buy, buy, buy. Then the *Wall Street Journal* monitored his taped-message hotline on Meltdown Monday. With prices falling sharply at 10:30 a.m., Prechter told callers that the market might bottom out at 2100. Two hours later, he thought the bottom would be found at 1800. By the end of the day, Prechter was "predicting" that prices would drop to 1500. This "expert" could do better tossing a coin.

One way to shut down the casino would be to introduce a special tax on short-term stock transactions. That would reduce the incentive for computer program trading to wreak havoc on Wall Street, and it might discourage some fly-by-night takeover artists from gambling on companies. This measure should be welcomed by corporate America since the takeover mania forces managers to focus less on running a productive and efficient company and more on spending millions in self-defense.

You'll hear criticism of this idea, because a lot of Human Dust Cloths get rich off the takeover mania. The people who really benefit from corporate takeovers are the investment bankers and lawyers who promote the deals. In the 1988 bidding war between Macy's and Campeau Corporation over which shark would gobble up Federated Department Stores, the law firms and investment bankers involved on both sides received more than $200 million for 11 weeks of paper-shuffling.

Pry Politicians' Fingers Off The Economy

In some areas we need closer governmental oversight of financial institutions. But I mean *responsible* government. I don't think that Lifetime Politicians consider themselves responsible for anything but their own skins. In almost every problem area of the economy, we find their fingerprints, and what's worse, they actively oppose efforts to turn things around.

Politicians obstructed the fight to clean up the banking industry, even though it was their deregulation that caused the mess. Speaker of the House Jim Wright intervened with the

FSLIC in 1985 and 1986 on behalf of several home-state Texas savings and loan associations. Four executives of those institutions have since been indicted on fraud charges. And when the FSLIC tried to sell off insolvent associations, members of Congress from Texas reportedly tried to influence bids for friends and political associates.

By far the most dangerous political manipulation of the economy is carried out by the Secretary of the Treasury, through that office's ability to influence the Federal Reserve Board and its decisions on the prime interest rate and the country's money supply. We have a long history of administrations abusing these levers to create artificial good times during an election year. And most years after an election, we pay the price in inflation, recession or swollen budget deficits.

Running the Economy by Remote Control

For James Baker, Reagan's second Treasury Secretary, the campaign always came first. His entire background is political. He was George Bush's campaign manager in his 1970 Senate race and his 1980 Presidential bid. He ran for state office himself in Texas in 1978 (and lost). Did that background prepare him to supervise the economy objectively in 1988? David Stockman wrote that in White House budget meetings, when Stockman had a calculator by his side, Baker had a TV remote control; at 6:30 every afternoon, "the meeting shifted from the policy problem in the numbers to the political problems on the screen."

In February 1988, Assistant Treasury Secretary Michael Darby sent a confidential letter to top Fed officials, twisting the Federal Reserve's arm to shovel more money into the economy to prevent a slump before November 1988. We only got to read about it after the letter leaked to the press. Asked about the political aspects of the letter, Treasury Secretary James Baker replied that his assistant was "just setting forth some rather academic ideas and arguments." Yeah, right.

Jerry Jordan, chief economist at First Interstate Bancorp, warned in *Fortune* magazine: "Here's the Treasury Department leading the easy-money parade! It scares the daylights out of the whole world."

Incredibly, the Federal Reserve Board isn't pressuring banks to increase their reserves against debt. Instead, according to the *New York Times*, the Fed made a few quiet telephone calls to bank presidents around the country discouraging them from increasing their loan reserves. Why? The Fed's seven governors, who are appointed by the President and are subject to political pressures from the White House and Congress, are afraid of panic and political fallout if the biggest banks admitted that billions in loans were down the drain.

The public has a right to panic! You can't keep putting off sound fiscal policy without courting economic disaster. Things really are out of control, and the feel-good politicians have kept the bad news hidden for too long. It's time to revoke their authority over our economy, and every American citizen has the power, and the obligation, to do just that.

THE BOTTOM LINE

Unlike Ronald Reagan, who liked to make everybody feel good, I don't pretend that it will be a piece of cake to put our economic house in order. On the contrary, it's going to hurt.

We could be in for hard times. I don't have a sugar-coated pill. The medicine is not going to be pleasant.

I have presented a few ideas for reform, summed up as back-to-basics economics. But there is one last point to be made, and it is not addressed to the government. You and I are the only people who can end the crazy idea that Uncle Sam has to guarantee everything under the shining sun. Life just doesn't work that way. We have winners and losers. When the losers insist on reclaiming their losses from the taxpayer, we wind up with unfairness and economic chaos. And when those in control of the system yield for political reasons, we all lose.

To tell you the truth, I am optimistic about our ability to solve our economic problems in the long run. But I know it's one thing to talk a good fight, another to wage it. The path to economic stability is a jungle of thickets. The one hopeful sign is to understand that all those thickets were planted by us, and we can summon up the machete power to get rid of them.

Our best hope is to boot out the leaders we have today, who are like the customer in that Fram oil filter commercial. You remember. The auto mechanic holds up a new oil filter in one hand and a broken piston rod in the other, and says, "You can pay me now, or you can pay me later."

PART III

★

FOREIGN POLICY:
THE SEARCH FOR PEACE

CHAPTER 17

★

World Boss

As a superpower, the United States confronts the danger of international conflict every day. But as citizens, we are also confronted with a huge amount of information each day demonstrating the confusion and complexity of the outside world. Can our foreign policy possibly be wise and effective if we ourselves can't understand it?

Over the last twenty eventful years I've spent a lot of time thinking about our country's role in the world. I have settled on two overriding concerns: how to prevent the Big One, and how to prevent or at least stay out of the Little Ones. This chapter will take us through a tough examination of where we stand on those two issues—and why.

PLAYING CAPTURE THE FLAG

Remember the heated debate in 1987 over our naval presence in the Persian Gulf? A year later our ships were still plying the waters there, braving the straits. The average American, though, had lost interest in the debate, and ignored the operation as long as no violent reminders confronted him or her on the nightly news.

What bothered us so much about reflagging foreign ships as American? The critics pointed to the illogical nature of escorting Kuwaiti oil tankers as if they were our own. We aren't the biggest customers of Kuwaiti oil; the Japanese are by far, with the West

Europeans close behind. We get only 1 percent of our imported oil from Kuwait, while the Japanese get 31 percent of theirs. So we weren't protecting our own energy lifeline, but someone else's.

We made no serious and carefully thought-out decision. We didn't consult with the world's other superpower about the program. Instead, we showed the flag, reacting to Iranian threats and bombast with a hasty leap into the Gulf. Congress was dragged along, kicking and screaming about President Reagan's refusal to adhere to the War Powers Act. All of a sudden, we had more than 30 ships in the area, including the battleship Missouri—even though we were afraid to send her through the Strait of Hormuz for fear she'd be sunk!

The convoys cost the taxpayer almost $10 million each day, according to the Center for Defense Information. It turns out that we have been spending two dollars for every one dollar's worth of oil that the convoys bring out. For no good reason, we seemed intent on challenging the Iranians to another deadly game of Capture the Flag.

To many, here was another costly and open-ended commitment by an administration bent on intervention. Back in the 1960s, I wasn't exactly a fire-breathing liberal but I did have early doubts about our involvement in Vietnam.

I remember an incident in the late 1960s at the Commonwealth Club, the San Francisco private club where I once rubbed shoulders with California's power elite. Our "distinguished visitor" one day was Nguyen Cao Ky, the premier of South Vietnam.

Premier Ky told us how badly the Vietnamese people wanted democracy, the real message being "please keep sending your Marines and your dollars." What a snake-oil salesman that guy was. He never mentioned, of course, that he represented a military council that had overthrown a civilian government, or that his government was repressing the democratic rights of Buddhists and others. I wanted to ask him about allegations that he personally was involved in dope-dealing, but my question was drowned in the waves of applause he was receiving.

All at once, though, a group of young protesters made it into the building, climbed to the balcony and began to disrupt the speech. There they were, chanting antiwar slogans and calling for peace...and I thought it was great. Some of the other members were furious, and I even heard one say that the protesters "should be shot."

How could he miss the irony? These kids were protesting because their friends, brothers, cousins *were* being shot—in Vietnam. I cheered the protesters on, and the very next day I resigned from the Commonwealth Club.

The Johnson administration's actions and the response of the public 20 years ago are fundamentally the same as they are today. Only the names have changed: then Ky, now Panama's Noriega accused of drug smuggling. Then, American G.I.'s streamed into Cam Ranh Bay, now into Honduras.

So the question remains: why are we in the Persian Gulf, in Honduras, everywhere? Why do we still engage in these expensive, open-ended adventures around the globe, just inviting crackpots to take a shot at us? We can't afford such adventures. The human and financial costs are too high.

TRYING TO RUN THE WORLD

In 1945 the United States accepted its world leadership role, recognizing that in the wake of World War II it was the most powerful nation on earth. This was quite a step. For 150 years, we had followed a basically isolationist foreign policy, ever since George Washington's Farewell Address warned us to avoid "entanglement in foreign alliances."

Pearl Harbor and the war forced us to see our security not in continental terms, but on a global scale. After every other war in our history, we had demobilized. But something had changed this time—our thinking. We were intoxicated by our capabilities. We were one of the few countries not on our knees. When the war ended, our global outlook didn't.

We have mixed four elements in our postwar foreign policy. First, we have used *traditional diplomacy*, under the general management of our State Department. Second, we have pursued our international aims through *foreign aid*, using gifts of money to other countries to influence their internal and foreign policies. Third, we have maintained awesome *military force*. And fourth, we have engaged in worldwide *covert operations* by a network of intelligence agencies.

Table 3—World cop: U.S. gunboat diplomacy since 1945		
1946	Trieste, Italian-Yugoslav waters	Navy warships
	Bosporus Straits, Turkey	Navy carrier task force
	Greece	Navy carrier task force
1948	Trieste	Navy warships
	Nanking-Shanghai, China	Marines
1950-53	Korean War	United States and allies fight large-scale ground war
1954-55	Taiwan	Five Navy carriers, Marines
1957	Quemoy and Matsu, Taiwan	Four Navy carriers, Marines
1958	Venezuela	Navy warships plus Marines
	Indonesia	Navy's Seventh Fleet, Marines
	Beirut, Lebanon	14,000 soldiers
1961	Dominican Republic	Navy warships and planes
1962	Thailand	5,000 Marines
	Cuba	Cuban missile crisis, 180 Navy warships
1963	Haiti	Navy warships, Marines
1964-75	Vietnam War	The longest war in American history
1964-73	Laos	Air Force bombing missions
1965	Dominican Republic	21,500 U.S. troops assist in the overthrow of leftist government
1967	Middle East	Six-Day War, the Navy's Sixth Fleet off Syria
	Congo	Air Force C-130 missions against antigovernment rebels
1970	Cambodia	U.S. ground invasion, secret B-52 bombings
1975	Cambodia	Air Force, Navy, Marine forces rescue merchant ship *Mayaguez*
1980	Iran	Delta Team commandos infiltrate Iran to rescue hostages
1982	Libya	Sixth Fleet naval exercises cross Qadhafi's "Line of Death"
1983	Beirut, Lebanon	1,800 member Marine task force deployed, withdrawn after barracks bombed
	Grenada	Marines and Army forces invade, overthrow government
1986	Libya	Air Force bombs Tripoli, Benghazi
1987-88	Persian Gulf	Two Navy carrier task forces in the area; tit-for-tat strikes against Iran

In general, we have not mixed these ingredients very well. Frankly, we do a lousy job. Our international interests are distorted when we overemphasize the military side of foreign policy and neglect peaceful diplomacy. That distortion began soon after the war.

As the Cold War began, President Harry Truman replaced the utopian idea of international organization and peace-keeping with a more nationalistic policy. Instead of focusing on collective security through the United Nations, policy-makers baptized the United States "the world's policeman." Table 3 shows the United States' involvement in gunboat diplomacy since 1945.

The United States has since built a worldwide network of 374 military bases and installations in 21 countries (not counting our 871 bases here at home). The Coalition for a New Foreign Policy, a liberal research foundation, calculates that only 12 percent of our military spending goes to defend actual U.S. territory. Obviously our troops overseas are defending our interests, but we have allotted most of our military resources to foreign commitments.

That effort is matched by the Soviet Union, so that today you are far more likely to see an American or Soviet soldier in a foreign country than you are to see a diplomat (see Tables 4, 5 and 6). People around the world identify the United States not with Hollywood or democracy, as in the old days, but with a military presence. That attitude would have shocked Americans before World War II.

Table 4—Troops abroad: United States and Soviet Union		
United States total	**525,600**	**(including 64,400 afloat)**
• Western Europe	354,000	(27,200 afloat)
• Far East/Asia	143,800	(33,000 afloat)
Caribbean/Latin America	19,300	
Cuba	2,500	(Guantanamo Bay)
Honduras	120	
Puerto Rico	3,600	
Panama	9,300	(900 afloat)
Other Caribbean	3780	
• Middle East/Africa	7,000	(3,000 afloat)
Sinai	1,100	
Egypt	1,300	
Saudi Arabia	390	
Diego Garcia	1,300	
Other Middle East	4090	
Other areas	1,500	(300 afloat)

Soviet Union total	711,710	
• Eastern Europe	500,000	
• Far East/Asia	190,900	
Afghanistan	118,000	(began withdrawal, 1988)
Mongolia	65,000	
Vietnam	7,000	
Laos	500	
Kampuchea	200	
India	200	
• Caribbean/Latin America	8,210	
Cuba	8,000	
Peru	160	
Nicaragua	50	
• Middle East/Africa	12,600	
Algeria	1,000	
Angola	1,500	
Congo	100	
Ethiopia	1,500	
Iraq	600	
Syria	4,000	
North Yemen	500	
Libya	2,000	
Mali	200	
Mozambique	300	
Other Africa	900	

Table 5—Superpower military bases abroad*

United States	Soviet Union
American Samoa	Afghanistan
Ascension Island	Czechoslovakia
Azores	East Germany
Bahrain	Hungary
Belgium	Mongolia
Bermuda	Poland
Cuba	Vietnam
Diego Garcia	
Greece	
Guam	
Iceland	
Italy	
Iwo Jima	
Japan	
Netherlands	
New Zealand	
Panama	
Philippines	
Puerto Rico	
South Korea	

United States (continued)

Spain
Turkey
United Kingdom
West Germany
*Both sides have more than one base in many countries

Table 6—Superpower military advisors abroad	
United States	**Soviet Union**
Argentina	Algeria
Australia	Angola
Bolivia	Cape Verde
Chile	Congo
Colombia	Ethiopia
Costa Rica	Guinea
Dominican Republic	India
Egypt	Iraq
El Salvador	Kampuchea
Guatemala	Kuwait
Haiti	Laos
Honduras	Libya
Indonesia	Madagascar
Jordan	Mali
Kuwait	Mauritania
Liberia	Mozambique
Morocco	Nicaragua
Oman	Nigeria
Paraguay	North Yemen
Saudi Arabia	Peru
Somalia	Sao Tome/Principe
Thailand	South Yemen
Tunisia	Syria
Venezuela	Tanzania
Zaire	
Zambia	

POLITICS AND POLICIES

The foundation of our foreign policy for 40 years has been containment, defending any country facing Soviet aggression. But the direct U.S.-Soviet Cold War has lessened over the years. Why has globalism expanded to dictate a full-scale "world cop" role for the United States? Politics, that's why.

Today's Lifetime Politicians aren't the first to discover that foreign policy can be used for political purposes. The young Representative Abraham Lincoln criticized President James Polk in 1846 for his war with Mexico. Polk was trying to look tough and divert attention from his embarrassment over our northern border with Canada, where Polk had backed down on "Fifty-four-forty or fight."

Today, aggressive globalist thinking is the rhetoric of American politicians because it sounds tough, determined, and "Presidential." Candidate Ronald Reagan demonstrated that he would conform to that familiar mindset in 1979 when he said, "We must resist any unpeaceful act wherever it may occur." One of his transition team members wrote in a memo before Reagan's inauguration that "no area of the world is beyond the scope of American influence." And under President Reagan, our globalist tendencies made us the swaggering bully, knocking chips off shoulders around the globe.

But it's wrong to heap abuse on Ronald Reagan for his foreign policy. He merely tried to rebuild the containment consensus that was ruptured by Vietnam and detente, and he tapped into a popular xenophobic current exploited by so many other Presidents and candidates before him. Aggressive globalism has traditionally had a nonpartisan appeal, its roots lying in both the Truman and Eisenhower administrations. Reagan followed in the footsteps of John F. Kennedy, whose inaugural address promised to "pay any price, bear any burden, meet any hardship, support any friend, oppose any foe, to assure the survival and success of liberty."

Just as Barry Goldwater and George Wallace earlier expressed a resentment against "those foreigners," Richard Gephardt in 1988 echoed popular indignation at the economic success of Japan and South Korea, and Albert Gore tried to win conservative votes with a tough stance on Central America down South.

SIMPLE ANSWERS ARE COSTLY

Globalist thinkers are indulging in a very simplistic view of international affairs that doesn't recognize the complex changes taking place in Third World countries. They don't understand how different our actions look to the rest of the world.

When the average American hears, for example, that November 4 is now officially celebrated in Iran as "Death to

America Day," he or she is baffled, or merely amused. Iranians are celebrating the day they took our diplomats hostage in 1979, and we are facing many more indignities like that around the world. We can no longer afford to be amused.

Global militarism seductively proposes simple answers to complex problems, with predictably chaotic results. The United States supposedly learned a lesson in Vietnam—that we can't run the world. But did our decision-makers really acknowledge that?

In 1983, we put 1,800 lightly armed Marines in the middle of a vicious religious and tribal war in Beirut. Why—just to show the flag? The result was the barracks bombing and the senseless loss of 241 young lives. And then the Pentagon announced that the surviving Marines were being "redeployed" back home. In the end, we had accomplished nothing for our losses except an utterly useless carnage of our finest young men. Our troops deserve better thought and planning than that, but we continue to ignore the obvious lessons of such fiascos.

THE PARKING-LOT PASSION

Patriotism is a very strong emotion, and most Americans have it in a healthy amount. But some people are susceptible to a hyper-patriotism, with manifest pride in our ability to beat up somebody else. It's the old Rambo syndrome, but it's a lot older than the movie. Abraham Lincoln enjoyed telling people about the old loafer who said to him, "I feel patriotic," and when asked what he meant, exclaimed, "Why, I feel like I want to kill somebody or steal something!"

Politicians play to this weakness of ours. I have to go back to Ronald Reagan again to demonstrate this point. When he ran for Governor in California, he called for an all-out war on Vietnam, declaring: "We could pave the whole country and put parking stripes on it and still be home by Christmas."

On various occasions I have encountered friends with this mentality, and have been shot down when I tried to introduce a little calm, reasonable reflection. "Don't confuse me with facts," they seem to say. Well, that's all I'm trying to do with this book: provide some facts and draw some reasonable conclusions from them. Then we can rebuild our foreign policy sensibly.

The M-1 Mentality

For a lot of us, giving up on the idea of unrestrained world power is a difficult adjustment to make. A friend I met at the 1988 Masters golf tournament told me, "In 1945 I had an M-1 rifle on my shoulder, and all these German prisoners of war and civilians under my command. When I said move, they moved! If they got out of hand, I had every right to shoot them. I tell you, I had more respect as a private with an M-1 than a general has today."

I know that some of the conclusions I make are hard to accept. We refuse to admit, to ourselves or to anyone else, that the job of keeping the world safe is too big for one nation, even if it is one of the two great superpowers. Just the attempt is very expensive. We can't afford it. Further, it is an exhausting exercise, and we no longer have the stamina for it, or the leadership. Finally—and most crucially—we have found that trying by ourselves to keep the peace in a world of nuclear weapons is a very dangerous and bloody enterprise. Aside from any questions of morality, it just doesn't work.

THE "LOGIC" OF AN ARMS RACE

The prime exhibit in this exercise in futility has to be the furious race between the United States and the Soviet Union to see who can design and build the bigger stockpile of arms. We had good reason to suspect the Russians when Stalin was at the helm. The subjugation of Eastern Europe and the threat of a Soviet invasion into Western Europe were real and frightening in the late 1940s and early 1950s.

But a lot has changed in the last thirty years. It seems obvious to me that the new Soviet leaders are unwilling to risk their positions for a cause as elusive as "world revolution." They see the competition with the United States as one between two great powers, jockeying for influence and power—but not to the death. The competition has to have limits.

The arms race has no limits. Did it matter that there were enough nuclear weapons in 1968 for each side to destroy each other at least four times over? No, that would have been too rational. We kept on building.

Even the terrible implications of the phrase "Mutually Assured Destruction" (MAD) didn't stop the superpowers. MAD means each side has enough missiles to blow up the other side, even if the other side launches first. Then, the theory is, there's no advantage to ever launching a strike, since neither side can win. That would seem to be a good reason for both sides to feel secure in the knowledge that the other side would never be suicidal enough to launch an attack. But, no, that's also too rational.

ALIENS IN THE KREMLIN

Today, after the changes the Soviet Union has seen in the past decades and with the openness introduced by Mikhail Gorbachev, we have fewer and fewer reasons for the suspicion and hatred that marked the Cold War.

Yet the rhetoric continues. Jimmy Carter said early in his administration that we could now be "free of that inordinate fear of communism" which kept Americans captive for so many years. Even so, his successor in the White House did more than any President since Truman to hold us hostage to his distrust of the "evil empire." While running for the 1980 Presidential nomination, Reagan said, "I wouldn't trust the Russians around the block. They must be laughing at us because we continue to think of them as people like us."

People like us? Are they from outer space? How many Russians had Reagan met in 1980? No wonder he softened his tone after meeting with Gorbachev in various summits. He even signed the treaty on medium-range weapons that started the process of nuclear disarmament. But Reagan and his conservative cohorts said that the reason negotiations advanced this far is that the United States hung tough and built up a powerful military capability that frightened the Soviets.

I don't believe that for a minute. I think that any chance we have today for a disarmament accord stems from the new thinking introduced by Gorbachev, who realized, as we should, that the arms race is suicidal for the Soviet Union, the United States and the whole world.

Since Gorbachev rose to the top in 1985 he has been the leader in the diplomatic drive to disarmament, and Reagan has only been reacting. The handwriting was on the wall a few years ago and Gorbachev has sent constant signals, but we have blown billions of dollars because our leaders refused to perceive the unfolding changes. Only after a trip to the Kremlin itself was President Reagan able to admit that the Soviet Union was no longer an evil empire. I'm glad he finally dropped his dogmatic rhetoric, but the episode doesn't say much for our long-term planning and forethought.

Bombs Away

There are now 50,000 nuclear weapons in the world. The two superpowers have a combined total of 17,640 megatons of nuclear firepower. That is equivalent to the explosive power of 5,820 World War II's. That's right; if you add together all the bombs dropped in that entire war, including the two atomic bombs dropped on Japan and the tons and tons of bombs rained down on Germany, and multiplied all that by 5,000, you would almost equal the power of our nuclear arsenals today.

Of course many people on both sides do not want to see an end to the arms race. There are strong economic forces behind military buildups. In the United States, defense contractors are among the largest employers in the country and therefore enjoy massive clout in Washington, where reason rarely triumphs. The same situation prevails in the Soviet Union. There the Defense Ministry and the branches involved in defense production are among the most powerful players in that heavily bureaucratized government. Their words count at the Politburo level as much as our defense contractors' words count in the Pentagon and the White House.

LEADERS CAN BE CAPTIVE TOO

One of the most discouraging aspects of the whole situation is the frightening lack of political will on the arms control issue. It has been easier to wail about the Russian threat. Either by scare tactics—"The Russkies are coming!"—or by posing as the calm arms expert, the wily politician manipulates the uninformed citizen. The result: we remain captive to a deadly arms race no one but the arms makers can win.

Nikita Khrushchev, who was tossed out of the Kremlin in 1964, wrote in his memoirs about a candid conversation he had with President Eisenhower during a summit visit to Camp David:

> [Eisenhower:] "Tell me, Mr. Khrushchev, how do you decide the question of funds for military expenses? Perhaps first I should tell you how it is with us....It's like this. My military leaders come to me and say, 'Mr. President, we need such and such a sum for such and such a program.' I say, 'Sorry, we don't have the funds.' They say, 'We have reliable information that the Soviet Union has already allocated funds for their own such program. Therefore if we don't get the funds we need, we'll fall behind the Soviet Union.' So I give in. That's how they wring money out of me."

> [Khrushchev:] "It's just the same. Some people from our military department come and say, 'Comrade Khrushchev, look at this! The Americans are developing such and such a system. We could develop the same system, but it would cost such and such.' I tell them there's no money; it's all been allotted already. So they say, 'If we don't get the money we need and if there's a war, then the enemy will have superiority over us.' So we discuss it some more, and I end up by giving them the money they ask for."

Khrushchev tried to get a handle on the Russian military-industrial complex, but the Brezhnev gang who bounced him from power were true Lifetime Politicians. They made a compact with the military, getting its political support in exchange for more military spending. The result was a massive Soviet military build-up in the late 1960s and early 1970s. In short, the Soviet Union has its own set of Lifetime Politicians and bureaucrats whose interests are in continuing hardline policies that hold the Russian people captive.

If the American people and the Russian people could ever get together, they might decide that the common enemy is the careerist politician, whether he or she is sitting in the Kremlin, the Congress or the White House. We have had enough of the experts and professionals. In the next chapter, I'll lay out enough information on our Pentagon to enable every American to make his or her own decisions. Bring on the amateurs!

CHAPTER 18

★

Pentagon Follies

It's expensive to be the world boss. For one thing, you have to stay armed to the teeth. The last defense budget submitted by Jimmy Carter in 1980 was for $160 billion. The first thing Ronald Reagan did was ask for $20 billion more. By his last year in office the defense budget was nearly $300 billion.

This is escalation with a vengeance for equipment that often doesn't work. On top of that, it tells you where our priorities are: destructive weaponry rather than peace efforts. We spend only about $4 billion a year on our State Department.

Do we really need such blockbuster expenditures to protect us from the Soviet Union? I doubt it. But the problem is that no one really does know, including the people who are lobbying for bigger and bigger military spending. We, the public, aren't normally given enough information to make a good call. And so in this vital area, as in other areas we have discussed in this book, we are captive to the politicians who claim to know how much we need to spend.

THE SPENDING RACE

The major determinant of our defense spending seems to be what the Soviet Union is doing. How do we know what they are doing? We don't. But we have people who guess at it. This leaves a great deal of room for our politicians to exploit that uncertainty for their own ends.

One story is revealing. In 1955, at Air Force Day ceremonies in Moscow, Soviet leader Khrushchev bluffed the United States into believing that the Russians had gained a superiority in bombers. Charles Taylor, a U.S. military attache, counted 28 Soviet Bison jets flying overhead, more than double the number we thought they had. My god, we had a "bomber gap." Many years later, after building the B-52, we learned that the Soviets had circled their bombers at least twice. Who knows how many deceptions or mistakes of this kind have motivated us to strengthen our arsenal? It's like a Marx brothers movie.

Lifetime Politicians are perfectly happy with the farce. It helps them win campaigns. When John F. Kennedy found out that his charges during the 1960 campaign about a "missile gap" were wrong (we had 30 ICBMs, they had fewer than five), he kept plugging the issue anyway. It made the Eisenhower-Nixon administration look weak, and it made him look tougher to voters who might be worried about his liberalism. That's why we got a military buildup under Kennedy—not because we needed one.

U.S. Defense Spending ($ billions)	
1960	48.1
1965	53.5
1970	81.7
1975	92.3
1980	134.0
1985	252.8
1986	273.4
1987	282.2
1988	277.0
1989	299.6 (authorized)

Things are a little better these days. We now have satellites and electronic surveillance systems to count weapons and troops under Soviet command. We monitor their missile tests and training exercises. Our analysts also read Soviet military journals, where they are laying bare their innermost secrets, right?

Estimating Soviet military strength is still not an exact science. We are not good at identifying and evaluating *emerging* Soviet weapons before they are deployed. We don't know what goes on inside Soviet research and development laboratories.

We're not good at estimating inventory levels of munitions, spare parts and replacement equipment.

Our estimates of Soviet military spending are also sketchy. The Soviets publish their budget but we can't put much faith in it. They engage in "creative bookkeeping" by fitting components of military expenditures under other categories. (Of course, our Pentagon does that, too.)

MONKEY SEE, MONKEY DO

When our analysts try to make Soviet figures comparable to ours, we enter a never-never land. For example, the United States pays its volunteer recruits $600 a month, while the Soviets pay their conscripts the equivalent in rubles of about $6.50 a month. Yet we estimate Soviet manpower costs as if they were paying as much as we are. So it's not surprising that we get inflated reports of Soviet military spending.

All in all, our intelligence apparatus walks a tightrope, mixing what we know for sure with what we can only guess at. By extrapolating from past trends we can sometimes adjust for present uncertainties. But this entails a wide margin of error: some of our current estimates of Soviet research and development programs go back to data last published in the 1950s!

In the end, the CIA and the Defense Intelligence Agency work together to draft the National Intelligence Estimate (NIE), which has a major influence on our spending decisions. The NIE, using the imperfect techniques already cited, often overestimates Soviet spending, and that in turn stimulates our spending. The rationale is: when uncertain, make the "worst-case" scenario.

In 1976, a defector provided an actual Soviet defense budget to our government, the only one we'd ever seen. It seemed to indicate that previous CIA estimates of Soviet spending were too low by 50 percent. Ronald Reagan, then running for the Presidency, picked up on this "gap" to show how defenseless we were. But the facts were something else. The information didn't change our estimates of Soviet military capability. We were right about the hardware they had, we had just overestimated their efficiency. It was costing them twice as much as we had thought to produce the military equipment they had. They are terribly inefficient, and who can be surprised at this news?

While they may spend a larger chunk of their GNP on military spending than we do, our GNP is about twice theirs. Besides, we would be better off focusing not on spending but on what is actually being produced. Whichever way you look at the rationale for defense spending, you soon realize that a lot of people are shooting in the dark.

THE IRON TRIANGLE

A combination of ignorance, greed and politics yields the "Iron Triangle," an epithet coined by defense critic Gordon Adams to describe the incestuous relationship that ropes together the Pentagon, defense contractors and members of Congress in an unholy alliance to drive up military spending. Each side of the triangle benefits: the military services get to buy the big weapons they want, the politicians get defense plants for their districts and the contractors receive billion-dollar awards to build the stuff. They bargain together to see how they can each serve their parochial interests rather than jointly serving the national interest.

The political-military link in the triangle is tight, rooted in the congressional committees that oversee (or overlook) Pentagon affairs. Melvin Price, an Illinois Congressman first elected in 1944, found the golden key to Lifetime Politician status in 1974 when he became chairman of the House Armed Services Committee. By making his committee a rubber-stamp for the Pentagon, Price was able to funnel military contracts into his home district and use PAC money from the contractors in his campaigns. In 1988, like many lifers, he died with his boots on. He was in the middle of his 22nd term in office, 83 years old and still making important decisions about defense.

Pure politics often gives us weapons we don't need and can't afford. In 1982, the Pentagon and White House were agreed that the aging A-10 Thunderbolt attack plane could be phased out. Great, we'd save money. But then Representative Norman Lent of New York heard about it. The A-10 was made in his district, and he wanted to fight for the jobs it meant. Lent complained to the White House. Did President Reagan decide the issue on the national security merits? No. He needed Lent's vote on a completely different issue: his 1982 tax bill. Reagan traded the A-10 for the tax vote, lifer Lent stayed popular in his district, and the rest of us footed the bill for a plane we didn't need.

A successful Lifetime Politician learns quickly that election day can be a referendum on how well he or she has served the defense industry. In California, an estimated 30 percent of the manufacturing workforce work directly or indirectly for defense contractors. All those jobs have to be protected, or else the member of Congress will look like a failure. So our representatives in Washington bring home the Pentagon bacon. California's Senator Pete Wilson brags in his speeches that his votes on the Senate Armed Services Committee helped bring 600,000 new jobs to the state. Those jobs build more planes, tanks and submarines, not because we need them, but because Pete Wilson needs the votes.

Even liberals reverse their priorities when it comes to local defense spending. California's other Senator, Alan Cranston, forgot his die-hard liberal sympathies when it came to the B-1 nuclear bomber. He voted for the B-1 because its California jobs translate into votes. Check the voting on a defense appropriations bill—and you will see that it crosses party lines, but there's usually a 100-percent correlation between "yes" votes and the congressional district where a particular weapon is going to be made. Hey, who cares about the national pocketbook when local jobs are at stake?

ALL-AMERICAN SOCIALISM

Americans looking at the Soviet Union often claim that we have a fundamental advantage because we enjoy free competition, which sparks creativity and quality. But whoever made that claim hasn't looked at our weapons procurement. They would quickly find that there's not a lot of competition.

First of all, too much government money goes to the 25,000 defense contractors. Naturally, this makes them greedy for more and too lazy to look for business in the civilian sector. The top 10 defense contractors (by amount of Pentagon contracts received) in 1987 were:

1. McDonnell Douglas
2. General Dynamics
3. General Electric

4. Lockheed
5. General Motors
6. Raytheon
7. Martin Marietta
8. United Technologies
9. Boeing
10. Grumman

Maybe you, or a relative, work for one of these companies. You might be scoffing at my use of the term "socialism" to describe defense contractors. But six of the top 10 relied on government orders for more than 60 percent of their total business in 1986. Two of them—General Dynamics and Lockheed—did more than 85 percent of their business with the Pentagon. With that kind of dependency, it's hard to see these companies as still functioning in a private enterprise system. They are the welfare queens of American business. Only a fool would believe that this high level of government business makes them lean, mean and competitive.

You Have to Spend Money to Make Money

Defense contractors keep their welfare checks coming in by using a PAC-money whip on politicians. In the 1986 congressional elections, Common Cause found that the PACs of the top 10 gave nearly $3 million to candidates. Almost half of that went to incumbents sitting on the House and Senate Armed Services committees or the defense subcommittees of the House and Senate appropriations committees.

One consequence of the noncompetitive defense business is that the procurement process suffers. Theoretically, when the Pentagon starts to develop a weapon, competition is spurred by a request for proposals (RFP) from contractors. However, during the design phase that precedes the RFP, one or more of the major contractors usually gets a head start on the competition by working closely with Pentagon officials. And invariably that firm is the first choice when it comes time to assign the contract.

Because of this distorted sequence, the contractors often take part in determining the military needs that they will later try to fill. They obviously have tremendous incentives to identify needs that enhance their profit-making potential. One official from North American Rockwell said: "Your ultimate goal is actually to write the RFP, and this happens more than you might think." When the request-for-proposal process miraculously results in specifications for a particular weapon that look virtually identical to a bid one contractor has submitted, the Pentagon will usually remove the contract from competitive bidding and award it on a "single-source" basis. As it stands now, only half of the Pentagon's procurement money is spent through competitive contracts. So much for our free enterprise system.

There's nothing unpatriotic about questioning the way our military works and pays for itself. In fact, the result of our current system is massive fraud and, ultimately, a weaker national defense. Nine of the top 10 contractors were under federal investigation in 1987 for fraudulent billing, and most of the investigations are uncovering new outrages. I'm not just talking about the $700 coffeepots and the $3,000 toilet seats. The entire system of collusion and corruption is at fault. When Lockheed is accused of $281 million in overcharges, McDonnell Douglas of $130 million in inflated charges, and General Dynamics of millions as well, something is fundamentally wrong.

The shenanigans at Northrop show why we should be concerned if we want a strong defense. The company got half of its total 1987 revenue from one project, the Stealth bomber, but now there is a federal suit underway alleging false billing of $400 million by Northrop on the Stealth. On another Northrop contract, the Defense Department had to withhold more than $130 million in payments for MX missile guidance systems because they didn't work. Meanwhile, the Stealth bomber can't fly because of Northrop's shoddy work, and 12 of our 30 MX missiles sit in silos unlaunchable because they have no guidance systems.

There are plenty of examples to back up my criticism of the Pentagon. I'll just take a quick pass through five horror stories. I don't want to pretend here that I am a military expert because I'm not. But I have done a fair amount of research, and it seems clear to me, as it will to you when you look at the evidence, that when it comes to defense spending the experts are not part of the solution. They are part of the problem. Hold on to your seat as you read these tales about five of our most critical military systems. Abbreviated as they are, you will get the flavor.

Minesweepers? Who Needs Those?

We tend to build not what we need but what contractors and politicians want—flashy, big-ticket items. For the U.S. Navy, that means big, expensive aircraft carriers, which produce more jobs than smaller ships and are impressive at photo opportunities. Right now the Navy has 14 carriers; the Soviets have none. But the Pentagon wants to keep building more, with four new carriers scheduled for the 1990s. They will cost $3 billion each by the time they are finished—and $15 billion each counting their planes and escort ships.

However, when it comes to what we actually need the Navy for, $15 billion for a single carrier is questionable. In our Persian Gulf action recently, for example, we needed minesweepers. But minesweepers are smaller, and not as flashy—and nowhere near as expensive as carriers. How many minesweepers does our Navy have? Exactly three. The Soviet Union has 125.

Long-Range Bombers—But Can They Fly?

The B-1 is a famous flying white elephant. It has been in development for more than 15 years and still isn't able to do the job it's supposed to do: penetrate Soviet air defense radars and drop highly accurate bombs.

The technology involved in the B-1 dates back to the late 1960s and early 1970s. Back then the planes were supposed to cost $41 million each. But the design was delayed for years as Air Force generals and contractors added more and more expensive "bells and whistles," particularly in the form of complicated electronics. Unfortunately, those expensive add-ons are also the hardest to get to work, and the plane has been plagued by problems.

Jimmy Carter had the courage to cut the B-1 out of the defense budget in 1979. One reason he was able to do it is that we had started to develop another long-range bomber design, even more advanced than the B-1. That was the Stealth. But Ronald Reagan arrived on the scene in 1981, and he regarded any weapons system as sacred and vital—even if it doesn't work or is obsolete. He reinstated the B-1 program, only now we're paying a little more than the original $41 million. Now the B-1 goes for $278 million each.

Is it worth it? I've talked to Air Force pilots about the plane, and they tell stories of aerial tankers lined up waiting hours for take-off, because the B-1's aren't ready to roll. The plane is still unstable in flight, its electronics systems jam each other into uselessness, and the Soviets have had almost 20 years to figure out how to stop the B-1 from crossing its borders.

But, as Hedrick Smith reported in the *New York Times*, the Pentagon arranged for B-1 subcontracts in more than 400 of the 435 congressional districts, so it is no surprise that the one place the B-1 flies is through Congress. Lifers won't admit that the B-1 isn't a bomber. It's a bomb.

Jack in the Box

Recently I was thinking of buying a Silicon Valley electronics company. Their executives kept trying to impress me with the sophisticated and innovative work they were doing for the Pentagon. They interrupted one meeting to bring in a suitcase from the trunk of their car, and opened it to reveal an unbelievable jumble of tangled wires, cables and high-tech thingamajigs. The company president said: "You're looking at the guidance system for the B-1 bomber." So much for security. (I didn't buy the company.)

Then there's the son of B-1. Stealth is the nickname for the B-2 Advanced Technology Bomber, which uses a lot of secret techniques (including futuristic fuselage shapes, nonmetal materials and special paints) to escape radar detection. The idea was that Soviet air defense radar would be blindsided by an incoming Stealth aircraft.

It's not certain yet that this technology will work. We saw before that Northrop isn't making it easy to test the plane because they can't produce a working prototype. But we are still planning to build 132 of the bombers for $59 billion. That's a mind-boggling $450 million per plane. A billion here, a billion there—it adds up.

Why do we have such trouble getting these weapons off the ground? In World War II we designed and built thousands of planes in months but that was before the age of "high-tech." We put a big bomb in a simple aircraft, flew it over an enemy city and dropped it. Pretty simple, and it worked. The complexity of today's high-tech weapons marks them for failure or at least constant trouble. These systems are designed in a laboratory dream world of optimum conditions. It's different in the real world. In our F-111 raid on Libya in 1986, seven of the nine planes couldn't drop their bombs properly because of mechanical or electronic malfunctions.

Another Big-Ticket Fiasco: The MX Missile

Here's a program that was on the Pentagon drawing boards for a decade before it was endorsed in 1979 by Jimmy Carter, who needed to demonstrate that he had a little Rambo in him. To appease conservative Senators and others who opposed the SALT II treaty, Carter announced he would spend $40 to $60 billion on an MX program, which was supposed to give us the capability of raining nuclear warhead missiles on Moscow. Ten years later the MX is still far from operational, although it is eating up a lot of our money.

One bizarre problem is finding a home for the MX. It was originally designed to be based in a "secure mode"—that is, in a way that would guarantee it couldn't be destroyed by a Soviet first strike. To do that we talked first about putting the powerful weapons on mobile tractors. That seemed to irritate people who didn't fancy nuclear missiles being carted around the countryside.

Then came the "racetrack" idea: clusters of MX missiles on underground loops, each loop covering more than 30 square miles. Missile-bearing trains would be able to stop anyplace on the circuit and fire away. This was promoted as a good plan because the Soviets wouldn't be able to predict where the missile would be at any specific time, so they wouldn't be able to target it. (You think I'm kidding, but I'm not.)

For some strange reason no states came forward to offer their land for nuclear racetracks. Stymied, the Reagan administration came up with "Dense Pack," which called for the placement of MX missiles in silos clustered close to one other. This theory held that if the Soviets targeted these silos, the first warhead they sent would explode and its blast would destroy the rest of the incoming Soviet warheads. The "experts" called this "warhead fratricide." Make sense? Well, lots of other people thought that sounded pretty nutty, too. Dense Pack must refer to the wallets of the consultants who dream up this stuff.

Now we have decided to put the MXs into the old Minuteman silos, which is odd because the vulnerability of the Minuteman silos was the original reason for building the new missile. It's crazy to be spending billions on what is basically a first-strike weapon when we can't even find a safe place to put it.

Just like all the other gold-plated weapons, we can't get the darn thing to work right. Former Northrop engineers charged on "60 Minutes" that the company knowingly used cheaper defective parts in the nose-cone computerized systems. Get that: *knowingly* installing defective parts on a nuclear missile! A lawyer for the engineers stated that the MX was "as likely to land in Chicago as in Moscow."

Space Stations: Pie in the Sky

Here's one about future spending, not just money we've already blown. We are planning to build a "space station" that will be primarily for military use. In making this proposal in his 1984 State of the Union address, Ronald Reagan called it a futuristic "expansion of the American dream." He estimated the cost at $8 billion. By 1988, just four years later, the cost estimate was $32 billion. What happened? The contractors were turned loose with "feasibility studies." A billion here, a billion there....

In the face of this exploding cost, it becomes tougher to admit that the entire project is being pursued only because of the wishes of the many defense contractors involved and because the National Aeronautics and Space Administration needs to salvage a reputation tarnished by the Challenger disaster. John Pike of the Federation of American Scientists put it this way: "The space station may not be good for science, but it is good for McDonnell Douglas."

The Ultimate Escalation: Star Wars

This is the big ticket to end all big tickets. It proves beyond doubt that anything can be justified on the altar of "national security." Ronald Reagan announced the Strategic Defense Initiative (SDI) on March 23, 1983, explaining it as a research program to discover whether it is possible to use emerging technologies to track, intercept and destroy ballistic missiles *before* they reached us. Shoot them down on their way over here, in other words. As a Buck Rogers concept, SDI quickly became known as Star Wars.

First, I have to tell you how expensive this is. It puts the B-1 bomber and the MX missile to shame. The President initially asked for $26 billion for a five-year program. By 1988, the program had ballooned to a projected $90 billion. That, remember, is just for the "research"—$90 billion to test if the ideas will work.

Actually putting SDI into operation, assuming we find in the laboratory that it will work, might cost as much as *one trillion dollars*. Who's going to pay for that? That's a pretty hefty investment for a country with a huge budget deficit. We will have to jack our taxes sky-high to pay for this sky-high program.

Already the taxpayer is paying a bundle for the concept, without having increased our national security one bit. To date, we have spent $12 billion on SDI, and we're spending almost $4 billion a year now. I suppose it might be worth it if we knew for sure that it would work. But we have no idea how feasible it is. We just have the usual interested parties—Pentagon officials and their handmaidens, the defense contractors. According to the Pentagon, more than 700 contractors take slices of the SDI pie, including about 100 of our top universities.

Those contractors aren't about to tell us honestly if the scheme will actually work. At the Lawrence Livermore National Laboratory, managed by the University of California at Berkeley and recipient of more than half a billion dollars in SDI contracts since 1983, top physicist Edward Teller has even been accused of spreading falsely optimistic information about Star Wars to Washington policy-makers, just to keep the funding train on track.

It doesn't take much imagination to see that Star Wars represents another escalation in the international game of "chicken." It assumes that the Soviet Union has an interest in one day dispatching nuclear warheads in our direction. So we'll put up a shield to block those invading missiles. But that will surely provoke the Soviets into countermeasures. They will work on their own Star Wars system. They will think of ways that they could overwhelm our defensive system, no matter how advanced it is. Escalation to meet escalation.

Aside from that consideration, Star Wars is deemed unworkable by most experts who do not have a financial or political stake in the program. A perfect shield that would not allow leakage even in an attack of thousands of warheads from a determined adversary? So perfect a guard is inconceivable.

It is not worth detailing all the difficulties here; a few will suffice. A comprehensive SDI umbrella would consist of boost phase, postboost phase, midcourse, reentry phase and terminal defense layers. These terms refer to different parts of the trajectories of the incoming missiles. To be successful, a system would have to destroy a large number of missiles right after they took off from the Soviet Union—in the boost phase. And then this initial retaliation would have to be backed up by all the other layers.

The biggest technological problem is coordinating all these layers so that they are working together and accurately readjusting themselves to the type of attack we are dealing with. Coordination would require tremendous computer capabilities. We would need improvements in computer speed, reliability and durability, all things that might be on the technological horizon but are not here now. The phone company can't even get its national computer network to work perfectly.

The problem boils down to this. The exotic kill mechanisms—lasers and particle beams that we see on TV in displays that look remarkably like video games—may be feasible after a great deal more research. But the Soviets can and surely will modify their offensive threat to respond to our Star Wars program. The history of military technology says they will probably be able to counteract almost anything we build. Anyway, SDI would do nothing to protect us against warheads launched from Soviet submarines off our coast, since their low trajectories put them out of SDI's reach. We can expect a few of those.

The Moon Didn't Shoot Back

Sidney Drell, a top physicist and the head of the Stanford Linear Accelerator down the road from me, has an answer to SDI advocates who say, "The skeptics said we couldn't go to the moon, too." Drell points out that while our scientists had the time to gradually combat the physical principles standing between us and the moon, the moon did not shoot back. Why would the Russians be so obliging?

If we build SDI, consider the scene in space. Star Wars will require satellites floating in orbit, completely vulnerable to Soviet attack. To protect them, we would have to build a set of killer satellites that would attack the Soviet weapons attacking the SDI sensor satellites that would be concentrating on the Soviet missiles attacking our people. What a scenario to contemplate! It's a nightmare.

I'm sorry to get into such a technical discussion of a weapons system. It's a tactic I didn't want to employ in this book because I wanted to concentrate on the root problems we face as a society rather than specific policy issues. But the Strategic Defense Initiative represents such a culmination of all the problems we have discussed so far that I felt it was important to spell out some of the details.

I understand why the Lifetime Politicians and their rich-PAC contractor cronies would want to build Star Wars. After all, here in California alone SDI meant $4.9 billion in new Pentagon spending from 1984 to 1987. That's a heck of a lot of money, and the lifers can point to that as good for our state.

But space weapons aren't good for us, and I'm surprised that a lot more people aren't up in arms (so to speak). Perhaps the most distinguished critic of SDI is Dr. Robert Bowman, former director of the Air Force Space Research Division who was in charge of SDI-type research under Presidents Ford and Carter. Why is he opposed to a program he used to direct? Bowman, a nuclear engineer and an Air Force pilot who flew 101 combat missions in Vietnam, charges that the Reagan White House changed SDI's focus from peaceful research to an aggressive arms race.

According to Bowman, the original idea of the strategic defense program at the Pentagon was to monitor closely what the Russians were doing in space warfare, making sure that they were not getting ahead of us. But, he said, the Reagan team's anticommunist ideologues transformed the program into an active drive to change the strategic balance of power. "Star Wars has nothing to do with defense," Bowman concludes. "It is a blatant attempt to regain absolute military superiority through the development of new offensive weapons disguised as a defense. It is the most gigantic fraud ever perpetrated on the American people."

The bottom line on this fraud is that we are now investing billions of dollars in a program when we're not sure what it will turn out to be, we're not sure it can be built, and it looks as though whatever it turns out to be will actually decrease our security in the long run, provoking the Russians to respond in the ultimate escalation.

RUSSIAN SPIES IN THE PENTAGON

No, there aren't any Russian spies in the Defense Department (that I know about), but sometimes these Pentagon mistakes make you think that decisions on our weapons and money are made by hostile agents.

In fact, the Iron Triangle is made up of people whose interests are not necessarily synonymous with the national interest. The sharpest edge of the triangle is the revolving door syndrome: officials who shuttle between the Pentagon and the defense industry. An official who leaves the government can give inside information to a contractor that helps to secure awards. In return, the official is highly compensated either as an executive of the company or as a consultant.

The traffic goes both ways, according to the late Admiral Hyman Rickover, long the Navy's most outspoken officer: "the great difficulty in conducting defense business is that the top [Pentagon] officials come from industry and have an industry standpoint." Ronald Reagan's two secretaries of defense, Frank Carlucci and Caspar Weinberger, were both with the Bechtel Corporation, a defense contractor, before their Pentagon service.

DOORS FROM NOWHERE TO NOWHERE

The revolving door isn't only open to the very top officials. The same lateral movement goes on in the management levels below the Cabinet secretary.

For example, just look at the ping-pong career of Thomas K. Jones, who was a rising young analyst for Boeing in their Strategic Programs division. In the early 1970s he made one pass through the revolving door into the Pentagon, serving on the Nixon administration's SALT I negotiating team. Then it was back to Boeing in 1974 as "Manager of Program and Product Evaluation" (there's nothing like a tour of duty in the Pentagon to cinch a promotion in private industry). With his Washington contacts he helped the Seattle-based aerospace company secure Pentagon contracts for studies on the effect of nuclear blasts on civil defense shelters.

When the Reagan administration moved into Washington, Jones once again made his way back into the Pentagon, as Cap Weinberger's "Deputy Undersecretary of Defense for Research and Engineering of Strategic and Theater Nuclear Forces." And—surprise!—while Jones was in that position, Boeing received many more contracts in his field of interest—how to fight and survive a nuclear war.

All those turns in the revolving door seem to have made Jones a little dizzy. One of his valuable insights, disclosed to Robert Scheer of the *Los Angeles Times*, was that people could easily survive a nuclear war. Just "dig a hole," he advised, "cover it with a couple of doors and then throw three feet of dirt on top...it's the dirt that does it...if there are enough shovels to go around, everyone's going to make it." You can imagine what a sweetheart he is to the nuclear arms industry, not to mention shovel manufacturers.

Until we can slam shut the revolving door, we'll never get anywhere in Pentagon reforms. When the House Armed Services Committee tried to investigate Northrop's abuses on the Stealth contract, the company defended itself by hiring the former head of the Justice Department's defense-contract fraud division.

So reforming the military is not going to be easy, but we can't afford not to try. Our national investment priorities have been turned upside down because of the influence defense contractors have on the budget process, plus the skyrocketing costs of military hardware (see Figure 13).

Instead of spending money to help the needy and the disadvantaged, and provide a stable economic environment for the rest of us, Lifetime Politicians pour money into the military sinkhole. We're not building hospitals, highways, bridges and new industrial plants because we're buying the B-1, MX, and more aircraft carriers.

In addition, our scientific research is increasingly being diverted to military ends. Because of this massive shift in priorities, our competitiveness in civilian areas suffers, since nonmilitary industries can't get long-term research and development investment capital. The huge effort placed behind Star Wars symbolizes that priority. With decisions like these, the lifers are making a crucial mistake that we'll pay for long into the future. But then, they've never been known for their long-term planning.

Figure 13—Have we been shortchanging everyone but the Pentagon?

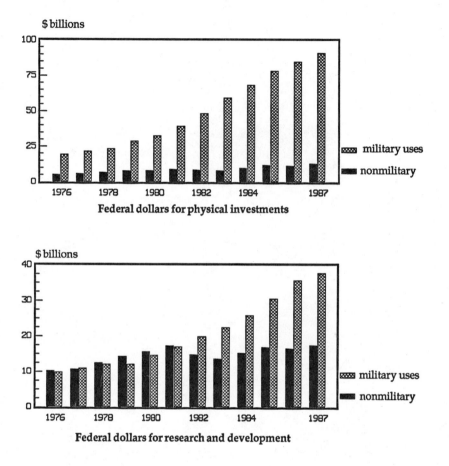

In the last chapter of this section, I'll lay out some ways to end this nonsense. Right now, let's move on to the Central Intelligence Agency and covert operations. I think we'll find some Lifetime Politicians wearing trenchcoats.

CHAPTER 19

★

Behind Closed Doors

Why are we captive to forces we don't even see? We are rather new to covert operations, but they have become stitched into the fabric of power that emanates from Washington. They are not easy to examine because they are by definition secret, by nature insidious and often, by exemption from the ordinary rules of conduct, illegal. We need to keep tabs on these cloak-and-dagger types who are out there executing foreign policy on our behalf. They don't ask our permission.

Like foreign aid, covert operations in foreign countries are an attempt to influence and control events according to the prevailing administration's desires. We occasionally hear about operations that are botched. But there are a lot of successful forays, missions that accomplish their goals, that we never hear about because we are not supposed to. Mum's the word. Here, though, is a small sample of various covert actions we know were undertaken by various government intelligence agencies between 1947 and 1988:

> **1947, Eastern Europe**—The Central Intelligence Agency (CIA) was formed by the Truman administration. It began setting up guerrilla movements in Albania and the Ukraine to "roll back the iron curtain." The job was bungled. Almost none of the funds, equipment or agents sent into these countries were seen or heard of again.

> **1950-53, Poland**—The CIA set up an underground apparatus in the early 1950s, funded by millions in gold bullion. Agents

sometimes slipped out to the West to report—and ask for more money. It took the CIA several years to discover that the Polish secret service had almost from the beginning co-opted the entire project and was making quite a bit of money from it.

1953, Iran—The CIA instigated the overthrow of the Mossadegh regime after it had nationalized the oil fields and squeezed out U.S. and British business interests. The agency returned the Shah to power as part of a deal that broke the monopoly of British Petroleum and introduced American oil companies into Iran for the first time. The great masses of Iranian people regarded the Shah as our puppet—and you know what eventually happened.

1954, Guatemala—The CIA sponsored a coup d'etat by a small group of rebel soldiers. Armed and trained by the agency, they toppled the regime of Jacob Arbenz Guzman.

1958, Indonesia—The CIA supported an unsuccessful rebellion.

1960, U.S.S.R.—Francis Gary Powers was flying a spy-plane mission when the Soviets shot down his plane and captured him. At first, President Eisenhower denied that the CIA was involved, claiming the U-2 "strayed" into Soviet airspace. When the Soviets produced the pilot, Eisenhower had to admit the truth. Powers stood trial and confessed to being a CIA agent.

1961, Cuba—President Kennedy carried through with an Eisenhower administration plan to invade Cuba, using expatriate Cubans trained by the CIA to make it look like a nationalist attack and not an American invasion. The landing at the Bay of Pigs was a disaster and a humiliation for Kennedy. Other CIA-sponsored assassination attempts on Castro followed, as well as the hunt for and eventual execution of Che Guevera, Castro's right hand man.

1961-64, North Vietnam—The CIA organized guerrilla and small boat attacks, arming and directing thousands of Vietnamese soldiers in "irregular" units. The agency also established a massive intelligence and interrogation system—"Operation Phoenix"—which reached into every South Vietnamese village.

1962, Laos—After a Geneva accord prohibited foreign troops in Laos, the White House directed the CIA to move operatives into that country to wage a "secret war."

1963-65, Belgian Congo (now Zaire)—The CIA became involved in civil war here. Agents bought and sold Congolese politicians and supplied money and arms to their supporters, including B-26 bombers, which carried out missions against insurgent groups the United States did not favor.

1970, Chile—President Nixon and the CIA attempted to fix the Chilean election. U.S. business interests were concerned that a Marxist government led by Allende would jeopardize their position if he were elected. The CIA attempted to thwart the election process and was ultimately involved in Allende's death and a coup d'etat.

1971, Cambodia—President Nixon began secret bombing with Air Force and CIA involvement.

1975, Angola—The CIA began supporting the FNLA, one of three liberation movements fighting to gain control when Portugal left the country. Russia, Cuba and China supported other movements.

1980, Iran—President Carter mounted a secret mission, coordinated with covert agents, to rescue American hostages. The plan failed, proving to be a great embarrassment to Carter and helping to elect Ronald Reagan, who later sold arms to the people who had taken these hostages.

1982-88, Nicaragua—The CIA created, and began to arm and train, the *contras* in Honduras and Costa Rica. In 1983 the CIA mined harbors in Nicaragua. The action was first denied by the Reagan administration and then attributed to the *contras*. Only later did the news surface that this act of war was undertaken by the United States.

The CIA isn't the only U.S. agency for covert operations. During the Reagan administration, the CIA was expressly forbidden by the Boland amendments to support the *contras*. However, the White House sidestepped this prohibition through the National Security Council, which operates at the President's behest. The Iran-*contra* scheme involved not only the NSC and CIA but personnel in the State and Defense departments and an underworld of retired generals and intelligence agents in the arms and "security" business. (If you and I had kicked the arms-for-hostages idea around for a few hours, we would have seen its stupidity. How could our brilliant leaders have been so dumb?)

Covert activities have clearly increased over time, as they always do. If you count all the agencies and military departments involved in intelligence activities, we're spending more than $20 billion a year on our secret foreign policy. The CIA's budget alone is now believed to run about $1.7 billion a year, which would qualify it as a Fortune 500 company.

That's a lot of money for secretly meddling in other countries, especially by a nation that is a proponent of freedom and open democracy. *Newsweek* has reported that in the Reagan era CIA funding increased 17 percent a year while funding for the State Department went up 8 percent. When diplomacy gets the short end of the stick and spies get free rein, you need to be concerned because it means you don't know what's happening. And that bothers me.

When the CIA was formed in 1947, it was supposed to function primarily as an intelligence agency, gathering and analyzing information. "Covert operations" weren't stressed. Unfortunately—but not surprisingly—the agency quickly attracted rogue elements. Many of them had been involved in espionage during the war and had liked it. Some were impressed by the Soviet NKVD, the forerunner of today's KGB, and wanted to develop an American equivalent. A lot of the subsequent activities reflected the James Bond thinking inevitable when an open society condones and finances a secret arm.

COVERT ACTIONS AND PRIVATE MOTIVES

Former CIA director Stansfield Turner wrote in his book, *Secrecy and Democracy: The CIA in Transition,* that in 1973 his predecessor, James Schlesinger, asked the agency's employees to inform him of any improper activity that had come to their attention. The resulting report was 683 pages long. That was well before William Casey's freewheeling reign. Imagine how long such a report would be today.

Don't forget, though, that it is usually the President who initiates or at least approves covert operations. To get around congressional oversight of the CIA's mischief, President Reagan even authorized other agencies under his personal control (like the NSC) to conduct clandestine activities. In the wake of the Iran-*contra* scandal, a bill was proposed in Congress that would require the President to notify Congress immediately of all covert operations. Reagan, not surprisingly, promised to veto any such bill.

Looking over the record, I think the key lesson is that most of our failures cannot be attributed to faulty equipment or bad luck. More often the blame lies with misguided policies and loose cannons in the halls of government.

I see a lot of similarities between the flaws in our espionage and the follies in the Pentagon. Both worlds are corrupted by the heavy hand of politics. William Casey had been Ronald Reagan's campaign manager in 1980, and he followed in a long line of CIA directors whose policy advice was slanted. President Ford appointed George Bush to the top CIA spot. Bush had been a member of Congress and head of the Republican party under Richard Nixon, so I wouldn't exactly consider him an impartial intelligence professional.

Then there's the history of ties between the CIA and American corporations abroad, which Senator Frank Church, who chaired the famous committee in 1975 that exposed CIA assassination plots, called an "incestuous relationship." Experts have written entire books about such private abuses of our foreign policy, ranging from the "Seven Sisters" oil companies' role in the Mossadegh overthrow in 1953 to ITT's role in the overthrow of Allende in 1970.

WHY DO THEY CALL IT "INTELLIGENCE"?

Countless times we have had people making policies or triggering covert operations who knew very little about what they were trying to do. Too often they paid too little attention to the history or culture of target countries. An example of this ignorance was passed along by NBC anchorman Tom Brokaw, who recalled being briefed by Ollie North on Nicaragua's supposed reliance on Cuban military advisers. Using CIA satellite photographs, North assured Brokaw that a baseball diamond in Nicaragua confirmed the presence of Cubans because everybody knows how crazy the Cubans are about baseball. It had somehow escaped Colonel North's attention that if there's a baseball-crazy country in the world, it's Nicaragua.

I'll grant you that a lot of our mistakes come from something deeper than just stupidity, but that's for the next chapter. I don't know about you but I am angry that we can't even find intelligent spies to do our dirty work.

C H A P T E R   2 0

★

Why We Bet on the Wrong Horse

In 1974, I took my family to Spokane to see the World's Fair. We visited the Iranian pavilion and saw a film of the Shah's wedding, which cost $25 million. The wedding was full of the most unbelievable displays of wealth and opulence. After the film was over, I told my family that the Shah wouldn't be around much longer because a leader living so lavishly could not last when his people were so poor. You didn't have to be a CIA analyst to make that prediction. But apparently nobody in our government saw it coming.

This is the kind of miscalculation we make over and over again. As a result, I'll venture another prediction. I think the odds are good that we will blunder into another conflict in the Third World. Maybe it won't be as nasty as the Vietnam War, but it still could be pretty awful. The two top candidates in the 1980s have been Iran and Nicaragua.

As I write this, we have more than 30 ships bumping into each other in the Persian Gulf. And for five years in the 1980s we fought a "low intensity" battle against Nicaragua. In plain English, we were at war with both countries. We hired mercenaries to do our fighting in Central America and let our jets and battleships do the talking in the Gulf. Either one of these situations could—and might still—escalate into a costly war that would take a heavy toll in American lives.

I think it's useful to go back in time, as we did earlier in examining our position as world boss. I want to understand why we became a power that believes in meddling in the affairs of other countries. This question is too important to blame simplistically on one political party or the other. It's the way we as a nation *think* that is at fault.

Americans have traditionally thought about the outside world in two ways: sometimes we've been isolationist, and sometimes interventionist. Before World War II, most of us were satisfied with being a shining—but isolated—beacon for the rest of the world. We preferred to stay home and not get involved elsewhere.

In fact, in the old days Republicans called themselves the party of isolationism, warning against entanglement in international rivalries. Prior to the bombing of Pearl Harbor, most Republicans opposed FDR's efforts to support Britain and France in their war with Nazi Germany. Talk about noninterventionism! People were arguing that the potential loss of Europe to fascism was not worth getting involved in a foreign war.

But World War II changed all that. By 1945, there was a rough area of agreement among top Democratic and Republican politicians that we were not going to relinquish the prominent position we had gained in the world. Since then, three misguided principles have undergirded American foreign policy. Those principles, which you can identify every single day in your newspaper, have worked together to get us into trouble time and time again.

WE'RE NUMBER ONE!

First, there's American *exceptionalism*, with its roots in our own revolution and frontier mentality. It gives us the audacity to imagine ourselves with unlimited interests, unlimited capabilities, and as the only nation that knows what's right for those folks in the rest of the world. Before World War II, we truly believed that if only other countries would copy our sterling example, all the world's problems would be solved. After the war, we added an aggressive missionary spirit. We felt compelled to spread our wisdom to all corners of the globe.

This arrogance led us into a lot of places where we didn't belong. Vietnam was the most obvious and destructive example, but there are dozens of others. In the 1980s, the Reagan administration decided that it knew the government of Nicaragua was wrong for its people.

ONE-SIDED CHESS GAMES

The second notion is that the United States can manage any crisis with a careful application of *gradual escalation*. We assume that a small, calculated display of American resolve is enough to make rebellious Third World nations or insurgents quake in their boots. If a slap on the wrist doesn't bring proper obedience, we hit a little harder. Inevitably we move to a greater and greater commitment of resources and, finally, we face the possibility of all-out war.

The faith of the Kennedy, Johnson and Nixon Cabinets in gradual escalation contributed to the Vietnam debacle. An original commitment to prop up a shaky regime against a communist insurgency led to economic aid and military support for the South Vietnamese, which in turn led to U.S. ground troops, which led to bombing raids in the North, which led to a full-scale war.

The same process continues today. Our 1987 commitment to escort tankers in the Persian Gulf led to an extraordinary buildup of the U.S. naval presence there. When some tankers struck Iranian mines, the United States responded with a "restrained" attack on a couple of Iranian oil platforms. What happens if the Iranians get lucky and sink a destroyer? Won't we ever learn that people from other cultures may not think in the same "rational" manner as our so-called experts? Khomeini and Ho Chi Minh had one thing in common—thought processes radically different from ours.

BETTER DEAD THAN RED

The third and most important misbegotten axiom of U.S. foreign policy is *uncompromising anticommunism,* which drives us into one disaster after another. Our commitment to anticommunism has caused us to betray our values time and time again in our relations with the Third World.

In 1949, just before our ally Chiang Kai-shek was chased out of mainland China, communist leader Mao Tse-tung sent his right-hand man Chou En-lai to sound out State Department officials about the possibility of better relations with the United States. The Chinese were already having trouble with Stalin's Soviet Union, and by the 1960s there was a complete rupture. But in 1949 we were so doctrinaire that we assumed all communists were the same. Anticommunists at home were already flinging charges of "who lost China" at the State Department. We ignored the overture. We paid the price when we ended up fighting Chinese soldiers in Korea. And we were estranged from the world's most populous country for more than 20 years.

The same obtuseness eventually got us into Vietnam. Everybody remembers the names Ho Chi Minh and General Giap—the communist leader of North Vietnam and his military commander, who led forces against the Americans in the 1960s.

Few people remember that both Ho Chi Minh and Vo Nguyen Giap were once pro-American. At the original ceremony proclaiming Vietnam's independence from France in 1945, Ho quoted from Thomas Jefferson and our Declaration of Independence, and Giap saluted the U.S. flag as a Vietnamese band played the "Star-Spangled Banner." That scene seems so bizarre today that it is almost inconceivable. Both men looked to the United States as a symbol of liberty and self-determination and wanted warm relations with us.

But in the 1950s we backed France when it tried to recapture its old colony. Paris and Washington didn't like Vietnam's radical tilt, so Ho Chi Minh turned to Moscow and Peking for support. Our anticommunism blinded us to the opportunity of maintaining relations with a leftist Third World country. I don't have to remind you of the results.

Those two missed opportunities—in China and Vietnam—cost us tens of thousands of young lives in devastating foreign wars. How on earth could we allow ourselves to pay such a bloody price for an abstract principle like anticommunism—especially when our analysis of the political situation was way off base?

When simplistic anticommunism combines with a total misunderstanding of politics in Third World states, you get a misguided policy. In his 1980 campaign, Ronald Reagan told a reporter for the *Wall Street Journal:* "the Soviet Union underlies all the unrest that is going on. If they weren't engaged in this game of dominoes, there wouldn't be any hot spots in the world."

This was clearly the perspective of an ideologue, someone who reduces complex matters to black-and-white simplicities. I'll admit that his years in the White House brought some change in Reagan's outlook, but he came kicking and screaming to the table. The political motivations that propel our foreign policy on this devil-theory avenue are still strong. The rhetoric of one political campaign still sounds like all the ones before.

I'm not soft on communism, but why can't we have a little more faith in our own system? Are we really in a perpetual state of siege? One direct result of this anticommunist fervor is that we usually end up backing the wrong people around the world.

WITH FRIENDS LIKE THAT....

I can imagine a President being proud to stand beside impressive allied leaders like Winston Churchill, Charles deGaulle, Margaret Thatcher, or Corazon Aquino. We don't "always" back the wrong horse. But why would a President choose to stain our flag by linking us with brutal thugs and con men? The Hall of Shame includes Noriega, Pinochet, Marcos, Somoza, the good old Shah, Papa Doc and Baby Doc Duvalier, and a whole parade of South Vietnamese bad guys.

Tin-pot tyrants take advantage of our paranoia. They milk us for as much money—and military equipment—as they can get. These dictators may not even be any tougher on communism than the democratic regimes they overthrew. They just paint a tougher image and cleverly pick our pockets. The Third World's brand of Lifetime Politicians (and I mean *Lifetime*) have pulled this scam for years, and it works.

It is no mystery why we end up with characters like Manuel Noriega of Panama. His own former aides admitted to Congress that Noriega had been on the CIA's payroll for years. He got that money because our unelected tribe of national security experts in Washington believed his boasts of confronting the red menace in Central America. But a confidential Panamanian document from Noriega's "Presidential Advisory High Command," reprinted in

Newsday in 1987, laid bare the farce. In the document's own words, Panama would "convince the Pentagon, without the State Department's knowledge, of an imminent communist threat unless they renew economic and military aid."

She Asked, "What Was Your Name Again?"

Early in 1988, I called the CIA's public affairs division (they're listed) and asked about reports that Manuel Noriega had been paid $200,000 a year by the agency in years past. A spokeswoman told me she could "neither confirm nor deny press reports, because we find that just helps the opposition." I thought we were trying to help the Panamanian opposition. She probably meant the Russians, but they already know we're that stupid. Maybe she meant American taxpayers, who might oppose paying the dictator of Panama the same salary we pay the President of the United States.

So the Noriega government was not only going to play the Pentagon against the State Department, it was going to use a "threat" of communism as blackmail for more U.S. dollars. The Panamanians knew that the Pentagon would go along.

That is one way we become captive Americans. Our anticommunist delusions allow these idiots to hold our foreign policy for ransom, and Washington's disinformation keeps individuals like you and me prisoners of the experts who keep reassuring us.

We keep paying the price, every time one of our staunch anticommunist friends breeds a radical revolution because of the dictator's corrupt oppression. The leader's power base doesn't rest with that country's people but with the armed forces and Washington, D.C. When the leader gets thrown out, the people who do the throwing despise us as the sponsor of the old regime. It's a pattern that has been repeated again and again. We shoot ourselves in the foot and lose any chance of playing influential roles in those countries. There is a very simple lesson to be learned here: our support for dictators almost always undermines American interests in the long run.

BUT WHAT HAVE YOU DONE FOR ME LATELY?

Our foreign aid program works in tandem with our foreign policy—that is, we give money to nations deemed to be "on our

Figure 14—How much foreign aid do we give to other countries?

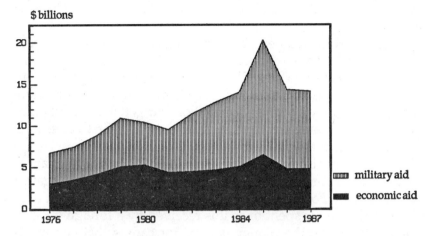

side." American foreign aid began during World War II, when we gave roughly $50 billion to 38 countries. After the war the money really started to flow, as politicians saw a new way to throw money at problems.

Between 1946 and 1987 our foreign aid totaled $328 billion. Most of that money had some geopolitical motivation: we were trying to buy political affection. After the devastation of the war, $13 billion went to Western Europe under the Marshall Plan, to keep those countries from going communist after the devastation of the war. Since the end of the Marshall Plan in 1952, the countries that have received the most are Israel, Egypt, South Vietnam (not anymore, of course), South Korea, India, Turkey, Pakistan and Taiwan.

In 1987, the top five recipients were Egypt, Israel, Turkey, Pakistan and El Salvador. Common sense will tell you that we didn't shower aid on those countries just because of their economic needs. If true need were our most important criterion, Ethiopia would be first on the list.

Turkey is high on the list because of its vital role in the North Atlantic Treaty Organization (NATO) and its slavish commitment to our anticommunist theology (never mind that it represses the Kurds). Pakistan shares a border with Afghanistan, where rebels were making life difficult for the Soviet-backed government and the invading Soviets. Israel has been near or at the top of the list of aid recipients since its creation in 1948. Egypt is one of our few friends in the Arab world, and we basically had to buy their agreement to the 1978 Camp David peace accords with a guarantee of future aid. (Then we had to pacify the Israelis with more money.)

El Salvador has been busy putting down left-wing rebels. According to a study released in 1987 by the Congressional Arms Control and Foreign Policy Caucus, the United States gave El Salvador foreign aid in the amount of $608 million, which was more than that country's entire $582 million budget. The El Salvador government must think that it's now our fifty-first state, with Uncle Sam's open wallet ever obliging.

The study also pointed out that three of every four dollars of that aid was spent on the El Salvador government's war against the guerrillas. For the most part, we exercise little control over how our money is spent once it is received by a foreign government. Sometimes the money is used for causes that contradict our own foreign policy goals. For example, we give Egypt $2 billion in aid a year. Although that money was originally intended to give Egypt a feeling of security in its "peaceful" relationship with Israel, Egypt uses it to maintain a standing army of 500,000 troops. What's more, Egypt gives $1 billion a year in arms and ammunition to Iraq. So much for America's attempts to stop all support for the Iran-Iraq war.

So, get this picture: while the Iranians were secretly receiving American arms via Israel, Iraq was receiving American military support via Egypt. Then they used our weapons and ammunition to kill each other. How come the President and Congress never explain these facts of life to us? Because they don't fit their stereotypical view of the world as consisting of communists on one side, freedom-lovers like ourselves on the other side. I think the professional politicians are afraid of common sense.

NO METHOD IN OUR MADNESS

Most U.S. foreign aid is military rather than economic (see Figure 15). No wonder we never seem to get anywhere in the fight against world hunger. Even though we send vast amounts of aid, we don't attack problems in a socially or politically responsible way. Money for weapons does nothing to alleviate poverty.

When the Lifetime Politicians look for places to cut foreign aid, it is not surprising they leave big recipients like Israel and

Figure 15—Have our foreign aid priorities changed under Reagan?

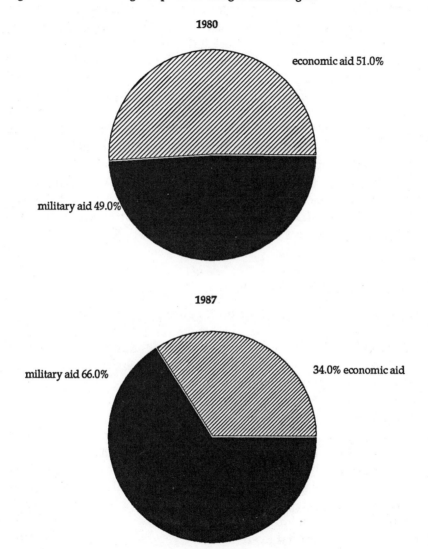

1980

economic aid 51.0%

military aid 49.0%

1987

military aid 66.0%

34.0% economic aid

Pakistan alone. They're afraid of their domestic constituencies, or afraid to stop propping up another "anticommunist" despot. So they go after those too weak to protest, although they need the money most. In 1988, economic aid to 19 poor Third World countries in Latin America, Africa and the Pacific was eliminated entirely. Israel and Egypt went untouched.

Pakistan got even more aid in 1988 than the year before. It doesn't seem to make much difference that Pakistan's ruler, General Zia ul-Haq, is a virtual military dictator. Meanwhile, Pakistan's neighbor, India, the world's biggest democracy, gets the short end of the stick. While India has nine times the population of Pakistan, it receives one-tenth the economic assistance its neighbor gets: only $35 million for 1988.

Why the difference? India prefers neutrality in foreign affairs, while Colonel Zia says he's on our side. A Reagan administration official told the *New York Times* in January 1988, "Let's face it, the CIA and the Pentagon, and not the State Department, set American policy in South Asia."

How shortsighted can we be? Extreme poverty and social inequalities are only driving the Third World closer to upheaval. If we don't help them now, or help them to help themselves, we'll pay later in a big way.

COUNTING ON DUMB LUCK

One common denominator in our foreign policy woes has been ignorance about the outside world. Our Vietnam experience showed that we knew nothing about that country or the people we were fighting—or even the people we were trying to "save." And the same goes for many other countries: the Philippines, Nicaragua, El Salvador, Mozambique, and—closer to home— even Mexico.

For most of us, general knowledge of foreign affairs is very thin. We've all heard the horror stories. In a recent test of college freshmen, 95 percent could not locate Vietnam on a world map. In a nationwide survey, 63 percent of Americans couldn't name the United States and the Soviet Union as the two countries involved in the strategic arms reduction talks.

Our educational system hasn't yet decided to make world affairs a priority subject. One statistic tells me a lot about our predicament: 22 million Soviet citizens are studying English, but only 42,000 Americans are studying Russian. This is a shocking imbalance in countries with roughly the same population. How can we even negotiate with the Russians, much less build a peaceful and commercial relationship with them, if we don't speak their language and understand their culture?

A lot of us are too cozy here at home in America. You can't ram new facts into a closed mind. The ideologues among us don't want fresh ideas. Their slogans and mindsets satisfy them completely. Conservatives and liberals both spew the same tired cliches about international affairs. The inflexible mind has plenty of simple answers—but they are not really answers, and we should not settle for them anymore.

STOP PLACING BAD BETS

If we are trying to promote democracy around the world, we need to learn the lessons of the past decades in the Third World. "Elitist strategies," where the United States promotes a favored client as long as he espouses anticommunism, do not work. When we try that, countries tend to lose their democracy and slip into dictatorship, while the economy is drained by corruption and mismanagement.

We need to stop supporting characters like Ferdinand Marcos and start supporting broad-based strategies of democratic development. We must stress education, health and agricultural assistance and self-help without regard to politics or military strategy. Doing so would be in the mainstream of American traditions and would help us to reassert our moral leadership.

I have some more specific proposals in the next chapter, but I don't want to leave this subject without registering once again my shock at an American foreign policy that induces us to support people whose sole virtue is anticommunism. We need to stand for something positive.

CHAPTER 21

★

Can We Wage Peace?

You know by now that nothing annoys me more than so-called experts claiming they know how to solve problems better than the rest of us with common sense. All other problems pale compared with the need to avoid a nuclear confrontation with the Soviet Union. It's the ultimate bottom line. But the experts have not shown any ability to reduce the danger, and I'll be damned if I'm going to keep listening to their smooth reassurances.

I'm no great brain, and I have no formal experience in international relations or high-level defense policy. But beneath the surface, most people have more going for them than they realize. ROTC was my big thing in college; I got straight A's there for two years and was named a "Distinguished Military Student." And although I was a psychology major in college and (with two jobs) a mediocre student, I got an A in the one quarter of Russian that I took. I also got an A in a quarter of Russian geography. I used to think they would come in handy in the Big One. Thank God we never had it.

I know it's difficult for most of us to relate directly to the issues of war and peace. We feel helpless. "What is it, after all, that I can do?" But the research I have done convinces me that this is too important an issue to leave to the politicians and experts. We have to register our thoughts, feelings, ideas and opinions about the absolute necessity for the United States and the Soviet Union to thrive in a state of peaceful coexistence.

The most promising development on this front has been the recent change in the Soviet leadership. The emergence of Mikhail Gorbachev demonstrates a willingness by the Russians to look at old questions in new ways. Our own leaders must meet that change by demonstrating a similar readiness. To some extent, we are already doing that. Instead of continuing to denounce the "evil empire," Ronald Reagan walked with Gorbachev in Red Square and negotiated the first step in a nuclear disarmament treaty.

It might even be a wise move to admit that a lot of the initiative in the new relationship is coming from the Soviets, instead of trying to take all the credit, as politicians like to do. Who takes the credit is not important. We have an incredible opportunity here. We must seize the moment.

A NEW WAY OF THINKING

We are so used to the Cold War and the paranoia that went with it that many of us can't believe the Russians mean it when they say they are for peace. But the signs are increasing that this is for real. Gorbachev's ascent to power was followed by disarmament negotiations, a military pullout from Afghanistan, new cultural exchanges, exit visas for dissidents, invitations to U.S. companies to participate in Soviet-American joint ventures and a new era of openness called "glasnost." Moscow is even getting a McDonald's. So there's more than rhetoric going on here. Actions speak louder than words.

That doesn't mean, of course, that we should disarm. But I think we must realize that without hope and trust, we will never break the mutually hostile stalemate that was created. Unfortunately, the Russian people are like us in one way—they have not had their say. Our hope should be that with glasnost they will enjoy more freedom to express their concerns and ideas for the future. In both countries, the two most powerful in the world, the people have to make end runs around the politicians.

In making that end run, we have to keep our eye on the ball, which basically comes down to "waging peace." It doesn't take a lot of explaining to describe waging war. We all know, from bitter experience, what that means: death and destruction to the other side. Waging peace is more complicated because we are not used to doing it. Like anything new, it's strange. We have to think seriously about it before we can feel comfortable.

I have been spending time with the concept of waging peace, and while I don't pretend to have all the answers, I want to make a start at stimulating your thinking by suggesting some of the possibilities conjured up by this prospect. If you will let your mind roam, I am sure lots of other possibilities will surface. This is an exercise for all citizens. We need to break our dependence on politicians and academics for fresh ideas. Theirs are familiar—and we know they don't work. So here goes.

Emphasize Diplomacy Over Militancy

Every time we have a problem around the world, we bring out the gunboats or we set up covert operations. Bobby Ray Inman, former deputy chief of the CIA, has stated that covert actions get started when the White House is frustrated with diplomacy. In the nuclear age we must develop the patience for diplomacy and what it entails: painstakingly long negotiations, endless proposals and counterproposals, and at least some mutual respect.

One bit of advice any former President could give to a successor would be to strengthen the State Department's role in foreign policy. Every year the State Department gets only about three-tenths of 1 percent of the federal budget; the Pentagon gets a quarter of the whole thing! Frank Devine, a retired Foreign Service Officer and former ambassador, has written that scrimping on diplomacy causes "persistent erosion of Foreign Service ethic, morale and capability."

Our armed forces are two-million strong, but we only have 16,000 diplomats. Instead of spending $15 billion for one of the aircraft carriers the Navy wants to build, we could double the State Department's $4 billion budget and increase the number of American diplomats.

We could also encourage diplomacy by decreasing the size and authority of the National Security Council (NSC) staff. Such a move would improve continuity in our policies because in most administration transitions the whole NSC staff is changed while only the top political appointees at State are replaced. The Foreign Service carries on as a body of career professionals. A strengthening of State over the NSC will lessen the volatility of administration change-overs and provide the new President with more experienced advice and long-term planning.

Yes, diplomacy can be a frustrating business—and the striped-pants brigade in the State Department has long been an object of scorn in American political life. But believe me, it beats guns—and I'll take it anytime over nuclear bombs.

Rein in the CIA

We will always need the capability to act covertly in international affairs. But there is no reason to allow those activities to be launched for partisan political reasons, run by incompetents and hidden from accountability.

First, the public and Congress must insist that the director of the CIA be someone of the highest personal integrity and professional competence. When William Casey had his confirmation hearings in 1981, Senators softpedaled his previous troubles with the Securities and Exchange Commission during his Wall Street career. They also ignored the fact that he had been Ronald Reagan's campaign manager and was tied to Reagan's partisan interests, not to professional independence. Casey was a sure bet to get involved in questionable adventures. If the lifers on the Hill had had any spine in 1981, they would have run Casey out of town.

Second, we have to insist on strict accountability for covert operations. This isn't as difficult as it sounds, and if future CIA directors and Presidents have any scruples they will uphold their legal commitments. The notification requirements are not unreasonable. Under the 1980 Intelligence Oversight Act, a President has to notify six legislators before a covert operation has been launched—the majority and minority leaders of the House and Senate, and the chairs of the Intelligence committees. After a covert affair, the President is supposed to inform the rest of the Intelligence committee members "in timely fashion."

In the Iran-*contra* affair, the White House didn't notify anybody. Admiral Poindexter claims he didn't even notify the President of the United States. I don't believe this. We can't let another administration get away with that kind of behavior.

Third, we have to cut down on the number of covert operations overall. There are reliable estimates that the CIA maintains at least 3,000 operatives overseas. According to CIA Officer John Stockwell, "officers energetically go about seeking opportunities" for covert actions, since that's how they get promoted. Great—3,000 officers, all running around the world stirring up trouble. That is what gets us our bad name abroad. Let's concentrate on waging peace instead.

Be a Leader, Not a Boss

I go along with what Dick Nixon has said about our relations with the Soviets: we can never be friends, but we can't afford to be enemies. In the future, both countries are still going to pursue their own interests, but we have to concentrate on gaining advantages with smart negotiating, not with more weapons.

Gorbachev is already getting the jump on us in the new peace competition for world leadership in the 1990s. He has recognized that by being out in front with new arms control proposals and diplomatic initiatives, the Soviet Union could gain the upper hand in world opinion and look like the world leader.

Notice I said world leader, not world boss. The Soviet Union has been pulling back from its own interventions. They are finally realizing their aggressive mistake in Afghanistan and are even pressuring Vietnam to get out of Cambodia. More and more, the Russians are laying a new diplomatic foundation for their foreign policy. In 1986 the Soviet Union announced it would start paying its full share of the United Nations budget and would pay its overdue $197 million bill for U.N. peacekeeping forces around the world.

We've been lagging behind in the new peace race. When the Soviets finally turn towards the U.N., we back away. The United States owes over $400 million to the organization, including $62 million for peacekeeping, but we're not paying. The Russians look good to the rest of the world, we look cheap.

I'll give you another example of how we miss opportunities to gain through peaceful competition. During the 1987 Washington summit, Gorbachev made an offer to President Reagan to cut off Soviet military aid to the Nicaraguan government if the United States would end military aid to the *contras* and the rest of Central America.

On the face of it, that's not a fair deal for us. But did we respond with cleverness and shrewd negotiating? Did we present a strong counteroffer to their opening bid? No. The White House completely dismissed the proposal as "absolutely unacceptable" and "ludicrous." That's not negotiating to win. That's still talking like a world boss.

If we really want to gain the respect of the world, we have a lot of peace cards to play against the Russians. For example, the Soviet Union still refuses to publish its real military budget, keeping the world suspicious about Soviet intentions. Meanwhile, we have the most open society in the world. We should keep pressuring the Soviet Union toward more international glasnost.

Our best peace card is human rights, where the Soviets still have a contemptible record. Another advantage for us is the prospect of peaceful change in Eastern Europe, where Gorbachev's glasnost is beginning to weaken the Soviet hold. Captive nations can't be held down forever.

No TV? That Can't Last

Communism forces unbearable social and economic conditions on the people of Eastern Europe. But the human spirit never dies. Just ask the Rumanians. Their standard of living is atrociously low and falling, homes are barely heated, the streetlights aren't lit, and television only broadcasts for two hours a day. Finally, in November 1987 thousands of workers in several cities took to the streets in violent protest. The spirit of Solidarity is alive and well throughout Eastern Europe, and changes are coming whether Soviet leaders and their puppets like it or not.

We would be missing an historic opportunity to advance global human rights if we were to miss the signals of change in Poland, Hungary and Czechoslovakia. If we can draw those nations peacefully into the world community and reassure the Soviets that they too are welcome, we will have won the Cold War without firing a shot.

Have More People Exchanges

The best way to break down barriers is to leap over them and get to know the people on the other side. It sounds simple. So why don't we do more of it with the Soviet Union? An idea that has been suggested is to exchange all the kindergarten children in the United States with kindergarten children in Russia for one year. That is too impractical, but it would certainly give pause to anyone even thinking of an attack on the other country. Introducing American and Soviet children to each other's way of life would reduce the xenophobia that now characterizes those perceptions.

But many ideas along this line would work. Exchanges of college students, family exchanges, cultural and athletic exchanges are ways to reverse the climate of suspicion and fear. These are not even costly exercises. So what's holding us back?

Open Trade Channels with the Soviet Union

The world's two great superpowers should be natural trading partners. There's an enormous potential here for dollars and good will. Ask the farmers of the Midwest, who lost more than $10 billion in grain sales after Jimmy Carter slapped an embargo on shipments to the Russians because of the invasion of Afghanistan. Trade sanctions almost always hurt American business and the American worker or farmer more than they hurt the Soviets. In that case they ended up getting all the grain they needed from Argentina. Why does it so often look like our allies are undercutting our policies? They're not, they just have a better handle on things.

In 1986, we exported only $1.2 billion worth of goods to the Soviet Union, a drop in the bucket compared to our sales to Western European countries. The Soviet Union could be one of the greatest markets in the world for American goods. And once the Soviets reduce their military establishment and start making more consumer goods and food, the United States could be a valuable market for their exports.

Waging peace through diplomacy and trade would be the competitive prelude to a brighter era of cooperation between the superpowers. Enlightened leaders on both sides might actually respond to the wishes of their people and work together against what Carl Sagan has called "common enemies." Sagan writes that we could collaborate on "joint projects of great scope and vision, [for example] in relief of starvation, especially in nations such as Ethiopia, which are victimized by superpower rivalry....[or] in fusion physics to provide a safe energy source for the future."

It makes sense to me. But none of this will happen until we can get control over the biggest machine ever built by man, the global military-industrial complex.

Cut Defense Spending

Back in chapter 16, in the section on economics, I concluded that the only place for truly dramatic budget cuts was in our defense spending. If we wage peace, then we're not going to have to pay for war.

Nikita Khrushchev wrote in his memoirs, "I keep coming back to my own feeling that we should go ahead and sharply reduce our own [military] expenditures, unilaterally. If our enemy wants to go ahead inflating his military budget, spending his own money right and left on all kinds of senseless things, then he's sure to lower the living standards of his own people." Khrushchev only talked like that after he was yanked from the Kremlin. He was no longer a Lifetime Politician, so he thought with a lot more common sense.

In a world spending $1 trillion a year on military forces, and more every year, we all need to start using our common sense. I'm not afraid of being accused of being soft on communism or a wimp on defense. Many Americans are waking up to the fact that it is not unpatriotic to question the Pentagon's budget and stand for peace. In 1981, only 7 percent of the public favored reducing military spending, but by 1987 that figure had increased to 38 percent.

I'm not paranoid about the Soviet war machine, even if it looks pretty good from a bean-counting standpoint. War is more than firing beans back and forth. The evidence shows major problems in Soviet combat readiness, quality of training and reliability of their soldiers.

Believe it or not, non-nuclear forces of NATO and the Warsaw Pact nations are in relative balance. Early in the Reagan buildup, General Frederick Kroesen, commander of U.S. Army forces in Europe, testified: "It disappoints me to hear people talking about the overwhelming Soviet conventional military strength. We can defend the borders of Western Europe with what we have. I've never asked for a larger force."

At the nuclear level, all we really need is a secure retaliatory capability—for both sides. That means we don't need all the missiles and bombs we have. We don't need to disarm totally to ensure our security, but on the other hand we don't need a first-strike capability or a total defense either. By first strike, I mean weapons like the MX and Trident submarine D-5 missiles which are designed to be used first in a nuclear war. That kind of Pearl Harbor scenario is not the American way.

We can rely instead on a strategy of sufficient nuclear weapons to deter any Soviet attack. Since we need only a fraction of our current arsenal to destroy the Soviet Union completely, we can junk the rest. Deterrence has worked and can work in the future, as long as the arms race is ended and the numbers start going down instead of up.

The Soviets see things the same way now and Gorbachev has announced a new nuclear doctrine of "reasonable sufficiency," which means they will no longer build for superiority.

In the wake of huge budget deficits and a looming recession, in 1988 the Pentagon finally seemed willing to consider budget cuts. Once Cap "the Shovel" Weinberger was gone, the new Defense Secretary Frank Carlucci and Congress found $23 billion they could trim.

That was not nearly enough. The Army cut only 10,000 troops from its active force of more than 780,000 (a reduction of barely more than 1 percent). The Navy mothballed 16 old frigates, out of a total U.S. fleet of more than 500 ships. There was no major overhaul, no rethinking of what we need and don't need. When we already have all the nuclear weapons we'll ever need, we're still planning to build five more nuclear subs—plus the MX missile.

Let's get serious. To really cut the defense budget, we can't just trim the edges. We have to change our entire military blueprint, and we have to give up our attachment to big-ticket weapons. Almost half (45 percent) of the Pentagon's budget goes to buying new weapons or to research on future weapons (see Figure 17).

Think Small, Not Big

In our obsession with the Soviet Union, we built up a military machine designed to fight a superpower. One result is that in the conflicts more likely to break out—small scale battles—we have been notably unsuccessful. In a classic case of overkill, we used big B-52 bombers in Vietnam, bombing Viet Cong guerrillas in the jungles from 30,000 feet. We build monsters like the B-1 and Stealth bombers and sophisticated fighter planes like the F-16s. They're great for air shows and, maybe, for the war to end all wars, but they're not too flexible. The F-111 was built to attack

FIgure 17—How does the Pentagon spend its budget?

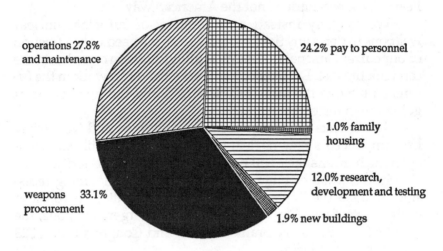

operations 27.8% and maintenance

24.2% pay to personnel

1.0% family housing

12.0% research, development and testing

weapons 33.1% procurement

1.9% new buildings

Total 1986 Department of Defense budget: $281 billion

huge Soviet industrial complexes and naval targets, not something as small as Qadhafi's tent.

When the most immediate danger we face is not Gorbachev's ICBMs but Khomeini's terrorists, does it make sense to be spending $4 billion a year now, and billions more in the future, for a space-defense system? We can easily cut SDI spending down to $1 billion a year in research funds—and that's probably still too much. And settling for a retaliatory nuclear capacity means we don't need the first-strike MX missile, or first-strike Trident submarine missiles.

One more place to think small: personnel. One-fourth of the entire Pentagon budget goes for personnel pay. A lot of that pork can be sliced. Would you have guessed that 1.1 million *civilians* work for the Defense Department? Eliminating some of these paper shufflers won't handicap G.I. Joe if he meets Ivan on the battlefield. I have an even better idea for cutting personnel costs, but I'm saving it for the last section in this book.

For some reason, small-minded Lifetime Politicians have a hard time thinking small when it comes to our armed forces—one more reason to get rid of the lifers.

Make Our Allies Carry More of the Load

It makes no sense for the United States to continue to carry the full load for other nations. As part of our resolve to wage peace through diplomacy, we should cut back on our military expenditures—and seek more support from our allies. The United States currently spends 6 percent of its GNP on defense while the European NATO countries average 3.5 percent and Japan, 2 percent. They don't spend a lot because we do. Melvyn Krauss, an economist at New York University, argues that our willingness to pay for worldwide bases "has robbed allies of the incentive to defend themselves."

We can give them that incentive. If the government brought home half of the 217,000 Army troops stationed in Europe and demobilized them, we could save over $4.5 billion. Mikhail Gorbachev has already expressed his willingness to negotiate for mutual reductions in the troop strengths of both East and West in Europe. Let's take him up on it.

One way to save defense dough that Pentagon experts always mention but never implement is better coordination of allied weapons production. When we say that, we usually mean that Europe should just buy weapons made by American manufacturers. For example, in 1988 the Reagan administration proposed that the allies jointly develop and produce a jet fighter known as the Hornet 2000, a new version of the U.S. Navy's F-18 Hornet. But Britain, West Germany, Italy and Spain would have to scuttle their own program, known as EFA—for European fighter aircraft.

The idea was promoted to the Europeans by executives of McDonnell Douglas, the builder of the F-18.

But our contractors are never willing to give up a little gravy when the Europeans try to persuade us to buy their products. As a result, five different tanks (with different shell sizes and spare parts) are now being built in the NATO countries. An attempt during the Carter administration to get the German-made Leopard II—the best of the lot—accepted as NATO's standard tank design foundered in the halls of Congress, where politicians preferred an inferior tank design whose parts were made in their districts.

Build Baby Carriages, Not Bombs

We have to end our war economy. This crucial step should be a top priority for the next President. For one thing, our budget can no longer stand the strain of immense military spending. Our economic health won't rebound and enjoy vigorous growth until we shift research and investment funds from defense industries to civilian sectors.

The Soviets already have a head start on us. After the 1987 U.S.-Soviet treaty on intermediate nuclear forces, a Soviet official announced that "we are now transferring the Votkinsk machine-building plant [which produced the banned SS-20s] from military production to peace production, to a people's economy." The plant now produces washing machines and, of all things, baby carriages.

The Center for Economic Conversion, located in Silicon Valley and surrounded by the defense electronics industry, has researched the problem for American industries. In an interview for this book, CEC Director Michael Closson told a fascinating story about a defense contracting firm in Connecticut called Kaman. In the 1970s Kaman built helicopters for the Pentagon but had trouble competing with the major aerospace firms. So management looked for other products to manufacture. First they thought of the obvious, and for a while the company made windmills.

But the company's president, a talented amateur guitarist, realized there was a market niche for a high-quality, mass-produced guitar that could compete with Japanese imports. He put his engineers to work; they were vibration specialists because vibration is a major problem with helicopters. And sound is nothing more than high-frequency vibration. They were able to design a new sound box for an innovative (and very successful) guitar. So Kaman has begun to replace helicopter sales with sales of the "Ovation" guitar. Make music, not war.

We Did It Before
At the end of World War II, the United States had 13 million workers in defense industries. We reduced that number to 600,000 in 18 months. We need a repeat performance now, and this is one race with the Soviets I wouldn't mind us running. We'd both win.

It won't be as easy to convert the war economy as it was in 1945 because we don't have the pent-up demand for goods and services we had then. But we have an enormous potential today in other areas. We desperately need to increase our exports to all parts of the world to reduce the trade deficit. There is no reason why factories now geared to making sophisticated military equipment could not be retooled and regeared to make products that Europeans, Asians and Africans want to have. As living standards in the developing countries (including Russia and China) rise, there will be the same demand for goods and services that we had at the end of World War II.

Put a Contract Out on the Contractors

Converting our economy from war to peace won't happen overnight. And we'll still need a healthy defense industrial sector to provide the better weapons systems of the future. But we don't need to be the dupes we have been, paying for fraud and enormous waste.

The biggest reform we can implement quickly is to end single-source contracts. They make up almost half of today's weapons deals. When arms makers battle head-to-head for a contract, prices go down and quality goes up. The open marketplace is that simple.

We can make a real dent in Pentagon spending with competition. General Dynamics used to have a monopoly on the Navy's Tomahawk cruise missile, and the price was more than $1 million each. In 1985 the Navy took away the single-source contract and allowed McDonnell Douglas to bid competitively. By 1987, McDonnell Douglas was providing 60 percent of the Pentagon's Tomahawks, and the price per missile had fallen to $653,000.

But you really have to watch the Pentagon. When the Air Force allowed Hughes Aircraft to compete with Raytheon for the Maverick air-to-surface missile contract, it saved money. But the taxpayer didn't see that savings because the Air Force turned around and used it to buy 3,357 of the missiles, instead of the original 2,000 ordered.

Come on, pass the savings on to the ultimate consumer— the taxpayer. We should be using the money we save elsewhere, not for more weapons.

Eventually, I'll be able to glance out my 12th-floor Silicon Valley office window and judge if we're succeeding in retrieving our defense policy from the special-interest contractors. From my window, I can see the headquarters and various plant buildings of major Pentagon contractors. Every time I look out, they have expanded.

Stop Arming the World

We are the biggest arms seller in the entire world, which may surprise you (see Figure 18). Before World War II, we used to pillory the "international arms merchants" for promoting the First World War and then the rise of Hitler. Now our corporations, in partnership with the federal government, sell arms all over the world, to good *and* bad guys.

Figure 18—Who sells the most arms around the world?

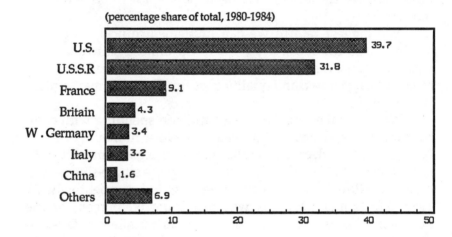

(percentage share of total, 1980-1984)

U.S. — 39.7
U.S.S.R — 31.8
France — 9.1
Britain — 4.3
W. Germany — 3.4
Italy — 3.2
China — 1.6
Others — 6.9

The Reagan administration planned to sell $15.2 billion in weapons around the world in 1988, a huge increase from $11.7 billion the year before. On top of that, $2 billion in weapons exports were sold directly by American arms manufacturers.

Arms sold to nations at war or coping with rebellion do nothing but aggravate their problems, and if the weapons are given as military aid (a lot are), they aggravate our budget crunch. In 1988, President Reagan pressed Congress for a hefty amount in military aid for Saudi Arabia. Doesn't Saudi Arabia happen to have a few billion dollars of its own? Whenever hostilities heat up for one of our clients, we hear urgent requests for more money and arms. That just exacerbates the overall budget deficit and takes us further down a military path in international relations.

Our leaders keep demonstrating their failure to drop the old ways of thinking. In the fall of 1987, the U.N. held a conference on using the money saved in disarmament to stimulate Third World development. The conference was in New York, and 148 nations were represented. The Soviets even scored points with a personal message from Gorbachev to the meeting.

Guess which country boycotted the meeting, on the grounds that disarmament and economic development should be treated as separate and unrelated goals. Guess which country even criticized the conference's $1.2 million price tag. That's right—the same country that spends that much *every two minutes* on its military—the United States.

Fight a Real War—Against Drugs

If we want to use our military hardware for something, let's use it for something productive. The Cold War mentality has blinded us to the *real* threat we face from outside our borders. It's not communism. It's drugs.

Do we see Presidents airlifting troops to Colombia to fight the forces of the Medellin drug cartel, which by all accounts has brought the Colombian government to its knees? Do we see the same level of rhetoric devoted to the dangerous tentacles of a drug conspiracy as to the dangers of communism, even though the threat is far more real? Already it reaches into the governments of Colombia, Panama, Honduras, Cuba, the Bahamas and others. When our politicians blind themselves to the realities of what is going on to our south, we end up like Oliver North, justifying the use of CIA planes for drug shipments because of a "larger" anticommunist goal.

It is time we stopped focusing on commies instead of cocaine. First, we need to get tough: smugglers should face the death penalty and dealers should get mandatory 25-years-to-life sentences. Second, we need the military in this fight. According to the Drug Enforcement Agency, 48 percent of all the cocaine seized in the United States was smuggled by private planes. (Another 11 percent actually came in on commercial airliners.) Our Air Force isn't used to protect us against these poison-carrying planes. And the Navy isn't concentrating on drug-smuggling ships. In a $282 billion Pentagon budget in 1987, only $67 million went for surveillance of narcotics trafficking.

The one service we do have to protect us against the drug invasion, the Coast Guard, had its budget cut by $103 million in

1987. That's the same year the Pentagon's budget was increased by $9 billion.

Let's get our priorities straight here. The odds of a Soviet invasion are decreasing, while our drug problem is skyrocketing. If future Presidents feel they have to show the flag somewhere, why not on our own borders against the real bad guys: drug smugglers. The smugglers we see on "Miami Vice" may be able to outgun the cops, but never the U.S. Army. *That's* the war we should be waging.

WAR NO MORE

Those are some of my ideas. I am sure you will have others. The key point is the raising of our peace consciousness. We must get used to the idea of war being obsolete and we must communicate that idea to our politicians.

It will be an uphill fight. A whole network of people and institutions thrives on the arms race. The Iron Triangle hates the idea of waging peace. In a recent issue of *Defense News*, stock market analysts noted their fears that a superpower arms control agreement would drive down the prices of defense industry stocks. E.F. Hutton's Gary Reich said, "These stocks are going down because of the outbreak of peace."

The unelected national security experts like to sound pessimistic, arguing that many years will be needed to negotiate adequate agreements. Their career paths are at stake. Their Russian equivalents are also against arms control, even though Gorbachev favors it. And on both sides, I don't see many politicians addressing the need to wage peace. They have too much at stake in the system as it now runs, as destructive as it might be.

The first task, then, is to energize people like you and me. When we let our leaders do the thinking for us, and stop calling them on their mistakes, we're through. The question was addressed nearly 200 years ago by one of our greatest leaders, Thomas Jefferson, who asked the important question:

> whether peace is best preserved by giving energy to the government, or information to the people. This last is the most certain, and the most legitimate engine of government. Educate and inform the whole mass of the people. Enable them to see that it is in their interest to preserve peace and order, and they will preserve them. And it requires no very high degree of education to convince them of this.

To which I say, "Amen." The United States and the Soviet Union currently spend limitless billions on weaponry, and they both suffer from a mindless waste of their resources. It is clearly in the interests of both to reach a level of trust and understanding that will permit cutbacks in arms spending and a refocusing on issues that are closer to people's needs.

The two superpowers could then work together to reduce conflicts in the rest of the world. If the Soviet Union and the United States could end their arms race, they could do *anything*. This may sound like a utopian dream, but that's because we have become inured to the mutual distrust that passes for international discourse today. The challenge to us all is surely to break those bonds.

PART IV

★

BACK TO OUR FUTURE

CHAPTER 2 2

★

The Lost Frontier

We stand at an interesting juncture today, as we move rapidly toward the end of the 20th century. On the one hand, Japan, a country we defeated in World War II, has emerged only a generation later as a world economic power. On the other, the Soviet Union has in Mikhail Gorbachev the most inspired leader it has had since the revolution of 1917, and his policies of glasnost and perestroika have kindled a national wave of exhilaration and upheaval.

Many Americans wonder why those two countries seem more dynamic today than our own, why their people seem more confident or excited about their future. It might be appropriate to pause here near the end of this long discussion and assess where we have come from as a country—and where we are going.

THE WAY WE WERE

During the first 100 years of our republic, America came close to its ideal in many ways. American citizens were imbued with the town-hall spirit of democracy and participation. People took their politics and civic duties seriously. We were far from perfect: women, blacks and minorities were typically excluded from the system, but at least for white male America, everybody had his say.

This was the age of the never-ending frontier. Prosperity was possible for anyone who worked hard and crossed over that next hill to find his promised land. Americans disdained the bad old world of Europe. We were above all that. We were the new and dynamic hope for mankind—or so we told ourselves.

In World War I we temporarily abandoned our isolationism and set out to make the rest of the world more like us. Woodrow Wilson told us we were fighting to make the world safe for democracy. In his crusade for the League of Nations Wilson wanted to create a world of peace, democracy and self-determination that would transcend the European balance-of-power politics. But the country didn't follow Wilson, it drifted back into isolationism.

Anyone who lived through the 1930s remembers Franklin Roosevelt with emotion. Even Ronald Reagan has spoken with genuine feeling of how much FDR meant to the nation. It took his inspirational leadership to return us to the path Wilson had pointed to two decades before. Roosevelt gave us the New Deal to rescue us from the Depression, and after Pearl Harbor he led us in war. Not since Lincoln had a President been faced with such trying times, and only by extreme good luck or the hand of God did we find a leader capable of meeting the crises of those days, though he led too long.

Notwithstanding that, before the war ended that same luck or hand from above took Roosevelt's wisdom from us when we needed it most to guide us in our new position at the apex of world power. It was instead Harry Truman and his advisers who shaped our role in the postwar world. They confronted the central problems of the time: security and prosperity for America and the world. The answers they devised still form the backbone of our responses to global problems.

The policies of the Truman administration were based on a vision of a new international system with two fundamental parts: one, a union of the free countries of the world in a political and military alliance against Soviet communism; and two, a liberal international economic order where goods and money could flow freely between nations.

In the glory days of the immediate postwar era, we had the power to recreate the international system in our own image. We could set world policies unilaterally but we also had to pay the high cost of world leadership. We rebuilt Europe through the Marshall Plan, resurrected the Axis powers and bound them to us in friendship, fought the continuation of colonialism, and generally made more friends than enemies.

The overwhelming world dominance we enjoyed after 1945 was a product of a war that devastated everyone but us. It couldn't last. In the 1950s, the price of world control kept rising as other countries began to rebuild from their wartime devastation and to compete with us. Even worse, our exalted stature at the top of the world began to change our way of thinking and our way of life.

Remember the Fifties? Those were good times. Too good, in fact. We began to forget the lessons of the depression and the war. We lost sight of the importance of pulling together, of working through adversity, of self-sacrifice. We grew more and more complacent.

After that, in the Sixties and Seventies, we seemed to evolve into three distinct nations: "Powerland," the Washington-New York hub of the political and financial elite; "Medialand," the California center that determines the good life and shows it to us on the big and little screens; and the rest of us out there in "Flyoverland," where we do our work, raise our families, and watch the aristocrats from Medialand and Powerland fly from coast to coast over our heads.

Are the American people—especially those in Flyoverland, who are too often ignored—able to handle the difficult times to come? We know bad times are coming, largely as a result of poor leadership. Is our culture still strong enough to withstand them?

I'M-OKAY-SCREW-YOU

Maybe we have become a free-ride society, asking not what we can do for our country but what we can squeeze out of it. Today, many Americans wallow in instant gratification. We waste more food, more resources, more energy in one week than most countries use in a year.

Many Americans are not able to live that well and deserve no blame. But Medialand sells the rest of us on the charms of a "Dink" lifestyle: Double Income, No Kids. Is that what we really want? Having children is out of style; it's "too expensive" and diverts our attention from accumulating more goods and more money.

Greed is making us forget some very basic lessons about our humanity. We're throwing compassion overboard in a headlong rush for monetary success. I learned recently from one of my young Stanford friends that the Graduate Business School at the university now teaches a course on ethics. Can 25-year-old MBA students be "taught" ethics? Why should they have to be? Can you get a B in ethics, or a C? Making the big bucks has become a national obsession, but what good will all this be if our economy collapses and society follows?

SO SUE ME

Our instant-fix obsession is incredible. Alcohol and drugs are used in epidemic proportions. Americans consume 60 percent of the world's narcotics. Our children grow up learning to turn to drugs when they face a problem or just to get a high. Scott Fuller, who is working with me on a homeless children's shelter in Silicon Valley, tells me that 36 percent of children in fourth grade across the country feel social pressures to drink. Fourth graders!

When total gratification no longer satisfies, we start whining and call a lawyer. We have become a litigious society. Everybody knows a lawyer or two. That's because we have 700,000 of them—two-thirds of the world's total. Japan has only 20,000. Maybe we should solve our trade imbalance with Japan by exporting lawyers. They'd be bankrupt in no time.

Our lawyers have a mission. They want every case, however trivial or unnecessary, to be as complicated and therefore as expensive as possible.

The regulation of society by law is no longer the goal, but merely a means towards more work for the legal profession. It was only 10 years ago that we first allowed lawyers to advertise their services. What a mistake that was. In 1986 lawyers spent over $47 million advertising on television. In your local Yellow Pages, the section under "Attorneys" is one of the biggest in the entire book, with full-page ads screaming, "YOU NEED A LAWYER!!!" Those ads entice us to go to court—"personal injury" cases, "damages for emotional distress." We are being conditioned to resort to the courts every time there is some sort of injury, real or imagined.

The lawsuit is replacing responsibility for our own actions, and if we refuse to show some responsibility it's no wonder our leaders avoid it, too.

The lawyer plague is just one manifestation of our societal ills. How would we react to another depression? Would we come to our senses and absorb the blow with the same distinction as our grandparents did? My hesitant answer is, we would. The American babies being born every day have what it would take to be just as smart, just as brave, just as compassionate and just as productive as their forebears. But the materialism of the past few decades has not prepared us well for challenges. We are prisoners of an unyielding individualism, and we've lost the kind of commitment to shared goals and values that pulled us through depression and war.

SCREW UP, WRITE A BOOK

Just when we need inspired leadership, we get sorry models to idolize. I call that the G. Gordon Liddy syndrome. The bookstores are filled with volumes written by people whose only claim to fame is their monumental failure. I don't want to read a kiss-and-tell book by a White House official kicked out for his unethical behavior. I don't need to see Fawn Hall hosting a television show, and I don't need Oliver North running for President—or anything. I have no idea why we idolize whatever low-life crawls across our TV screens. Benedict Arnold would be on the cover of *People* magazine today.

We need to reverse our political direction. The good people in Flyoverland have not been asked, much less told, to sacrifice for their country. But we certainly have not had good examples from our leadership to point the way. Thanks in part to Medialand, we know less and less about the qualities we should look for in a leader. Even the role models have been lost. In a recent survey of high school seniors, 52 percent could not identify Franklin Delano Roosevelt. That is pathetic.

DON'T LOOK BACK—SOMEONE MAY BE GAINING

Remember that I said we don't always bet on the wrong horse. One of our best bets ever was on Japan after the war, when we helped them up from defeat and urged them to follow our democratic, capitalist example.

Are they good learners! Never has a country risen so quickly from national devastation to such tremendous economic power. We were responsible in part, not only by giving them an example of aggressive growth, but also by prohibiting them from devoting their resources to their military. They offer a fantastic example of the transition from a war economy to peaceful production. Norman Cousins has pointed out that many Japanese wisely refuse our more recent pleas that they build up their military. "They know it is poor capitalism," he says, to make weapons that cannot generate profits.

Now it is the United States that isn't living up to its own model of success, and the Japanese will take every advantage of it. We're selling off our assets to them to finance our high living. I think we need to remember the Golden Rule: he who has the gold makes the rules. Robert Strauss, who negotiated with Japan as President Carter's special trade representative, told the *New York Times,* "When others control the money and you owe it, you dance to their tune."

What If We Let You Use the Pool?

Yo Kurosawa, a senior executive of the Industrial Bank of Japan, was quoted in 1987 as saying, "Why do we, people who live in rabbit hutches, have to finance the U.S. budget deficit to help Americans support a style of life with swimming pools and tennis courts?"

This isn't prejudice talking. I have made dozens of land deals with Japanese-Americans, and have found them to be the most honorable people I have ever dealt with. But Japan has a genuine competitive urge to pile up the chips in its corner. When we imposed more trade barriers on Japan in 1987, former Trade Minister Sadanori Yamanaka warned that "a cornered mouse may bite at a cat....it is possible that Japan will bite at the United States if and when Japan can no longer endure high-handed U.S. demands."

What difference does that make to you and me? Nicholas Brady, the head of the Presidential task force that studied the 1987 stock market crash, said one major trigger for the record plunge was when Japanese investors got worried about the health of U.S. currency. Brady said that "the Japanese, for their own reasons, sold an enormous amount of U.S. government bonds." Then, on Meltdown Monday itself, Japanese banks threatened to stop lending to embattled brokerage firms about to go under.

Have we let our society, our foreign policy and our economy decline so far that a foreign country can cause a stock-market crash? That's a little frightening. The Presidential task force was so troubled by the news that it wasn't even mentioned in the official report. The public's only knowledge came when Brady related the account to a private group in Washington, and it was mentioned in a story buried on page 30 of the *Wall Street Journal*.

Let's not get too apocalyptic. I'm not arguing that the Japanese will try another October surprise on purpose. The Tokyo stock market suffered when ours collapsed, too. I'm not expecting an economic Pearl Harbor.

But the Golden Rule is important. Remember how people around the world resented the economic power America wielded in the 1950s and 1960s? Our multinationals were everywhere, exerting influence in local politics and everyday life. Now the Japanese multinationals and banks are assuming that role—here in America especially. They're here in force in San Jose.

Washington has done a terrible job on equal trade policies. If our government cannot provide the leadership that we need to turn our country around and address the political and economic problems we are concerned about, we may end up a 21st century Third World nation.

WHERE IS OUR GORBACHEV?

No one imagined five years ago that the Russian people would be able to attack their problems so vigorously. "Russian" used to mean lazy, corrupt, backwards. Yet under Gorbachev they are in the middle of a vigorous national renewal. That spirit is sweeping countries behind the Iron Curtain, which someday will be lifted. Gorbachev wants to limit top party officials to 2 five-year terms, while the Bulgarians have limited their top leaders to 10 years in office. In 1988, Hungarians tossed out their leader of the past 30 years with a peaceful vote. If they can do it, why not Americans?

The American people are as ready as ever to march, if they have the right leaders. The crucial question is a hard one for Americans to swallow: where is our Gorbachev?

★

CHAPTER 23

National Service:
An Idea Whose Time Has Come

Have you ever noticed that the biggest American flag you see nowadays—sometimes the only American flag—is streaming over a car dealer's lot? Those monster flags trivialize patriotism. For a lot of kids today, cheering for Rambo passes for a patriotic experience.

Getting rid of Lifetime Politicians, putting our financial house in order and replacing militarism with diplomacy are three of the central reforms advocated in this book. But I also think we have to look beyond political reforms and do a little soul-searching. We can't just blame the politicians for everything, no matter how tempting it is.

Modern culture holds us back. Bound by the grip of TV, materialism and drugs, many of our young people no longer hold the American values of hard work, progress and national pride. But the youth are our future, and besides, we made them the way they are.

We don't fight harder to make them read. We over-protect them on the grounds of "wanting something better for them." We don't insist that they really learn about our history, our heritage, our democracy and institutions. I could go on and on.

It seems the more generations that go by, the more removed we are from the basics that made our country and our people great and unique. Every year we set loose an untrained, under-educated, unworldly, under-motivated group of 18-year-old men and women. Whether they're on their way to Stanford or the unemployment line, they are disadvantaged because of the lack of direction society offers. The kids don't know what they don't know.

It is up to us to get them off the streets and highways, out of the ghettos (of poverty or affluent excess), and off drugs and booze.

I don't claim to have a panacea. But I believe that one particular program offers us a path out of our cultural decline. Both as a symbol and a practical measure, it may do more to revitalize our political, economic and social institutions than any of the other reforms I have recommended. And it will bolster the other reforms and allow them to succeed. That program is mandatory National Service for every 18-year-old man and woman.

THE PAYBACK TO SOCIETY

You have seen in this book all the money we've not invested but blown. This may be the biggest opportunity for our government to invest in the future, and the return will be phenomenal.

National Service would put in place a program that would *require* a payback to society for all the benefits it confers. In return, it would revive patriotism and give kids some responsibility and pride in the contributions they can make to society.

It's not too much to ask of our pampered youth. You may not realize this but at least 87 countries have some form of obligatory service (usually military) for their citizens, usually around the age of 18. The United States, Britain, India, and Australia are the only major countries which don't require National Service. We need to study the best examples from the most workable models around the world, then add some good old American ideas.

I have thought long and hard about this idea—and I am as passionate about the need for National Service as I am about anything else in this book. Perhaps that goes back to my own days as an 18-year-old volunteer in a one-year Army program. I know what a motivating experience it was for me, although I didn't realize to what extent at the time.

I remember that back in the 1960s we had a huge, ongoing debate over the role of youth in American society. Young people were demanding an equal stake in the benefits of society—mainly, individual liberty (the right to do as you please). Not a bad desire, since that is the principle America is supposed to be founded on.

But young people aren't holding up their end of the bargain. We lowered the voting age to 18 in 1970, but by 1986 only 17 percent of the 18-to-30-year-olds were voting.

Today many young people are an undisciplined rabble. How could they be anything else, when their leaders and parents never tell them that there is an entry fee to society? That entry fee cannot simply be a birthright; something that's free is meaningless. I asked a woman at a party recently what she thought the entry fee to society should be. She said, "That's the dumbest question I ever heard."

Sex, Drugs and Rock 'n Roll

In 1979, a survey of Minnesota high-school students asked, "What do teenagers owe their country?" The majority answered, believe it or not, "Nothing."

Most people think that voting, paying taxes, and jury duty are the only things we owe to our country—and then they try to squirm out of all three!

There is a fourth fee. It is service to your country. When people hear those words they think of war, but National Service has very little to do with war. With a well-thought plan, we wouldn't need a grave crisis to hear our country's call.

MORE THAN A DRAFT

The ideal program would take every teenager, either at age 18 or immediately after graduation from high school (whichever came first), and place him or her in the National Service for at least one year or eighteen months.

Our military today needs only about 350,000 new soldiers a year. National Service would draw in around four million teenagers annually. So clear alternative paths to the armed forces would be available.

A National Service program would not be cheap. The Army figures that a military draft would cost $2.5 billion more than the All-Volunteer Force, while estimates of the direct cost of a full-blown mandatory National Service program range from $15 to $30 billion. On the other side of the ledger are the benefits. Right now more than four million American youths are unemployed, and most draw unemployment checks. Taking them off the welfare rolls might save up to $1 billion a year.

Military bases are already available all over the country. Some are empty, no troops at all, but are still maintained. Switching our priorities to waging peace would open them up for National Service use.

BOOT CAMP

The program would consist of three phases. Phase I would be Basic Training or boot camp for three months, to instill discipline and physical fitness. As anyone who has ever been in the service can tell you, those months give you a faith in yourself and in the buddy system that will be with you for life. In combat, soldiers don't fight for themselves, they fight because they don't want to let their buddies down. Working side by side in small units creates a feeling of mutual responsibility, and there's nothing like boot camp to teach that lesson.

Basic Training would include the best elements of the successful Outward Bound program, which teaches young individuals to survive in the wilderness and live off the land for days at a time. Grant Rogers, a friend in Los Gatos, California, has been running Outward Bound programs in the United States and abroad for decades, and he sings their praises for the self-reliance and confidence they inspire.

Rogers graduated from the Naval Academy and looks back in fondness on the rigors of his plebe year. He tells of approaching George Roberts, a former Academy classmate and now the president of Teledyne (a Fortune 500 company), for a contribution to Outward Bound. "George wasn't too familiar with the program and asked me what it was like. I said, 'It's like plebe year.' George responded immediately: 'How much money do you want?'"

It would be a snap to find retired military men and women, officers and noncoms, to volunteer their time and efforts to work with regular Army elements to implement National Service.

(That would keep costs down.) I'd like to lend a hand myself, to get back to basics and into shape.

IF I HAD A HAMMER

Phase II of National Service would be Trade Training, lasting another three months. Just like it says, this period would concentrate on the skills of the real world (and those that will be most needed in Phase III). We could teach carpentry, electrical skills, building and construction work, heavy equipment operation, and other vocational skills like computer training and health care. All the while physical fitness training would continue. The teenagers would be learning (almost subconsciously) about the importance of interdependence and Americans pulling together.

Phase III will be the big payback stage. We would now have a constant supply of disciplined and trained young people eager to work together for their country. They could be assigned, according to their interests and aptitudes, to attack a wide range of societal problems.

While some of the teenagers moved into the military services, the rest would be joining the Peace Corps or VISTA (Volunteers in Service to America, our domestic Peace Corps). Others would work on construction projects to rebuild our aging infrastructure—new dams, bridges and highways. The U.S. Forestry Service and a new Civilian Conservation Corps (from the New Deal era) would take thousands of youngsters into the wilds, working to protect our environment.

National Service would make available cheap talent in fields the government can't afford to fund in this deficit era: hospitals and caring for the aged, children's day care, ghetto school teaching and other inner-city work.

HARLEM, MEET THE UPPER EAST SIDE

Beverly Hills, meet Watts. It's important that National Service be non-discriminatory, just as it is in Switzerland, Israel and other countries. *You don't get out of it because you're rich or well-connected.*

Those who come from privileged backgrounds should take a breathing spell before they go on to their upper-crust colleges to give them some notion of collective interest beyond their personal goals. For those recruits coming from less affluent environments and slums, National Service could offer educational opportunities and avenues leading out of dead-end lives.

We are still in many ways a segregated society—by choice. Did you know that without a high school diploma, or with a criminal record, you can't even join today's volunteer Army? Can we afford to lose these dropouts before they've had a chance?

The best thing that National Service would give to the youth of America, whether from the suburbs of New Jersey, the farmland of Kansas or the beaches of Southern California, would be a chance to get out and see other parts of the country and meet other kinds of people.

I was always impressed by my melting-pot interaction with people from all levels of society in the Army. I had never before been taught the satisfaction of accomplishing something as a team, sticking together to get a job done. I learned it in the Army.

A fellow like John F. Kennedy, from a **wealthy** Boston family, whose father was serving as ambassa**dor to** Great Britain when World War II began, served in the Navy. There he came into contact with guys from various strata of society, and emerged from that experience with a more socially conscious and egalitarian outlook. I've always said, if you weren't in the service, your education was lacking.

A LEANER MILITARY

An obvious benefit would be widening the talent pool of the military. National Service would bring in better-educated recruits than today's all-volunteer force. In a recent conference at the Naval Academy, retired Army General William Dupuy noted that "the Army needs more quality than it has on board, more than it is now recruiting, more than it can get under current policy or current budgets."

Still another benefit would be the inclusion of young women in the program. Today's volunteer Army is only 13 percent female. National Service will give women, especially those from lower-income backgrounds, a head start into the workforce, on an equal footing with men.

Let the Kids Wage Peace

When foreigners think of Americans today, their main impressions are of soldiers at military bases and undercover CIA agents. National Service could support a massive overseas expansion of the Peace Corps, which currently has only 5,200 volunteers. Sending a hundred thousand young Americans to the Third World for a few months of hard work and help would do a lot for our reputation.

A more motivated young America, a better trained young America, means a more competitive America in the international economy. And our foreign policy would be rejuvenated also, since we could rely more on a vibrant people-oriented military suited to waging peace, instead of relying on gold-plated weapons which don't work.

REAL PATRIOTISM

Another big plus for National Service is the potential to inspire patriotism in our youth and enthusiasm for public service. To that end, we should incorporate in National Service a study program similar to the preparation our immigrants undergo before naturalization.

I was startled when I learned that natural-born Americans are far less likely to vote than immigrants who have gone through the citizenship process. Adults who apply for naturalization have to study the history, governmental institutions and political values of American democracy. That learning process, culminating in a final ceremony, is taken very seriously and new citizens have a high regard for political participation. If you absorb democratic values as an adult, you're better able to appreciate those values and more willing to practice them.

Let's use the opportunity of National Service to register 18-year-olds to vote and help them emerge better citizens. If we push our youth to excel through this program, they will emerge as leaders for business and the military—even for Washington.

THE METAMORPHOSIS

There is so much that our schools today don't teach kids, and much of what they do teach doesn't register. For most kids, only as adulthood approaches is life taken seriously. In my judgment, 18 is the age of receptivity. The individual is beginning to question, to wonder and to really want to know more about the outside world he or she will soon face. A structured environment at that age is the last chance to educate the American against becoming a captive American later.

In the social education which we give teens in National Service, we could provide them with an engaging approach to American history and values, and to basic facts about the rest of the world. At this age, young people are often unaware of the social problems in our cities and around the world. Let's use this opportunity to expand their sensitivity to the difficulties we're facing. That is how we'll get new ideas for solutions.

THE WIMPS IN WASHINGTON

This is just one more great idea which has not seen the light of day for political reasons. The lifers are afraid of voter reprisal. Every now and then a bill calling for a "study" of National Service is tossed into the hopper. Two such bills, in 1979 and 1981, were offered by two of my local Congressmen, Pete McCloskey (now retired) and Leon Panetta. They did not call for mandatory service, only "modified voluntary service."

Few Presidential candidates come out for National Service (Bruce Babbitt and Gary Hart did) because they don't want to lose the youth vote, even though it's not much of a vote. Even the Washington-based "Coalition for National Service," a non-profit group that lobbies for the idea, travels the politically safe route of promoting only a voluntary program.

I was interested—but not surprised—to discover that members of Congress, as individual members of the elite of America, are not personally high on military service. Washington author Donald Winter did a study in 1980 that looked at the members of Congress who belong to the "Vietnam generation." Only 14 percent had served on active duty anywhere in the military. For this generation as a whole, 28 percent had served in the military. So members of Congress were twice as likely as their contemporaries to have escaped military service. No wonder they are not big fans of National Service.

Some people say that parents would object to a National Service program. I don't believe it. They (and I mean *we*) are sick and tired of seeing rudderless children drift off into shallow lives with little or no direction. Parents will welcome it—for themselves and their kids.

National Service will reaffirm the values that made the United States possible in the first place.

CHAPTER 24

★

The National Think Tank

I was pretty rough on the kids in the last chapter, wasn't I? They're not the only ones who'll have to contribute to the great national renewal we need.

I began this book with my disappointment that the experts couldn't help me find answers, and in various chapters I've heaped a lot of abuse on the heads of so-called specialists. My criticism has centered on their inability or reluctance to contribute more to solving our problems. Like our leaders, they are captives of the status quo and are afraid of new ideas. They like things the way they are.

I have a couple of ideas on how the country can make the best use of expertise in an informal national think tank. Frankly, I prefer action by ordinary people like myself. But I don't want my Stanford friends to think I have forgotten them.

The key to using the collected wisdom of academics and other specialists is to diffuse their knowledge and put it to work in the public arena. And today there is no better way to do that than through television. The average household has its TV set turned on seven hours a day. We should be using at least some of that time to watch something worthwhile.

One of the few places we see academics on television is on the Public Broadcasting System. But PBS doesn't have the resources necessary to do the job as well as it could. Ever wonder why the best shows on PBS are British? That's because their government spends seven times as much on public television as we do.

We need to develop a showcase for our universities' foremost brains.

"The University of the Air"

Why not establish a cable channel solely devoted to broadcasting college courses? Videotaped lectures by the best teachers from campuses across the nation could be collected into an impressive offering of classes, especially history. People at home could watch whatever courses they wished at convenient times, with reruns around the clock.

There are a handful of educational channels, including a commercial cable network called the Learning Channel of Washington, D.C., which offer something similar on a limited scale. But to benefit the millions of Americans who never had the opportunity to attend college, we need a national program that would offer incentives for viewing. One such incentive might be an arrangement with community college systems to offer credits for the televised courses. A home examination scheme similar to correspondence courses would allow viewers to take the courses seriously.

The "University of the Air" would be a way for academics to combine their work in the ivory tower with teaching a broader spectrum of people. The most entertaining and dynamic lecturers might become celebrities, and every citizen would have access to this think tank.

I may be naive, but imagine how better informed American society would be after five years of broadcasts of the University of the Air. The captive American would have keys to freedom only a channel change away.

The National Long-Range Planning Board

There are no easy answers for many of the serious problems I've examined in this book. I've proposed some immediate reforms for our political and economic system, and I've pointed the way to more fundamental changes I think we need. But it is obvious that one crucial element is lacking from our current discussions of where the nation is headed, and that is long-term planning.

Everybody knows that the Soviet system of five-year economic plans is a joke. In one document, they try to designate exactly how much of every single product the economy will produce and the public will consume. The plan specifies everything from how many tons of steel the automobile industry will need to how many rolls of toilet paper people will use. Once it is presented, though, both industry and consumers alike treat the plan as fiction. The real economic activity involves getting around the inevitable shortages.

That's not what I'm talking about. I think we need long-term thinking about where our national economic priorities lie to avoid the short-term politicized process we use in Washington now. I believe we desperately need more foresight to deal with chronic problems like drug use and poverty, and to anticipate the cultural problems we will face in the future. And we could use a lot more deliberation on what the world of the next century will look like and how to map out our foreign policy accordingly.

In politics, economics and international affairs, we must have more intelligent planning than Lifetime Politicians are willing to do. One of the few praiseworthy leaders I call an "unelectable," Dan Evans of Washington state, has said honestly that "long-term planning in the Senate has come to mean eight to ten minutes."

You know my views on why I don't think we'll get worthwhile help from the brains in academia. Those authorities are part of the problem, because they are already tribesmen in the unelected political elite. We need an independent panel of astute women and men who could devote some serious, nonpolitical analysis to the perpetual issues that plague the United States.

I can say right off what the board *shouldn't* look like. Congress and the White House jointly set up a so-called National Economic Commission in 1988 to address "in an orderly, nonpolitical way" the budget and trade deficits. The Commission was the brainchild of two men who themselves would like to be President, Bob Dole and Mario Cuomo. Half its twelve members were named by President Reagan, half by congressional leaders in an attempt at bipartisanship. Does all that sound nonpolitical? Among those appointed were Bob Strauss, known as "Mr. Democrat" inside the Beltway, and Lee Iaccoca, whose economic ideas in the past have centered on government bailouts for Chrysler. President Reagan even appointed that paragon of fiscal insanity himself, Cap "the Shovel" Weinberger, whose budget-busting ways in the Pentagon were well known.

Another bad example we need to steer clear of is a group calling itself "American Agenda, Incorporated." This self-important, self-appointed group of D.C. insiders formed in 1988 and declared that it would prepare "options" for the next President to deal with problems like the deficit and arms control. What great minds were behind this gathering? None other than Jerry Ford and Jimmy Carter, along with some of their former Cabinet officials and advisers. Henry Kissinger and, of course, Bob Strauss showed up in this clique.

What a crock. If those incompetents had been on the ball while in office, we wouldn't be in the fix we're in now! We don't need a bunch of political hacks spewing 20/20 hindsight in the middle of an election year. They're just trying to maintain their Beltway influence, to remain players in the game of Washington power.

FOLK WISDOM

I'll tell you what a true long-range planning board should look like. It should be small enough to avoid deadlocked paralyzing debates, but large enough to allow a real diversity of views. The term of membership should be short, so that the body doesn't become a permanent bureaucracy of its own. You're in, you devote a reasonable period of time to creative meditation and dialogue, and then you're out. The members should be from different regions of the country, with different backgrounds and wide-ranging interests. They should be chosen because they are true achievers in their various fields, and I mean outstanding achievers. No resume-stuffers need apply.

Most important of all, the people chosen should have absolutely no political background whatsoever. None—at the federal, state or local level. That's an iron-clad requirement, with no exceptions. Members of any of the elected or unelected political tribes I've described earlier simply have narrow minds. Even if they aren't currently in political office, their thoughts are constricted to what they consider politically feasible.

The whole point of long-range planning is to let the intellect roam freely, without boundaries. How else will we ever get innovative solutions? Mikhail Gorbachev would never have gotten his perestroika program off the ground in the fossilized Soviet

Union if he hadn't kept hammering away at the need for new thinking, for looking at society with open eyes and a fresh perspective. I hate to say it, but we should be following his lead (on this point, at least).

YOU CAN'T IMPROVE ON THE ORIGINAL

When you think about it, the ideal model for the board would be the original Constitutional Convention of 1787. That body of 55 delegates from 12 of the original 13 states (Rhode Island didn't like the idea) truly worked miracles. Many of the members were serving in the Continental Congress, but that was then almost powerless—it couldn't raise money, had nothing to do with commerce or foreign affairs and was only a part-time body anyway. The convention delegates considered themselves anything but career politicians.

They were planters, teachers, ministers, lawyers of course, doctors and merchants. They were genuine achievers in areas besides politics. Their average age was only 44. The average U.S. Senator today is more than 10 years older than that.

In less than 100 working days, the Founding Fathers created a Constitution that would stand the test of time for two centuries and more. That is incredible testimony to the power of long-range planning. They did it through free-wheeling debate and reflection, and they had no campaign considerations inhibiting their thoughts. The convention put itself out of existence after a year.

I've said what a planning board should and shouldn't look like. The one detail I keep coming up short on is how to choose the members. Whom can we trust to choose people who aren't already part of the problem? The Constitutional Convention delegates were chosen by their state legislatures, but in today's world we wouldn't get the same exceptional quality that way. I don't think we can trust Congress, or academia or even the media to select distinguished nonpolitical achievers without the process becoming just another politicized Beltway horse race. And if we left it to popular vote, we'd end up with Oliver North and Spuds McKenzie.

Frankly, on this point I'm stumped. In our current state of affairs, I know what we need but not precisely how to get it. I promised in my opening explanation of why I wrote this book not to act like a politician with an easy answer to everything. I can't provide all the solutions alone, and I am not afraid to say so.

If the experts and the academics in America are so smart, let them figure out an answer. But just this once.

CHAPTER 2 5

★

Goodbye, Captive American
Hello, Active American

I spend some time down in Palm Springs, a watering hole for the retired rich of America. I enjoy the desert, but I like being with the people there less and less—there's a lot of dropping out going on down there. Many of them have essentially given up on America.

I recently asked one wealthy individual there for his feelings about the country's economic prospects. He told me, "As long as I keep getting the interest on my tax-free bonds, I don't care about anything else."

That's the trouble with most of us. National problems seem so overwhelming that we finally just give up in frustration and concentrate on our own self-interest. A lot of individuals have seceded from the country and from each other.

I believe that should change. When I started researching this book over 20 years ago, I would read a disturbing headline and think, "Why can't we address that problem?" I shoved clipping after clipping into a drawer with some scribbled notes on them. For a long time, that's all I did.

Finally I kicked the propaganda and feel-good tranquilizers that I had been fed and decided to do something to prove to myself that all my shining beliefs about the Founding Fathers and their legacy of democracy were not obsolete. The fact that you are reading these words now convinces me I was not wrong.

Americans do not have to be captive to mindsets or to power-hungry politicians. We can grab hold of our destiny and shape it towards peace, stability, prosperity and progress. We'll need the hard work and new ideas of each and every citizen.

THE FEAR FACTOR

With all we know about how we've been sold down the river, why isn't there a lot more outrage? Where is the cry for change? The answer is that a lot of us are like the Lifetime Politician, prisoners of the status quo. We are afraid of change even though stagnation is crippling us.

Lots of people just don't want to rock the boat because they are pretty happy with the way things are. The rich sure don't want to change things; they've got theirs. Middle-class people are busy enough trying to keep their heads above water.

Many others are genuinely afraid to speak out. They fear repercussions because they work in or have connections with large corporations, big law firms, the military or in government organizations—all part of the establishment. In the course of my research I have met many people who told me the truth about what goes on around them, but refused to let me publish their stories.

I was going to start this book with a blockbuster scoop, alleging a million-dollar bribe offered by a famous businessman to a former high government official. The story is true, told to me by an impeccable source with first-hand knowledge of the deal. But I had to scrap it. The friend who revealed it to me was afraid that the former official might retaliate against his business interests in some way, and I am certainly not going to compromise my friend.

Then I came upon another dynamite revelation, involving a man who had been connected with illegal U.S. government operations on behalf of private corporations. The individual provided proof of the incidents, but forbade me from printing the story. He was afraid of reprisals against him or his family.

I even stumbled upon allegations by top-level insiders that President Reagan knew all about the diversion of the Iranian arms money to the contras, and that his advisers were forced to choose between having him appear a fool or a liar when the episode became public. They chose to portray him as a fool. But the nature of my sources keeps me from trumpeting that bombshell disclosure to sell my book. Everyone is too afraid of acknowledging the fact that yet another emperor has no clothes.

I would like to reveal all these things, but in my journey of discovery I have hit some powerful minefields. I have made the best case I could about the decline of our institutions, blaming the stupid or unscrupulous individuals whom We the People have put in the seat of power.

I have to tell you, after writing this book I am more mentally and physically exhausted than I have ever been in my very active life. Social life—what social life? During the past year, even my business has become secondary, but then what good is success in business when your peace of mind is wrecked by worry about more important concerns?

Now, I've said it all. I've gotten this book off my back, and I'm no longer a captive. Are you?

What are you willing to give for your country? To begin with, are you willing to sacrifice your representative in Washington?

DRAW UP YOUR HITLIST

I've said before that we've been putting band-aids on cancers. Those cancers can be excised, but the politician you've been relying on isn't the surgeon. The Lifetime Politician is the problem. *You* are the surgeon.

If you are reluctant to take on your Congressman because you think he's doing a good job, just think of Lincoln, who lost many elections and was booted out of Congress. He had only served two years in Washington before becoming President. That's the up-or-out principle.

There is no Member of Congress so vital to our government's functioning that we can't do very well without him or her. The myth of experience is one of the most important principles in this book. We've seen what the experienced incumbents do. Their expertise does nothing to guarantee good government.

Every Lifetime Politician is now on my hitlist. Your own incumbent should be on yours.

We could all learn something from the business strategies of corporate raiders like T. Boone Pickens. They target a company, round up the financing to take over and "restructure" the firm, and then fire the top management. That strategy is what we need for American government. You have to vote out every incumbent, and then be on the tail of every *new* incumbent. Force him to grapple with our problems while he's in Washington and then get the hell out, back to a real job.

Find out what's happening in your congressional district long before election day, and speak up loud and clear about it. Take one night a week or weekends and work for a challenger! But demand of him or her this pledge: "I will serve one or two terms and then get out."

A friend of mine in the South told me his Congressman had first run promising only one term. I asked if he had kept his word. "Well, no, but he's a good man," was the reply. "No," I told my friend, "he's a liar."

Throw the bums out. Just think—you can baffle all the pollsters and their carefully designed campaign blueprints. You can frustrate the special interests and PACs, as all their big-money contributions to incumbents go for naught. We can recapture political power for the citizens in a second American revolution!

NO REPRESENTATION BY STAGNATION

You'll have even more of an impact if you get involved in local or state politics. Mountain View, a town a few miles from where I live, is one of the few communities in California with a "fresh blood" law. No one can serve more than two terms on the city council. As a result, politics is fun in Mountain View. During campaigns the town is alive with posters and flyers, and the townspeople flock to civic meetings and rallies. Candidates aren't remote figures to voters, they are neighbors and co-workers. Up or out.

Whenever I argue for ousting the permanent politician and restoring the citizen-representative, someone always gripes, "You're never going to get good people to run. Politics is just too dirty."

As things are now, that's right. Ordinary people are dissuaded from running because it has become a career choice, and for most of them not a very attractive one. But with term limits, we would witness a New Wave of politicians. Good citizens could be persuaded to take a few years off from their private careers and serve their country briefly in Congress.

I'm not proposing that we bar good people from politics, just that we prevent their careers from stagnating in one place. The man or woman who excels in a political office can move up and down the career ladder into other federal, state or local positions and won't be beholden to the same constituency. And there will always be qualified individuals to replace them.

If You Can Stand the Heat, Get in the Kitchen

After the success of his autobiography, Lee Iacocca says he got over 70,000 letters urging him to run for President. In his latest book, *Talking Straight*, he says he could do it and might win, but rejects the idea: "Politics is a profession. To be good at it, you've got to live it and breathe it." Lee is dead wrong on that one. We need to steal politics back for the people, not leave it a private club for careerists.

With the New Wave, we would get people with good old common sense into office, men and women who are not disenchanted or cynical about public service and who could make decisions without worrying about reelection all the time. We could develop an entirely new breed of political leaders from all walks of life. Individuals who prove themselves in private endeavors would see public office as a privilege and duty, without having to sacrifice their financial well-being, their careers and their family responsibilities.

New Wavers would be more accountable to their constituencies because their ties to the community would be unbroken. The old boys club will die as the New Wave continually brings new faces to Washington.

We should all be lucky enough to live in Vermont. They still have a true citizen's legislature there. It meets for only 90 days a year and the members are real people from all walks of life, not career politicians. The largest group consists of retired persons, while many are farmers, business people, professionals, teachers and insurance salesmen. An increasing number of homemakers are in the body. The laws passed by this legislature reflect common sense because the people who make them have to live with them in everyday life.

CATCH THE NEW WAVE

When I ask people why they don't want to run for office, they give three reasons. First, they don't think they are qualified. Wrong! You don't have to be a lawyer to be a good legislator. I am confident that a healthy cross section of the public would write better, more accessible laws than the loophole-ridden maze of legislation we get today. By their very mindset lawyers miss the big picture beyond the framework imposed by their training. That's why the word "legalistic" has a negative connotation.

Second, some successful business people say they won't try politics because of the question of financial disclosure. Tough disclosure requirements may be deterring some faint-of-heart or disreputable characters, but there are plenty of well-qualified citizens around who are not afraid of disclosure.

Third, people fear rejection. Deep down, no one really wants to go through the humiliation of losing a race. Just running for office is psychologically difficult. The nature of campaigning is that you continually beg other people for something—their vote, their money. I know how humbling that experience is from my work in local charities in the San Francisco Bay Area. Trying to raise money from friends and strangers is tough.

Once you take the first step and decide to run, the fear of rejection can become positive, spurring your efforts, making you work harder to win. Anyone who has been an achiever at the local level knows that good planning is at the root of confidence.

So start planning now for your New Wave sabbatical in politics. This book provides a grounding in the common sense of politics, economics and foreign policy for the New Wave politician of tomorrow. And if we can get public campaign financing, you won't have to beg for money. You'll be independent of the big-money lobbies and the professional politicians.

A MESSAGE FROM ADOLF HITLER

At the back of the book I offer some suggestions for further reading. Stay abreast of what's happening in Washington and around the world. The 1990s can be the era, finally, of the informed citizen because new technologies are making news and information available more widely than ever before. That revolution will help us counter the tide of PR and propaganda we've been getting.

But don't just listen and read. Think. Adolf Hitler, who created the most oppressive dictatorship ever known, once remarked: "What good fortune for those in power that people do not think!"

I believe all of us should devote more of our waking hours to productive thought and less to watching TV. Think skeptically as you hear and read volumes of information from Washington and around the world every day. How much of it is true? How much of it do you suspect is misinformation? Why would a member of the power elite want you to believe it? And what goes unsaid?

Think about the national reforms I propose; they are listed together as a checklist at the end of this chapter. Do they make sense? Will they address the problems? If not, improve on them!

After you think, make your ideas known to neighbors, friends and those in power, either as a member of the New Wave of politicians or in a simple letter to the editor of your local newspaper. You may think your letter will be lost in the crowd. Well, over the years I've read a lot of remarkable newspaper letters from fed-up men and women, and every one of them has had some impact on the way I think.

A MESSAGE FROM YOU

One night recently I was listening to Larry King's radio call-in show. One particular caller caught my attention with his opening words: "I'm the most uneducated man that ever called your program. It has taken me eight years to get the courage to call."

He went on to say that he was alone in his rented room with a hotplate, next-door to the car wash where he worked. Why had he called? Because, he said, even someone like him with only a fifth-grade education could see that something was desperately wrong with America.

The caller continued: "I was just sitting here thinking about the news and wondering why our country is falling apart. Why is there so little common sense in government?"

That single individual, by making that call and speaking his mind, impressed me tremendously. The moment he believed he had something worth saying, he had taken the first step toward becoming an active American. And his call gives each of us the most powerful self-help message there is: "if he can do it, I can, too."

For so long we've heard that the issues are too complicated for the common man. After reading this book you will never take that for granted again. Remember, this is still the land of the citizen-king.

Yes, most of our problems have been around for years, and we've survived. But we can't count on muddling through forever. Our economic and military predominance in the past allowed us a huge margin for error in our decisions and policies. We have piddled away that margin. The problems are more pressing and of greater magnitude, and the price of failure has never been higher.

There's no reason to think that you, as an individual, will have to perform a solo herculean task. This is not a job for Superman. People have the mistaken idea that a white knight will come along and lead us out of the woods. We don't need that. The problems are immense but we are all interdependent, and my efforts will be multiplied by your own and by those of your friends and community. Could anyone doubt our ability to overcome our difficulties if we harness the energy and imagination of 230 million Americans?

That's why each vote is so important. Look at it this way: Ronald Reagan won in a landslide in 1984, right? Wrong. Reagan got 55 million votes, Mondale got 38 million votes, and *Fed Up* got 90 million eligible voters to stay home.

I read an infuriating letter to the editor in the *New York Times* a while back. The paper had complained about low voter turnout in a New York primary, but the letter-writer said, "I think that's fine. The fewer people vote, the more my vote weighs." Do you want people like that to run this country for you? Are you ready to give up your birthright as a free American citizen to the elitists who have kept you tranquilized for so long?

I'm not. And I'm betting that you're not ready to throw in the towel, either. Your voice can help determine which path our country takes. In the regeneration of the American spirit, your personal efforts are vital.

People in other parts of the world have concluded we've lost that ability. Let's prove them wrong. Thomas Jefferson said, "a little rebellion now and then is a good thing." Use the ideas in this book. Let's stir up a little rebellion. It really is morning in America. This is our wake-up call for the 1990s.

CHECKLIST
FOR THE ACTIVE AMERICAN

---------------------------------- ★ ----------------------------------

Chapter 9
- Choose Presidents by substance, not form
- Elect the Unelectables

Chapter 10
- Limit congressional committees
- Give viewers the full picture of Congress
- Limit congressional terms
- Enact campaign finance reform
- Cancel the perks of incumbency
- End gerrymandering
- Establish President's question time
- Encourage shadow cabinets
- Crown an American king
- Start a motor-voter program

Chapter 16
- Introduce a wealth tax
- Raise consumption taxes
- Compete to win in the global marketplace
- Require separate congressional appropriations bills
- Trim farm subsidies
- Take Social Security out of the budget
- Reregulate the banks
- Increase banks' reserves to handle debt
- Tax short-term stock transactions
- Pry the politicians' fingers off the economy
- Take personal responsibility for your future

Chapter 21

- Emphasize diplomacy over militancy
- Stress accountability in covert actions
- Be a world leader, not a world boss
- Have more cultural exchanges with the U.S.S.R.
- Open up trade channels with the U.S.S.R.
- Cut defense spending
- Think small not big in weapons systems
- Make allies carry more of the load
- Convert the war economy
- Promote competition for defense contracts
- Stop arming the world
- Fight a real war—against drugs

Chapter 23

- Begin National Service

Chapter 24

- Broadcast a "University of the Air"
- Establish a national long-range planning board

Chapter 25

- Start your hitlist of incumbents
- Join the New Wave of politicians

SUGGESTIONS
FOR FURTHER READING

---------------------------- ★ ----------------------------

PART I. LEADERSHIP LOST AND FOUND

As a helpful overall guide to America's government I thoroughly recommend Robert Sherrill's book, *Why They Call It Politics*
(Harcourt Brace Jovanovich, 1979).

The Almanac of American Politics by Michael Barone and Grant
Ujifusa (National Journal, 1988) is an indispensable look at the
world of the Lifetime Politician. This book has profiles of every
U.S. Senator and Representative, their records and details on
their campaign finances. Beware: some of the stories are frightening!

The best source I've found on the funding of political campaigns
is Larry Sabato's *PAC Power: Inside the World of Political Action
Committees* (Norton, 1984). Another excellent book by Sabato on
modern elections is *The Rise of Political Consultants: New Ways of
Winning Elections* (Basic Books, 1981).

Roderick P. Hart's book, *The Sound of Leadership: Presidential Communication in the Modern Age* (University of Chicago, 1987) has an
important analysis of Presidential rhetoric.

Arthur Schlesinger, Jr.'s *The Cycles of American History*
(Houghton-Mifflin, 1987) is exceptionally enlightening, with in-
sightful anecdotes and a sweeping theory on the forces at play in
American political history.

Mark Green's *Who Runs Congress* (Dell, 1984) is a classic handbook for citizen action, with valuable tips on how to get more involved in government at the national and local level.

PART II. ECONOMICS: THE SEARCH FOR PROSPERITY

If anything is required reading about our economy, it is Peter Peterson's "The Morning After," in *Atlantic Monthly* (October 1987). This article is absolutely critical to understanding the state of our economy. Peterson's insights and his detailing of our mounting economic problems foreshadowed the Meltdown Monday fall of the stock market (the article came out just before the crash).

Alfred L. Malabre, Jr., presents a comprehensive view of the problems we now face with the twin deficits in *Beyond Our Means* (Random House, 1987).

Ravi Batra's *The Great Depression of 1990* (Simon and Schuster, 1987) shows the perilous parallels between the incidents leading up to the crash of 1929 and the crash of 1987.

Glenn Pascall's *The Trillion Dollar Budget: How to Stop the Bankrupting of America* (University of Washington Press, 1985) is a good overall description of our budgetary problems and offers scenarios to avoid total national bankruptcy.

A great way to scare yourself silly is to pore over the public documents published every year by the Office of Management and Budget. They'll try to push you toward their *United States Budget in Brief*, which they describe as "designed for use by the general public" with a "more concise, less technical overview." But the *Historical Tables, Budget of the United States*, is much more complete and tells the real story. (Both are available from the U.S. Government Printing Office, Washington, D.C.)

PART III. FOREIGN POLICY: THE SEARCH FOR PEACE

David Calleo's *Beyond American Hegemony: The Future of the Western Alliance* (Basic Books, 1987) presents the strong and clear argument that the United States is losing its position of world dominance, while the rest of the world (especially Japan and

West Germany) grows economically. Calleo examines the effect this will have (and is having) on our foreign policy and the health of our economy.

Barry Rubin's *Paved with Good Intentions: The American Experience and Iran* (Penguin Books, 1986) details our troubled relations in the Persian Gulf and elsewhere in the Middle East.

The Union of Concerned Scientists has produced two good books on SDI and its problems. The books are *Empty Promise: The Growing Case Against Star Wars* (Beacon Press, 1986) and *The Fallacy of Star Wars* (Vintage Books, 1984).

Joshua Epstein's *The 1988 Defense Budget* (Brookings Institution, 1987) presents a very persuasive alternative to the present defense budget, as well as making a number of suggested cuts to help our ailing economy.

I recommend James Fallows, *National Defense* (Vintage Books, 1981) as a general, searching analysis going behind the issues and beyond just the numbers and statistics. Fallows looks at our long-range defense strategies and how they can be improved.

John Mueller's *War, Presidents and Public Opinion* (Wiley, 1973) gives background on how recent Presidents have manipulated the public, and I recommend it for anyone interested in the effects the office of the Presidency has upon common people.

For a good argument on the damage wrought by covert operations (both internationally and domestically) see John Orman's *Presidential Secrecy and Deception* (Greenwood Press, 1988).

There is also the new *Breakthrough: Emerging New Thinking* (Walker and Company, 1988), a collection of contributions from 31 Soviet and American scientists and scholars. They focus on Gorbachev's proposals for "new thinking" and make their own arguments for finding a way to realize that war is obsolete. All royalties for this book go to the Beyond War organization.

If you are interested in the conversion of the war economy, I'd recommend reading *Plowshare*, a quarterly magazine published by the Center for Economic Conversion, Mountain View, California.

PART IV. BACK TO OUR FUTURE

To stay on top of all that's going on, it's best to read not only your local daily newspaper, but a national newspaper. And read the business section as well. You'll be surprised how much is going on beneath the surface.

I also think that the following magazines are absolutely indispensable (all are available at your local library or newstand). I like *The Washington Monthly* and *New Republic*, (both are fairly liberal); *National Review* and *American Spectator* (both conservative); and *Atlantic Monthly* and *Harper's*, which look at current affairs in depth.

INDEX